Mary Jane Holmes

The Tracy Diamonds

Mary Jane Holmes

The Tracy Diamonds

ISBN/EAN: 9783743319424

Manufactured in Europe, USA, Canada, Australia, Japa

Cover: Foto ©ninafisch / pixelio.de

Manufactured and distributed by brebook publishing software (www.brebook.com)

Mary Jane Holmes

The Tracy Diamonds

POPULAR NOVELS

BY

MRS. MARY J. HOLMES.

Tempest and Sunshine.	Darkness and Daylight.
English Orphans.	Hugh Worthington.
Homestead on Hillside.	Cameron Pride.
'Lena Rivers.	Rose Mather.
Meadow Brook.	Ethelyn's Mistake.
Dora Deane.	Milbank.
Cousin Maude.	Edna Browning.
Marian Grey.	West Lawn.
Edith Lyle.	Mildred.
Daisy Thornton.	Forrest House.
Chateau d'Or.	Madeline.
Queenie Hetherton.	Christmas Stories.
Bessie's Fortune.	Gretchen.
Marguerite.	Dr. Hathern's Daughters.
Mrs. Hallam's Companion	Paul Ralston.
The Tracy Diamonds. (*New.*)	

"Mrs. Holmes is a peculiarly pleasant and fascinating writer. Her books are always entertaining, and she has the rare faculty of enlisting the sympathy and affections of her readers, and of holding their attention to her pages with deep and absorbing interest."

Handsomely bound in cloth. Price, $1.50 each, and sent *free* by mail on receipt of price,

G. W. Dillingham Co., Publishers
NEW YORK.

BY
MRS. MARY J. HOLMES

AUTHOR OF

"TEMPEST AND SUNSHINE," "'LENA RIVERS," "THE ENGLISH ORPHANS," "PAUL RALSTON," "GRETCHEN," ETC., ETC.

NEW YORK
G. W. Dillingham Co., Publishers
MDCCCXCIX

COPYRIGHT, 1898, 1899,
BY MRS. MARY J. HOLMES,

[*All rights reserved.*]

The Tracy Diamonds.

CONTENTS.

PART ONE.

Chapter		Page
I.	The Prospect House	7
II.	The Cause of the Battle	15
III.	Uncle Zach and Craig Mason	24
IV.	Mr. and Mrs. Dalton	32
V.	The Tragedy	36
VI.	Expected Guests	49
VII.	The Tracys	57
VIII.	Alice	67
IX.	Waiting for T'other One	78
X.	Alice and Jeff	83
XI.	Alice and Craig	91
XII.	A Coquette	98
XIII.	On the North Piazza	105
XIV.	The Diamonds	115
XV.	The Drive	121
XVI.	The Return Home	132
XVII.	Progress	138
XVIII.	Browning	144
XIX.	What Time Told	157
XX.	In the Haunted House	168
XXI.	The Denouement	180
XXII.	What Followed	189
XXIII.	The Close of the Season	204

Chapter	Page
XXIV. Craig's Visit	212
XXV. In the Red School House	216
XXVI. The Last Act of Part One	222

PART TWO.

I. Fanny and Roy	228
II. Mrs. Prescott	239
III. Ancestry	246
IV. Inez	256
V. In the Yosemite	268
VI. At Prospect Cottage	275
VII. On the Road to Clark's	290
VIII. Mark Hilton	300
IX. Mark and Tom	308
X. Inez and Her Father	314
XI. Mark and Helen	320
XII. Fanny and Inez	330
XIII. The Sisters	337
XIV. Roy	343
XV. At the Last	356
XVI. Mark and Tom	363
XVII. In Ridgefield	370
XVIII. Dotty's Funeral	376
XIX. Odds and Ends	383

THE TRACY DIAMONDS.

PART I AND PROLOGUE.

CHAPTER I.

THE PROSPECT HOUSE.

The time was a hot July morning, with the thermometer at 85 in the shade, and rising. Not a leaf was stirring, and the air seemed to quiver with the heat of midsummer. The fog, which, early in the day, had hung over the meadows and the river, had lifted, and was floating upward in feathery wreaths towards a misty cloud in which it would soon be absorbed. Even the robins, of which there were many in the vicinity of the Prospect House, felt the effects of the weather and sat lazily upon the fence or the branches of the trees in which their nests were hidden. Only the English sparrows showed signs of life, twittering in and out of the thick ivy which covered the walls of what had once been a church, and was now used for public offices. It was a morning in which to keep quiet and cool if possible. "The hottest on record," Uncle Zach Taylor, the proprietor of the Prospect House, said, as he examined the thermometer and wondered "What on earth Dot was thinking of to raise Cain generally in such weather." The house was in a state of upheaval, and looked as if the annual cleaning was about to commence on a gigantic scale. In the back yard carpets were being beaten by two men, with the perspiration rolling down their faces, on the south and west piazzas furniture of every description was standing,—bureaus and washstands, tables, chairs and couches, with two or three old-time pictures in old-time frames. One was a representation of the famous Boston Tea Party. The Dartmouth, Elinor and Beaver were in close proximity to each other, their decks swarming with Indians breaking open chests and shovelling tea into the water. The others were family portraits, evidently husband and wife—she, small and straight and prim, in a high crowned cap with a wide frill shading her face—he, large and tall, with a black stock, which nearly touched his ears, and his forefingers joined together and pointing in a straight line at the right knee, which was elevated above the left. "A kind of abandoned position," Uncle Zach was accustomed to say to his guests when calling their attention to this portrait of his wife's great-grandfather, who assisted at the Tea Party, and gave, it was said, the most blood-curdling whoop which was heard on that memorable night. A blue cross on the figure of a man on the deck of the Dartmouth indicated which Zacheus had decided was his wife's ancestor.

He was very proud of the pictures. "Wouldn't take fifty dollars for em. No, sir,—and I don't believe I'd take a hundred. Offer it, and see," he frequently said. But no one had offered it, and they still hung in their respective places in the best room of the hotel except when, as was the case this morning, they were brought out and placed at a safe distance from the scene of confusion around them.

There were brooms and mops and scrubbing brushes and pails and the smell of soap suds in the vicinity of the wing at the west end of the hotel, where the fiercest battle was raging. Four women, with their sleeves rolled up and towels on their heads, were making a terrible onslaught on something, no one could tell what, for there was neither dust nor dirt to be seen.

"But, Lord land, it's Dot's way to scrub, and you can no more stop her than you can the wind. She's great on cleaning house, Dot is, and you can't control wimmen, so I let 'em slide," Uncle Zach said to a young man whom, after his examination of the thermometer, he found on the north piazza, fanning himself with a newspaper and occasionally sipping lemonade through a straw and trying to get interested in Browning's Sordello. After reading a page or two and failing to catch the meaning, he closed the book and welcomed Uncle Zach with a smile as he sank panting into a rocking chair much too large for him, for he was as small of stature as the Zacheus for whom he was named, and whose clothes he might have worn had they been handed down to so late a date as the 19th century. "This I call comfortable, and somethin' like it. How be you feelin' to-day? You don't look quite as pimpin as you did two weeks ago, when you come here," he said to the young man, who replied that he didn't feel pimpin at all,—that the air was doing him good, and in a short time he hoped to be as well as ever.

Had you looked on the hotel register you would have seen the name, Craig Mason, Boston, and above it that of Mrs. Henry Mason, his mother. Craig had never been very strong, and during his college course at Yale, had applied himself so closely to study that his health had suffered from it, and soon after he was graduated he had come to Ridgefield, hoping much from the pure air and quiet he would find there. Nor could he have found a more favorable spot for nerves unstrung and a tired brain.

Just where Ridgefield is does not matter. There is such a place, and it lies on the Boston and Albany Railroad, which keeps it in touch with the world outside and saves it from stagnation. It is a typical New England town, full of rocks and hills and leafy woods, through which pleasant roads lead off and up to isolated farmhouses, some of them a hundred years old and more, and all with slanting roofs, big chimneys and low ceilings and little panes of glass.

These are the houses from which the young generation, tired of the barren soil and hard labor which yields so little in return, emigrates to broader fields of action and a more stirring life, but to which the father and the mother, to whom every tree and shrub is dear, because identified with their early married life, cling with a tenacity which only death can sever.

A river has its rise somewhere among the hills, and there are little ponds or lakes where in summer the white lilies grow in great profusion, and where in winter the girls and boys skate on moonlight nights, and men cut great blocks of ice for the Prospect House, which in July and August attracts many city people to its cool, roomy quarters. The house was built before the railroad was thought of, and in the days when stages plied between Boston and Albany and made it their stopping place for refreshments and change of horses. It was called a tavern when Zacheus Taylor brought his wife Dorothy there and became its owner.

"Taylor's Tavern" he christened it, and that name was on the creaking black sign in large white letters, and the little man always rubbed his hands together with pride when he looked at it and remembered that *he* was the *Taylor* whose name could be distinctly seen at a distance as you came up the street either from the east or the west. "A kind of beacon light," he used to say, "tellin' the played out traveler that there is rest for the weary at Taylor's tavern."

It was a pleasant sight to see him greet his guests with the cheery words, "Glad to see you. How are you? All fired tired, I know. Walk right in to the settin' room. Dotty has got dinner most ready. Dotty is my wife, and I am Mr. Taylor," with a nod towards the spot where Taylor's Tavern swung. But if he were the *Taylor*, Dorothy was to all intents and purposes the *Tavern*,—the man of the house, who had managed everything from the time she took possession of her new home and began to understand that a clearer head was needed than the one on her husband's shoulders if they were to succeed. Her head was clear, and her hands willing, and Taylor's Tavern became famous for its good table, its clean beds and general air of homely hospitality. As years went by a few city people began to ask for board during the summer, and with their advent matters changed a little. There were finer linen and china and the extravagance of a dozen solid silver forks to be used only for the city boarders, and, when they were gone, to be wrapped in tissue paper and put carefully away in a piece of old shawl on a shelf in a closet opening from Mrs. Taylor's sleeping room. Uncle Zacheus submitted to the silver forks and china and linen, but when, as his wife grew more ambitious, she told him that "Taylor's Tavern" was quite too old fashioned a name for their establishment, and suggested changing it to "Prospect House," he resisted quite stoutly for him. The change would necessitate a new sign, and "Taylor's Tavern" would disappear from sight. It was in vain that he protested, saying it would be like putting away a part of himself. Dorothy was firm and carried her point, as she usually did. The sign was taken down and the sign post, too, for the new name was to be over the principal entrance to the house, as it was in cities.

The sign post Zacheus had carried to the barn and put up in a loft as a family relic and reminder of other days. The signboard with "Taylor's Tavern" upon it was laid reverently away in the garret in a big hair trunk which had belonged to his mother and held a few things which no one but himself often saw, for Dolly did not interfere with the trunk. Carefully wrapped in a pocket handkerchief was a baby's white blanket, and pinned on it was a piece of paper with "Johnny's Blanket" written upon it. Johnny was a little boy who died when only three days old and his father had taken the blanket and put it away in the trunk with some articles sacred to boyhood, such as a pair of broken skates, a woolen cap, a cornstalk fiddle, withered and dried, but kept for the sake of the brother who made it and who had sailed away to Calcutta as cabin boy in a ship which was lost with all on board. Giving up the sign was harder than any one suspected, and when he felt more than usually snubbed he would go up to the hair trunk and look at it with affection and regret and as nearly as he was capable of it with a feeling that it embodied all the real manhood he had known since his marriage and with its disappearance his identification with the place had disappeared, leaving him a figure-head known as Uncle Zach, or Mrs. Taylor's husband,

She was never really unkind to him. She merely ignored his opinions, and brought him up rather sharp at times when he displeased her. Henpecked him, the neighbors said, while he, called it "running her own canoe."

"Not very hefty," was the most she ever said of him to any one, and whether she meant mentally, or physically, or both, she did not explain. "Shiftless as the rot, with no more judgment or git up than a child," was the worst she ever said to him, and he accepted her opinion as infallible and worshipped her as few women are worshipped by the man they hold in leading strings. She had been his Dot, or Dotty, when she was Dorothy Phelps and measured only half a yard round her waist, and he called her Dot still when she weighed two hundred and could throw him across the street. What she did was right, and after the burial of "Taylor's Tavern" in the hair trunk he seldom objected to what she suggested, and when she told him she was going to improve and enlarge the house and make it into something worthy of its name, he told her to go ahead, and bore without any outward protest the discomfort of six weeks' repairing, when carpenters and masons, plumbers and painters, transformed the old tavern into a comparatively modern structure of which Mrs. Taylor was very proud.

"I can advertise now with a good stomach," she said, and every spring there appeared in the Boston papers and Worcester *Spy* and Springfield *Republican*, a notice setting forth the good qualities of the Prospect House and laying great stress upon its rooms and views. If the advertisement was to be believed, every woman could have a large corner room, with the finest view in all New England.

To some extent this was true; not all could have corner rooms, but all could have splendid views. If you faced the north you looked out upon what farmers call a mowing lot, where early in the summer the grass grew fresh and green, with here and there a sprinkling of cowslips, and later on lay on the ground in great swaths of newly mown hay, filling the air with a delicious perfume. Beyond were sunny pasture lands and wooded hills, and in the distance the church spires of North Ridgefield, with the smoke of its manufactories rising above the tree tops. If your room faced the east you looked up a long broad street, lined on either side with old-time houses, whose brass knockers and Corinthian Pillars told of a past aristocracy before the steam engine thundered through the town and the whistle of a big shoe shop on a side street woke its employees at six o'clock and called them to work at seven. Here, nearly touching each other across the street, are gigantic elms, which tradition says were planted on the day when news of the Declaration of Independence reached the patriotic town of Ridgefield. Liberty elms they are called, and they stretch along for nearly a mile from east to west, and, making a detour, spread their long branches protectingly across the Mall which leads into the Common. To the south is the railroad and the Chicopee winding its way through green meadows to a larger river which will take it to the Sound and thence to the sea whose waters bathe another continent. If your room was at the west you looked at your right on grassy hills, dotted with low roofed houses and on pastures where spoonwood and huckleberries grow. At your left the headstones of the cemetery gleam white among the evergreens and tell where Ridgefield's dead are sleeping, the tall monuments keeping guard over the gentry of brass knocker and Corinthian pillar memory, and the less pretentious stones marking the last resting place of the middle class, the bourgeois,—for Ridgefield draws the line pretty close, and blue blood counts for more than money. Near the willows and close to a wall so wide that the children walk upon it as they go to and from school are the old graves, whose dark, century stained stones have 17— upon them and are often visited by lovers of antiquity. Some of those who sleep there must have heard the guns of the Revolution and helped to plant the Liberty Elms which keep guard over them like watchful sentinels. The Ridgefield people are very proud of their old graves and their cemetery generally, especially the granite arch at the entrance with the words upon it:

"UNTIL THE MORNING BREAKS AND THE SHADOWS FLEE AWAY."

This arch, with its background of marble and evergreens, is a prominent feature in the view from the west rooms of the Prospect House, and it was in these rooms that the battle of brooms and mops and soap suds was raging so fiercely on the hot July morning when our story opens.

CHAPTER II.

THE CAUSE OF THE BATTLE.

Mrs. Taylor's advertisements had paid her well, bringing every summer a few guests from Boston and its suburbs, but New York had not responded, and until it did Dorothy's ambition would not be satisfied. Boston represented a great deal that was desirable, but New York represented more.

"Why don't you advertise in the New York papers?" Mark Hilton, the head clerk and real head of the house after herself, said to her, with the result that he was authorized to write an advertisement and have it inserted in as many New York papers as he thought best.

Three days later there appeared in several dailies a notice which would have startled Mrs. Taylor if she had seen it before it left Mark's hands. It did throw Zacheus off his base when he at last read it in the New York *Times*.

"Wall, I'll be dumbed," he exclaimed, setting his spectacles more squarely on his nose and running his eyes rapidly over the article. "Yes, I'll be dumbed if this don't beat all for a whopper. I shouldn't s'pose Dotty would have writ it, and she a church member! Mebby she didn't. Here, Dot,—Dorothy, come here."

She came and listened wide eyed while her husband read and commented as he read. The scenery of Ridgefield was described in glowing terms. "Hills and valleys for pleasant drives, two ponds and a river for sailing, rowing and fishing; many points of interest, such as haunted houses, and the like."

"That's all so," Zacheus said, "except the 'haunted houses.' There ain't but one, and that's about played out. Queer thing to put in a paper; but listen to the rest of the lockrum," and he proceeded to read a description of the house, which was nearly as fine as if a Vanderbilt had planned it. The *cuisine* was first mentioned as unsurpassed, and superintended by the lady of the house. "That's you, Dot," and Zacheus nodded toward her. "That's you, but what the old Harry is that *cu-i-sine* you superintend?"

Dot didn't know, and her husband went on to the rooms, which were palatial in size, handsomely furnished,

—hot and cold water,—with intimations of suites of apartments, each connected with a private bathroom and balcony. It didn't say so in so many words, but the idea was there and Uncle Zach saw it and disclaimed against it as false. "Hot and cold water," he said. "That's great; only two fassets, and them in the hall under the stairs near the dinin' room where it's handy for the teamsters to wash up before goin' to dinner; and what's them *suits* of rooms, I'd like to know, with baths and things? It's a fraud; only one bathroom in the house and that always out of gear and wantin' plummin',—and I've a good mind to write to the *Times* and tell 'em so. You didn't have nothin' to do with this, Dotty, did you?"

"No," she replied, glancing at Mark Hilton, who sat in the office listening to the tirade and shaking with laughter.

"I wrote it," he said at last, "and it is quite as true as most of the ad's you see, and those rooms in the upper hall which open together are suites, if you choose to call them so."

"*Sweets!* Who said anything about sweets? The paper called 'em *suits*," the excited man rejoined, while Mark explained the *sweets* and *cu-i-sine* which had puzzled Zacheus more than the suits.

"I wanted something to attract New Yorkers," Mark said, "and perhaps I did romance a little, but once get them here they'll be all right."

Partially satisfied with this explanation, but wondering why he should have mentioned the haunted house, with which, in a way, he was connected, and glad Dotty had nothing to do with the fraud, as he persisted in calling the advertisement, Zach gave up his idea of writing to the *Times,* and with his wife began to look for any result the advertisement might have. It came sooner than they anticipated in a letter from Mrs. Freeman Tracy of New York, whose grandfather, Gen. Allen, had lived behind the largest brass knocker and Corinthian columns in town and was lying under the tallest monument in Ridgefield cemetery. She had seen the advertisement, she wrote, and as she had, when a child, spent a few weeks with her grandfather, she had a most delightful recollection of the town and wished to revisit it. She would like a suite of rooms with bath adjoining for herself and daughter,—a smaller room near for her maid, and her meals served in her private parlor. She had just returned from abroad, and called it a *salon*, which puzzled Mrs. Taylor a little, until enlightened by Mrs. Mason, her Boston boarder, who, with her son Craig, was content with a table in the dining room. To be served in a *salon* was a new departure and if anything could have raised Mrs. Freeman Tracy in Mrs. Taylor's estimation, the *salon* would have done it. This, however, was scarcely possible. The granddaughter of General Allen was a guest to be proud of without a *salon*, and Mrs. Taylor was thrown into a state of great excitement and Mark Hilton was told to write to the lady that she could be accommodated.

Here Uncle Zacheus interposed, saying he should write himself, and he did write a most wonderful letter! He would be glad to see Mrs. Tracy, he said, and would give her the best the house afforded. That notice in the paper overshot the mark some, but was none of his doings, nor Dotty's either. Dotty was his wife. It was all true about the river and ponds and meadows and hills and views, but there wasn't but one haunted house as he knew of and that was tumblin' down. There was a good many places of interest, like old graves if she hankered after 'em, and an old suller hole where a garrison once stood, and as to the tavern, it was as good as they made 'em,—clean sheets, all the towels she wanted, spring beds, hair mattrasses, feathers if she'd rather have 'em, silver forks, too; none of your plated kind, and bread that would melt in her mouth. Dotty did all the cookin' and washed her hands every time she turned round. The rooms was large and furnished comfortable, with a rockin' chair in every one, and when they wanted to ride out in style he had two bloods, Paul and Virginny, which couldn't be beat. But them elegancies the paper spoke on was all in your eye. There was only two fassets of hot and cold water, and the hot didn't always work. There wasn't any *sweets*, such as he guessed she meant, but there was some rooms openin' together and jinin' the bath room, which she could have, and she could eat her victuals by herself if she wanted to. He told her he knew her grandfather well,—had watched with him when he was sick,—sat up with him after he died, and did a good many things at the funeral. Signing himself, "Yours to command, Zacheus Taylor;" he handed the letter to his wife for her approval.

She didn't approve at all, but for once her husband asserted himself and said it should go, and it went.

"We've heard the last from Mrs. Tracy we ever shall," Mrs. Taylor said, but she was mistaken. Within three days there came a dainty little note written by Miss Helen Tracy, the daughter, and directed to "Zacheus Taylor Esq., Prospect House, Ridgefield, Mass.," and was as follows:

"Dear Sir :—

"Your kind letter is received, and I hasten to write for mother and say that we shall be glad to become your guests. I know we shall be pleased, whether there are two faucets in your house, or ten,—one bathroom or twenty,—and you may expect us on Thursday, the —th day of the month.

Yours truly,

Helen Tracy."

Not in years had Uncle Zacheus been as pleased as he was with that note. It was his own, which he could open himself and keep. He usually went for the mail which he took unopened to Dorothy, although it might be addressed to the "Proprietor of the Prospect House." No one wrote to him; he was a cypher in the management of affairs and the correspondence of the house. But this note was directed to him personally. He was "Zacheus Taylor, Esq.," and "Dear Sir," and it made him feel several inches taller than his real height. He read it on his way home from the office, and then gave it to his wife with a flourish, saying exultingly, "I told you honesty was the best policy. They are coming without hot and cold fassets and bath tubs in every room. Read that."

Dorothy read it while her husband watched her, holding the envelope in his hand and taking the note from her the moment she had finished it. It was his property, and after showing it to Mark and giving his opinion of Miss Helen Tracy as "a gal with a head on her," he went up to the garret and deposited his treasure in the square trunk with Taylor's Tavern and Johnny's blanket and went down with a feeling of importance and dignity which showed itself in his going fishing after dinner without a word to his wife.

She was in a state of unusual excitement. She had heard of the Tracys as people who made a great show at Saratoga and other watering places and had never dreamed they would honor her. But they were coming, and her voice rang like a clarion through the house as she issued her orders and began to look over her linen and rub up her silver forks not in use. Four of them had been appropriated to the Masons. Four more were to be given to the Tracys,—possibly five,—as they were to have their meals in private, and paid handsomely for it. Finally, as the honor grew upon her, she decided that the whole eight were none too many for New Yorkers. They would look well upon the table, and she could hide them away at night from any possible thief. The rooms Mrs. Tracy was to have adjoining the bathroom were occupied when her daughter's letter was received, and were not vacated until the morning of the day when she was to arrive. Consequently, there was not much time for preparations. But Mrs. Taylor was equal to the emergency and took the helm herself and gave her commands like a brigadier general, first to her maids, then to the carpet-beaters, and then to a small, fair-haired boy whom she called Jeff, and who ran for dusters and brooms and brushes, showing a most wonderful agility in jumping over pails and chairs and whatever else was in his way, and further exercising himself by turning summersaults when there was sufficient space among the pieces of furniture crowding the piazza. A box on his ears from a maid in whose stomach he had planted his bare feet brought him to an upright position, and he stood whirling on one foot and asking what he should fly at next.

Mrs. Taylor, who was mounted on a stepladder and passing her hand over the top of a window to see if any dust had been left there, bade him go up town after

Mr. Taylor, who had been sent for a bottle of ammonia more than an hour ago.

"I don't see where under the sun and moon he can be," she was saying, when "I'll be dumbed!" fell on her ear and she knew the delinquent had arrived.

"I'll be dumbed" was his favorite expression, which he used on all occasions. It was not a *swear,* he said, when his wife remonstrated with him for using language unbecoming a church member. It was not spelled with an "a," and it only meant that he could not find suitable words with which to express himself when he must say something.

When he left for the ammonia he knew a cleaning up was in progress, but he had no idea it would assume so vast proportions, until he found the piazza blockaded with furniture and his wife on a stepladder arrayed in her regimentals, which meant business, and which for length might almost have satisfied a ballet dancer.

"Come down, Dotty; come down. You've no idea how you look up there so high in that short gown. Shall I help you? I've brought you a telegraph," he said, and his wife came down quickly, while he explained that he had stopped to talk with Deacon Hewett, and it was lucky he did, for he was on hand to get the telegraph the minute it was ticked off. He met the boy as he was leaving the office.

Mrs. Taylor took the telegram from him and read: "New York, July 15. To Zacheus Taylor, Esq., Prospect House, Ridgefield, Mass.: My niece is coming with me. Please have a room prepared for her and meet us at the 8 train instead of the 4.—Mrs. Freeman Tracy."

"If this don't beat all. Another room to clean. I'm about melted now," and Mrs. Taylor sank into a chair and wiped her face with her apron. "Where's Zach?"

she continued. "I want him to help move them things out of the northwest room, so we can tackle that next. Where is he, I wonder. Find him, Jeff."

Zach had disappeared. Mrs. Tracy's telegram, addressed to Zacheus Taylor, Esq., was of nearly as much importance as her daughter's note had been, and a second pilgrimage was made to the garret and square trunk where Taylor's Tavern and Johnny's blanket were hidden away.

"It kinder seems as if I was of some account to have them Tracys so respectful and callin' me 'Squire twice," he thought, and he went down stairs with a pleasureable sensation of dignity not common with him.

"Miss Taylor wants you," the irrepressible Jeff said, rolling round the corner on his head and hands like a hoop, and nearly upsetting Zacheus as he landed on his feet.

"What is it, Dotty; what can I do for you? It's most too hot to do much," Zacheus asked his wife, and in his voice there was something which made her glance curiously at him.

She had intended to "blow him up" for never being around when he was needed, but she changed her mind and replied: "I did want you to help move the bureau and things from the northwest room, but Jeff will answer as well. You look hot. Go and rest yourself on the north piazza with Mr. Mason."

The tone of her voice was nearly as exhilarating as Zacheus Taylor, Esq. had been, for it was not often that she spoke to him so considerately when on the war path, and it was with a feeling of great satisfaction that he took his way to Craig Mason and the north piazza.

CHAPTER III.

UNCLE ZACH AND CRAIG MASON.

CRAIG MASON was feeling tired and wondering how he was to pass the hot morning with no one to talk to and nowhere to go and nothing to see if he went there. His mother was spending the day at East Ridgefield, and, as most of the boarders in the house were men who had their business to attend to, he was rather lonely and sometimes wished he had chosen a gayer place than Ridgefield, where there was some excitement and now and then a girl to amuse himself with. Not that he cared particularly for girls as a whole. They were mostly a frivolous lot, fond of dress and fashion and flirting, and caring nothing for anything solid, like Browning. But they were better than nothing when one was bored. In college he had devoted himself to his studies and seldom attended the social gatherings where he would have been warmly welcomed and lionized, for his family was one of the best in Boston, and he had about him an air of refinement and culture which would have won favor without the prestige of family and wealth. The students called him proud and the young ladies cold and cynical. They did not interest him particularly, and, as he was not strong enough to join in the athletic sports of his companions, he kept mostly to himself in his handsome rooms and took his exercise behind his fleet horse, the only real extravagance in which he indulged. He had wanted to bring Dido to Ridgefield, but had been dissuaded by his mother, who said there were probably plenty of horses to be had,—that it might look airy and she hated anything like ostentation. So Dido was left at home and Craig had tried some of the stable horses and found them lacking. He had visited the library and the big shoe shop and had seen the crowd of girls and boys pour out of it at twelve and six o'clock, and wondered how he should like to be one of them, shut up in a close, smelly place for hours in company with Tom, Dick and Harry and their sisters. The last would have hurt him the most, for although courteous to every one, he was fastidious with regard to his associates and shrank from contact with anything common and vulgar, especially if there was pretension with it. Uncle Zach was ignorant and common, but he was genuine, and Craig had taken a great fancy to him. They had driven together a few times in what Uncle Zacheus said was the finest turnout in town, with his two blooded horses, Paul and Virginia.

"You've got to keep a sharp lookout or they'll take the bits in their teeth and run away with you," he said to Craig, who had expressed a wish to drive. "Mebby I'd better take the lines. Them white hands don't look strong enough to hold such bloods as Paul and Virginny."

Craig thought he could manage them, and wondered what Uncle Zach would say to Dido if he could once see her carry herself up hill and down with no sign of fatigue or need of a whip, while these plugs, as he mentally designated Uncle Zach's bloods, had to be urged after the second long hill and stopped of their own accord to rest after the third, while at the fourth Uncle Zach suggested that they get out and walk "to rest the critters." Craig took no more drives after Uncle Zach's blooded horses, but he went rowing with him on the river once or twice and always treated him with a deference which was not lost on the little man.

"He's a gentleman, every inch of him," Mr. Taylor

often said of him, and nothing could have pleased him better than his wife's permission to join him on the north piazza.

Craig was glad to see him. He had given up Browning for the time being,—had nearly finished his lemonade, and was quite ready for a chat with his loquacious landlord, who, after inveighing against the propensity of women to clean house when there was nothing to clean, and inquiring after Craig's health and declaring himself comfortable two or three times, commenced a eulogy on Ridgefield.

"The greatest town in the county, with the finest views and most notorious people and places. See that hill over there?" he asked, pointing to the west. "Wall, there's the suller hole where the Injuns pushed their wagons of blazin' hemp, and the garrison would have been burnt to the ground and the people scalped, if the Lord hadn't done a miracle and sent a thunder shower in the nick of time. One of Dot's ancestors was there shut up, so it's true. Dot's great on ancestory; goes back to the flood, I do b'lieve. She's got the door latch of that old house. I'll show it to you if you don't b'lieve it. Yes, 'twas a miracle, that shower, like the sun standin' still in one of our battles, I don't remember which. In the Revolution, wa'n't it, when Washington licked the British?"

Craig smiled and answered that he believed it was in the old testament times when Joshua was the general.

"Good land, I or'to know that, though I ain't up in scripter as I should be, seein' I'm a member in good standin', though I hain't always been," Uncle Zach replied, and continued: "You know the meetin' house across the street,—the Methodis', I mean,—not the 'Piscopal, where you go."

Craig said he knew it, and Uncle Zach went on: "I

belong there; so does Dotty. We joined the same day. Dot has stuck, but I've backslid two or three times. I repented bitterly, for I mean to be a good man, but I'll be dumbed if it ain't hard work for a feller to keep in the straight and narrer way and run a tavern."

Craig thought the share Uncle Zach had in running the tavern was hardly a sufficient excuse for backsliding, but he made no comment, and Uncle Zach went on: "I was goin' to tell you about some of the noted folks,—moved away now,—but always had Ridgefield for their native town. There's that Woman's Rights and Temperance Woman, Miss Waters. Everybody has heard of her from Dan to Beersheby. Good woman, too,—and lectures smart about women's votin'. I'd as soon they would as not. B'lieve the country'd be better off if they did, but I don't want 'em to wear trouses. Miss Waters did a spell, —then left 'em off, and I'm glad on't. Dot b'lieves everything she does is gospel, and I wouldn't like to have Dot wear my trouses, s'posin' she could get into 'em. A man or'to hold on to them, if nothin' more. Then there's another woman,—writes books, piles on 'em, the papers say, and if you b'lieve it some folks who came here are that foolish that they have my bloods, Paul and Virginny, and go over to see where she was born. An old yaller house, with a big popple tree at the corner. No great of a place to be born in, or go to see, but you can't calcilate what city folks'll do. I knew her when she was knee high and wore a sun bonnet hanging down her back, with the strings chawed into a hard knot. Knew her folks, too. She's a lot of 'em down in the cemetery. Good honest stock, all of 'em, and belonged to the Orthodox church; but you can't make me b'lieve she wrote all them books the papers say. No, sir."

"You mean sold," Craig suggested, and Uncle Zach

replied: "Mabby I do, but it amounts to the same thing. If they are sold they are wrote, and nobody ever wrote so many. No, sir. I'll bet I never read twenty books in my life, includin' the Bible. Hello, Mark, what is it? Does Dot want me?" and he turned to his clerk, who came round the corner with a paper in his hand.

Mark Hilton, who had been in Mr. Taylor's employ for three years, was tall and straight, with finely cut features and eyes which saw everything in you, around you and beyond you. Watchful eyes, which seemed always on the alert, and which might have belonged to a detective. Out of a hundred men, he would have been selected as the most distinguished looking and the one who bore himself with the air of one born to the purple rather than to the position of clerk in a country hotel. Nothing could be pleasanter or more magnetic than his smile and voice and manner. Craig had felt drawn to him at once, and, finding him intelligent and well educated, had seen a good deal of him during the short time he had been at the Prospect House. Uncle Zach adored him and treated him with a consideration not common between employer and employee. Pushing a chair towards him, he said: "Set down a spell and rest. It's all fired hot in that office with the east sun blazin' inter the winder."

Mark declined the chair with thanks, and passing the paper to Mr. Taylor said: "Peterson is here again with the subscription for the fence on the south side of the cemetery. I have been to Mrs. Taylor, who is too busy to see to it, and she sent me to you, saying you must use your judgment and give what you think best."

It was so seldom that Zacheus had the privilege of using his own judgment that he sprang up like a boy, and, taking the paper from Mark's hand, read aloud, "Thomas

Walker, ten dollars. Pretty fair for him. Miss Wilson, five dollars. Wall, I'll be dumbed if she's hurt herself with all her money. Why, the Widder Wilson could buy out Tom Walker fifty times, but she's tight as the bark of a tree. William Hewitt, five dollars. Hello, he's come round, has he? When they fust asked him to give towards the fence, he said, No. It was good enough as 'twas. Nobody outside the yard ever wanted to git in, and nobody inside could git out if he wanted to. Pretty good, wa'n't it? I guess I'll give ten dollars. I can afford it as well as Tom Walker. Widder Wilson, only five dollars. I'll be dumbed!"

He wrote his name with ten dollars against it and gave the paper to Mark, who, with a nod and smile for Craig, returned to the office, while Zacheus resumed his chair.

"Maybe ten dollars is more'n Dot'll think I or'to have giv," he said, "but I have a hankerin' after that cemetery. Johnny is buried there, you know."

"Who is Johnny?" Craig asked, struck with the pathos in Mr. Taylor's voice and the inexpressibly sad expression of his face.

Working hard to keep his tears back, he replied: "Johnny was our little boy who died when he was three days and two hours old, and with him died the best part of me. I'd lotted so much on what we'd do as he grew up. He'd been three-and-twenty if he'd lived, a young man like you, but I allus think of him as a little shaver beginnin' to walk and me a leadin' him, and many's the time I've thought I heard his little feet and have put my hand down, so—and taken his'n in mine,—a soft baby hand,—and called him sonny,—and I—I——"

Here he stopped, while the tears rolled down his cheeks, and Craig felt his own eyes grow moist with sympathy for this child man, who, after a moment, recovered himself and continued: "You must excuse my cryin'. I can't help it when I think of Johnny and all he'd of been to me if he hadn't died. I tell you what, I b'lieve I'd been a good deal more of a man if he'd of lived."

Craig had no doubt of it, and was trying to think of something to say when their attention was attracted to Mark Hilton, who was walking up the street.

"Look at him," Mr. Taylor said. "Don't he carry himself like a king! Sometimes I think Johnny might have looked like him, only not so well, maybe, and I don't b'lieve he would have been better to me than Mark. Do you b'lieve in hereditary?—b'lieve that bad blood trickles along down from mother to son, and son to mother, and busts out somewhere when you least expect it?"

"Yes," Craig said, "I believe in heredity and environment, too."

"Envyrimen? What's that?" Uncle Zach asked, and Craig replied: "As connected with heredity, it means surroundings,—education,—influence,—circumstances."

"Jest so," Uncle Zach interrupted. "You mean the way one is brung up will offset bad blood. Mebby, but I don't b'lieve in hereditary. No, sir! There's Mark now, —the best and honestest feller that was ever born,—right every way. His great-grandmother was hung, with three more men, and my grandmother went to the hangin', more's the pity,—but there warn't so many excitin' things in them days as there is now, with a circus and caravan every summer, and a hangin' was a godsend, especially as there was a woman in it,—a high-stepper, too. You see 'twas this way: You know about the haunted house half a mile from town, a little off the main road at the end of the lane?"

Craig had passed the house two or three times on his way to the woods beyond, and had looked curiously at its grey, weather-beaten walls and slanting roof, from which the shingles had fallen in places. Once he went close to it and looked through a window, from which every pane of glass was gone, into a large, square room, with a big fire-place in it, and had wondered if it were there the young wife had sat that stormy night and heard her name called, while outside in the darkness the awful tragedy was enacted. From the wide hearth some bricks were loosened, and, while he stood there, a monstrous rat leaped out, and, followed by three or four smaller rats, went scurrying across the floor, the patter of their feet, as they disappeared behind the wainscoting and jumped into the cellar below, making a weird kind of sound which timid people might mistake for something supernatural. Craig himself had experienced a creepy kind of feeling as he left the old ruin and went next to look into the well, which had been a part of the tragedy. An old bucket was still swinging on a pole after the fashion of years ago, and he let it down into the deep well and drew it up full of water, which he fancied had a reddish tinge of blood. Hastily pouring it back, he heard it fall with a splash into the depth below, and hurried from the place. He had not been near the house since, and had never heard the full particulars of the story, which, now that Mark was connected with it, had an added interest, and he asked Uncle Zach to tell it.

Getting out of his chair, Mr. Taylor walked briskly across the piazza, saying, "It's very excitin' and harrerin' in some places, and I must get braced up before I tackle it." After a few turns, he declared himself sufficiently braced, and, resuming his seat, began a story which I heard in my childhood, and which in many of its details is true.

CHAPTER IV.

MR. AND MRS. DALTON.

"You see, 'twas this way, and it happened nigh on to eighty or a hundred years ago. This tarvern wasn't built then. T'other one that was burnt stood further up the street and was kep' by—I can't think of his name, but he was one of Dot's ancestors. Beats all what a lot she has, and what a sight she thinks of 'em. Got 'em all in a book, somewhere; the one in the portrait who helped throw over the tea,—and the one who pushed the carts of hemp against the garrison. I've turned him wrong side up, I guess, but you know who I mean. She has him, door latch and all,—and the one who kep' the tarvern when Mr. Dalton,—Mark's great-grandfather,—brought his bride to town. She was handsome as a picter, they say,—with yaller curls down her back and blue eyes which looked as innocent as a baby's. She was proud as Lucifer; wasn't willin' to associate with any but the high bloods; walked as if the ground wasn't good enough for her to step on with her little morocco shoes. Dressed up in the mornin' as much as some do in the afternoon. But then she'd nothin' to do, for she had a hired girl, Mari, who waited on her as if she was a queen. Had a pianner,—the fust there was in town, and folks used to go up the lane and set on the wall to hear her play Money Musk and Irish Washwoman and Bonaparte's March, and some new things they didn't like so well.

"Mr. Dalton was a first-rate man, fine looking and a perfect gentleman. Mark must be like him, and mebby that's where your hereditary comes in. Everybody liked Mr. Dalton, and he had a kind word for everybody. He was rich for them days, and had some interest in the stages that run between Boston and Albany. The railroad wasn't here then. 'Twas all stages, three a day each way, and they stopped at the tarvern to change horses. Them was lively times, and Dot's ancestor made money hand over fist. Mr. Dalton paternized him a good deal. He used to go off in the stages sometimes and be gone a few days, but when he was to home he had nothin' to do and sat on the tarvern piazza a sight talkin' sociable with Dot's ancestor, smokin' and takin' a drink now and then and treatin' the other fellers. Everybody took a drink them days. W. C. T. U. wasn't born. Dot's one of 'em,—true blue, too. Don't keep it in her cupboard for little private nips and then go a crusadin' as some of 'em do. She hates it like p'isen, and if Johnny had lived she'd had him sign the pledge before he could walk. She'd no more let me sell toddy than she'd put her head in the oven. She's right, too. I shouldn't of backslid the last time if I hadn't took some black strap and molasses for a cold. I like the stuff, and only Dot and the thought of little Johnny keeps me from drinkin'. But to return to my story.

"I guess you'll think I'm goin' 'round Robin Hood's barn to git to it. Mr. Dalton worshipped his wife, and she 'peared to worship him, till there come up from Boston a dark complected man, a friend of the Dalton's,—St. John, they called him, and he was there half the time talkin' to Miss Dalton and playin' the flute while she banged the pianner. The rest of the time he sat on the piazza at the tavern smokin', takin' drinks oftener than Mr. Dalton, but never treatin' nobody. Mr. Dalton thought a sight of him. They was college chums,—Harvard, I b'lieve,—and when he went off on the stage he'd ask him to sleep in his house and see to Miss Dalton, who was timid,—the more fool he. And he did see to Miss Dalton, and drove with her and walked with her clear up to North Ridgefield, and didn't get back till after dark. Folks began to talk and the women pumped Mari, who wouldn't say nothin', she was so bound up in Miss Dalton.

"After a spell another feller appeared, St. John's vally they called him, and he brushed his clothes and blacked his boots, and walked behind him in the street, and went a good deal to the Dalton's,—sparkin' Mari, folks said, and I guess that was so. Wall, after a spell another chap appeared,—brother to the vally, they pretended. He didn't go to the Dalton's, but sat on the piazza and smoked and drank and swore about big bugs ridin' over the poor, and was an ugly lookin' cuss generally. Mr. Dalton was real good to him,—gave him money once or twice and tried to git him work. But he didn't want to work. It warn't that he'd come for.

"Wall, as I was sayin', things went on this way with St. John and his vally and his vally's brother comin' and goin', till folks was talkin' pretty loud and sayin' Dalton or'to be told, and finally Dot's ancestor,—the one who kep' the tavern,—up and told Mr. Dalton careful like what folks was surmisin', and hinted that St. John shouldn't go there so much. Mr. Dalton threw back his head and laughed the way Mark has when he don't believe a thing.

"St. John was his best friend; he'd known him since he was a boy, he said, and his wife was a second pen—penny—something——"

"Penelope," Craig suggested.

"I b'lieve that's the name; sounds like it, though who she was I don't know," Uncle Zacheus replied, and continued: "The next day what did Mr. Dalton do but go to Worcester in the stage and buy her a silk gown that would stan' alone, and a string of gold beads. Dot's ancestor's wife's sister, or aunt, I don't remember which, made the gown, and Miss Dalton wore it and the beads and a new bunnet to meetin' the next Sunday, lockin' arms with her husband all the way, and lookin' up in his face lovin' like with her great pretty blue eyes which had something queer in 'em, rollin' round as if watchin' for somethin'. I'll be dumbed if Mark hain't the same trick with his eyes, and that's all the hereditary he has from that jade. She'd heard what folks was sayin', but was jest as sweet and innocent as a lamb, and sent some flowers to Dot's ancestor's wife, who had said the most about her.

"Wall, I don't git on very fast, do I? but, as I was sayin', time went on, and it was summer again, and folks had kinder forgot. St. John wa'n't in town, nor hadn't been that anybody knew, unless it was Mari, who kep' a close mouth. The vally wasn't in town, nor the vally's brother,—no more his brother than you are. That came out on the trial.

"Wall, there was an awful thunder shower one night,— struck the Unitarian Church and knocked the steeple into splinters, and rained till the gutters run like a river, and you could almost go in a boat the street was so full of water. Mr. Dalton was at the tarvern when the storm came up, and waited for it to stop. It was dark as pitch, and they tried their best not to have him go home. But go he would. His wife would be anxious and not sleep a wink, he said, and about eleven o'clock, when it had nearly stopped raining, he started with a lantern, and that was the last he was ever seen alive.

"I'm gettin' to the p'int, and I shall have to take a turn or two more, for it is very affectin' as you go on."

He took a turn or two, and returned to his chair, saying, "I guess now I can stan' it to tell you the rest."

CHAPTER V.

THE TRAGEDY.

"Next mornin', about eight o'clock, Mari come to the tarvern to know where Mr. Dalton was, that he didn't come home.

"'He did go home,' says Dot's ancestor.

"'He didn't come home,' says Mari, 'and Miss Dalton is dreadfully worried for fear he's sick. Never slep' a wink, and kep' a candle burnin' all night.'

"I don't know what put it into his head to think somethin' was wrong, but he did,—Dot's ancestor, I mean, and why the plague can't I think of his name! I know it as well as I do my own. Here, Jeff, you rascal, come here," he called, as the boy came leaping across the end of the piazza like a young deer. "Go and ask Miss Taylor the name of her ancestor who kep' the tavern when Mr. Dalton was killed."

Jeff disappeared with a bound and summersault, while his master continued: "Queer boy that, but smart as a steel trap. He's descended from Mari, who lived with Miss Dalton. A good boy, but queer motioned,—never stands still. Jumps round like a grasshopper,—turns summersets, one after another, till it makes you dizzy to see him. Reads all the trash he can git hold of about pirates and Injuns runnin' through the bushes. Told the parson, when he asked him what he was goin' to be when he grew up, that he s'posed he or'to be a minister, but he'd rather be a robber. Dot thrashed him for that and shut him up in the back chamber without his supper. But, my land, he was out in no time. Clum' out of the winder, —slid down the lightnin' rod and went rollin' off like a hoop on the grass. Here he comes. What did she say, Jeff?"

"She said his name was Joel Butterfield, and she didn't see what you was borin' Mr. Mason with that story for," was Jeff's reply, as he went hippy-te-hopping away.

"Be I borin' you?" Uncle Zacheus asked, and Craig replied: "Not in the least. I'm greatly interested, and shall be more so when you get to the pith of the matter. Pray, go on. Mari had come to ask why Mr. Dalton didn't come home, and Mr. Butterfield, your wife's ancestor, suspected something wrong. That's where you left off."

"Jess so; Joel Butterfield; funny I couldn't remember his name. I did think of *cheese*. Wall, he was wonderful for smellin' a rat, jess like Dot; she's allus smellin' things when there's nothin' to smell. Says he,—that's Joel, I mean,—says he to Mari, says he, 'Was anybody to your house last night?' First she said there wasn't; then she said there was, but she didn't see 'em. 'Twas Monday, washin' day, and Miss Dalton's washin's was big; allus wore white gowns in the summer. Had two in the wash that day, and four white skirts, and Mari was tired and went to bed early and dropped asleep at once. Bimeby she waked up and heard a man's voice speakin' to Miss Dalton, low like. Thinkin' it was Mr. Dalton, she went to sleep agin, and didn't wake till mornin', but had bad dreams, as of a scuffle of some kind. When she asked Miss Dalton who was talkin' if 'twasn't Mr. Dalton, Miss Dalton said 'twas a stranger who wanted to see Mr. Dalton. She didn't know his name, but sent him to the tarvern, where she s'posed her husband was, sayin' he was to tell him to come right home, for she was afraid in the storm. This looked queer, and Joel and the bartender started post haste for the Dalton House.

"It was a beautiful mornin', but it had rained so hard

the night afore that the road in the lane was soft as putty, and they see plain the mark of wheels and horses' feet which went up to the house, turned round, went out of the lane and off toward East Ridgefield. Joel noticed it and p'inted it out to the bartender, whose name I don't know, and it don't matter,—he was no kin to Dot. They went into the house,—Joel and the bartender,—and found Miss Dalton fresh as a pink in a white gown, with a blue ribbon round her waist and a rose stuck in it, and she a workin' a sampler. Know what that is?"

Craig confessed his ignorance, and Uncle Zach explained: "They used to work 'em years ago in school, and at home on canvas with colored yarn or silk. Sometimes the Lord's Prayer; sometimes a verse of scripter, but oftenest the names of the family, and when they was born. Dot's got one, but she hid it away after she got to be forty. Wall, Miss Dalton set in a rockin' chair, workin' Mr. Dalton's name, and when he was born, and lookin' as innocent as the baby playin' on the floor. I forgot to tell you there was a little boy two years old, with eyes like his mother. That's Mark's grandfather. When Miss Dalton see Mari, who came in fust, she asked as chipper like, 'Did you find him? Was he there?'

"'No,' says Mari. 'It's mighty curis, too, for he started for home about eleven o'clock.'

"'Yes,' says Joel and the bartender, comin' in behind her. 'He started home at eleven o'clock. I'm afraid there's been foul play somewhere.'

"'Foul play,' Miss Dalton gasped, and her face began to grow white, and there was a scared look in her eyes, which rolled round as if lookin' for some place to hide.

"'Yes, marm,' says Joel. 'Foul play of the wust kind. Whose buggy track is that up to the door and back, and off to the east? Who was here last night? They didn't come to the tarvern.'

"Then she turned whiter, and wanted a glass of water, and told of the strange actin' man who had asked for Mr. Dalton, and began to wonder if anything could have happened to her John. The bartender had gone into the yard, and was lookin' round near the well,—one of them old-fashioned kind, with a curb and sweep and bucket. It is there now,—the well, I mean. Of course, there's been a new curb and bucket.

"'Great Scott' says 'ee, faint like and sick at the pit of his stomach.

"All round the well in the mud and grass was the tracks of men's feet, as if there had been a hard scuffle.

"'Come here, for Lord's sake,' he called to Joel, and Joel come and seen the tracks all aimin' for the well, and on the curb the muddy print of a hand as if some one had clung there fitin' for life, and right under the curb what do you think was hangin' on a nail?"

Zacheus was very dramatic and eloquent by this time, and pointed his forefinger at Craig, who was himself a good deal shaken, and answered under his breath, "Mr. Dalton's hat!"

"Oh, my land," Zacheus ejaculated, in some disgust. "A stovepipe hat on a broken nail! No, *sir!* The hat was found on the head of the vally's brother, and on the nail was a piece of Mr. Dalton's linen coat that everybody knew, and in the well stickin' up out of the water and kinder lodged on the stones was one of his boots with his foot in it! Joel was that faint when he seen it that the bartender had to hold on to him to keep him from pitchin' head fust inter the well.

"'Here's murder,' says'ee. 'Mari, come here.'

"She come, with her knees knockin' together and a lump in her throat as big as a goose aig.

"'Mari,' says'ee, 'where did you git water for breakfast?'

"'From the spring, over there,' pointin' to the orchard. 'Miss Dalton said she'd rather have the water from there, 'cause that in the well was low,' says Mari, her tongue so thick she could hardly talk.

"'Have you often got water from there,' says Joel.

"'No,' says Mari, and 'Yes, very often,' says Miss Dalton.

"She had come out to where the tracks was in the mud, and was white now as her gown and leanin' on to Mari.

"'Miss Dalton,' says Joel, 'your husband is in the well.'

"Then she screeched so loud that some of the neighbors heard her and come runnin' to see what was the matter, while she made as if she'd throw herself over the curb, but Joel catched her by her clothes and pulled her back.

"'Oh, John, John. Is he dead? Get him out, somebody,' she cried.

"'That's what we are goin' to do. Who'll go down after him?' Joel said, and, as no one offered, he pulled off his shoes and stockin's, and, tyin' a rope round his waist, went down himself, clingin' to the slippery stones, and got him up dead as a door-nail, with the marks of two big hands round his throat, as if he had been seized and choked till the life was out of him, and then been chucked into the well as the nearest place to hide him."

At this point Uncle Zacheus became so excited and agitated that he was obliged to wait a few minutes before describing more of the terrible scenes which shook the little village of Ridgefield to its depths that summer morning, when the dead man lay upon the grass in his dripping garments, a bruise on his forehead where he must have struck a stone in his fall, and a look of horror in his wide-open eyes as he lay with his face upturned to the sky.

"Oh, John, who could have done this?" Mrs. Dalton moaned, as she knelt beside him, her arms across his chest and her long curls falling over his swollen features.

Unnoticed by any one, the little boy, Robbie, had crept down the doorsteps and came toddling across the yard to the group by the well.

"Papa, mam-ma," he said, laying one hand on his mother's head and the other on his father's wet hair. "Papa, wake up. I's 'f'aid," he said, shaking the drops of water from his fingers and beginning to cry.

"'Twas awful," Uncle Zach said, resuming the story and dwelling at length upon the picture of the little boy stooping over his dead father and trying to wake him up. "Yes, 'twas awful, and, though I'll bet I've told the story over a hundred times, if I have once, I can never get over that part without somethin' stickin' in my throat and thinkin' what if it had been Johnny and me, with Dot makin' b'lieve. Oh—h," and he groaned aloud;—then continued: "'Oh, please somebody find the murderers,' Miss Dalton said; and Joel answered: 'You bet we will. We know 'em,' and he winked at the bartender.

"They'd got the coroner there and half the town come with him, for the news flew like lightnin', and the yard was full, and the fence was full,—the folks fightin' to git sight of the tracks in the mud, and the well and the mark of a hand on the curb and the piece of his coat on a nail, and when they couldn't do that they went and looked at the wheel tracks where the buggy turned in the lane, and then went back and fit agin to see the well. The women was mostly in the house where Miss Dalton sat wringin' her hands soft as wool and covered with rings, her white gown bedraggled with mud and her hair flyin' over her face, makin' her look like a crazy critter. I tell you she stimulated grief so well that she could almost have deceived the very elect, and folks at fust didn't know what to think. That Mr. Dalton had been killed was sure, and the verdict was wilful murder by somebody, and in less than ten minutes a posse of men with Joel and the constable started full run for Worcester. At a livery stable there they heard that a hoss driv' nearly to death had come in towards mornin'. Who brought him the stable man didn't know. It wa'n't the one who hired him the afternoon before, but he paid the bill,—a big one, too,—the hoss was so used up, and he wore a stovepipe hat. That was Mr. Dalton's, and the man was the vally's brother. I b'lieve I could have planned better than they did, for they left their tracks so plain behind 'em that before sundown they was all three under arrest and an officer on the way to Ridgefield to keep an eye on Miss Dalton and Mari. They found Mr. Dalton's gold watch in the vally's pocket and his wallet and twenty-five dollars in the pocket of the vally's brother. St. John was at a hotel with a cigar in his mouth, readin' a paper as cool as you please and mighty indignant at being suspected of murder. He pretended to be awfully shocked at the news. Dalton was his best friend, he said, and he'd no more harm him than he would himself. He knew nothing about the movements of the vally or his brother. He was at the hotel all night and could prove it. This was true, but the vally's brother gin him away by sayin' to him low, but so as to be heard. 'We sink or swim together; that was the bargain, and I've papers to prove it.' They found 'em on him, too, and the three was clapped into jail, and Joel and his men and the officer got back some time in the night to Ridgefield, which next mornin' was all up in arms wus than the day before.

"My grandmother lived here, and she said half the women was runnin' the street bareheaded, and some with their sleeves up and their kitchen aprons on, tellin' the news of the arrest to them who hadn't heard it, and then makin' a bee line for the Dalton house, where Miss Dalton still set in her muddy white gown, with her hair streamin' down her back, and she as cold and white as a block of marble. She'd set up all night; they couldn't make her go to bed, and when the men got back and she heard St. John was took, she turned blue, but never spoke nor stirred. In the room with her was the officer watchin' her and Mari, who was in hysterics most of the time. They'd laid Mr. Dalton out beautiful in his best clothes, and Miss Dalton had been in to see him. They tried to shet his eyes, but couldn't, and they was wide open, starin' at you, and when Miss Dalton see 'em she cried: 'Oh, John, John, don't look at me like that,' and fell down in a swound, and they didn't know for a spell but she was dead.

"They made him the biggest funeral Ridgefield ever seen, and folks come for miles and miles around. Why, Joel took in for drinks and keepin' horses more'n he'd took for months. 'Twas better than general trainin', or a cattle show for him. Miss Dalton sat like a stone with folks starin' at her as if they'd never seen her before, and that strange man always close to her. When she got back from the grave she was that wilted they had to carry her into the house and put her on the bed, where she lay, never movin', nor speakin', only moanin', like some dumb critter in pain.

"They took her next day, and the screetch she gin when they told her she was arrested was so awful that folks in the road heard it; then she froze up ag'in, except when she looked at her little boy. They say 'twas touchin', and made 'em all cry when she bid him good-bye, with him a sayin', 'Take, mam-ma; take me,' and clingin' to her dress she had on,—the silk one Mr. Dalton had bought her and the gold beads round her neck."

Here Uncle Zacheus' feelings so overcame him a second time that he could scarcely finish the story, and tell of Mrs. Dalton's farewell to her baby and home and Maria, against whom there did not seem sufficient evidence to warrant her arrest. She would be needed as a witness later, and was left with the child whom Mrs. Dalton entrusted to her, saying, as she took his little hands from her dress and put them in Maria's, "It is preposterous to believe they can find me guilty. But if the worst happens, and I never come back, take good care of Robbie, and tell him all the good you know of his mother."

Then like some tragic queen she turned to the officer, and, with a proud toss of her head, said to him, "Sir, I am ready."

She was all in black, with no color about her except the beads and her luxuriant golden hair, which showed under her widow's bonnet like a gleam of yellow sunshine as she was driven away from the home she was never to see again. The trial which came on quickly did not last long. There were not many witnesses, and few were needed, the case was so plain. Maria was on the stand until she lost her wits entirely, and what she said one minute she contradicted the next. Only one point of any importance was brought out by her evidence. Mrs. Dalton's name was Christina, which her husband shortened into 'Tina, and Maria testified that on the night of the murder, after she heard a man's voice speaking to Mrs. Dalton, she thought she heard, or dreamed that she did, some one call " 'Tina, 'Tina," in what she described "a gugglin'" voice, like one in distress or choking.

Up to this point Mrs. Dalton had sat with her face unveiled, her youthful beauty enhanced by her widow's weeds and her bright hair, telling upon the sympathy of the spectators. But when Maria repeated the name "Tina," as it must have been called that awful night by her dying husband, she covered her face with her hands and moaned, "Oh, Maria, in mercy stop before I go mad."

Then Maria broke down and was taken from the room for a time, nor could any amount of questioning afterwards wring from her a confession that she ever observed anything wrong between Mrs. Dalton and St. John. He liked her,—she liked him,—and they played and sang together a good deal when Mr. Dalton was home, and more, perhaps, when he wasn't. There was, however, sufficient evidence to convict Mrs. Dalton without Maria's. The papers referred to by the man called by Uncle Zacheus the "vally's brother," and whose real name was Davis,—a recent convict from state's prison,—contained a promise from St. John to pay Davis and his comrade, Brown, another convict, one thousand dollars to get Mr. Dalton out of the way. Davis, who, in spite of his unprepossessing appearance, was the least hardened of the two men, confessed that several plans had been suggested and talked over and abandoned, until he was getting tired and would have given up but for the thousand dollars, five hundred of which Mrs. Dalton had agreed to pay. The visit to Ridgefield that night was an accident. The horse had been hired to go to an intermediate town. On reaching it Brown had suggested going to Ridgefield to see how the land lay, as he expressed it. On hearing from Mrs. Dalton that her husband was at the hotel, and that she was expecting him home when the storm was over, they decided that this was their opportunity, as no one knew they were in town, and, waiting in the darkness and rain, they accomplished their work. Taken as he was by surprise, Mr. Dalton uttered no cry as they grasped his throat, except the words "'Tina, 'Tina," while the 'Tina called for gave no sign if she heard it.

She said she didn't, but few believed her. The evidence against her as an accessory to the murder was sufficient to convict her, and with the three men she was sentenced to be hung. Efforts were made to commute her punishment to imprisonment for life, but public opinion was strong against her, and with her coadjutors in the crime she suffered the penalty of the law.

After the execution, which was public and which hundreds attended, a half brother of Mr. Dalton came to look after the property in the interest of his nephew. In accordance with Mrs. Dalton's request repeated to Maria, who visited her once in her cell, the latter took charge of the little boy during his childhood, and for some time lived alone with him in the house, bravely fighting her nervous dread of the room where the body had lain, and her terror on wild, rainy nights when she fancied she heard her master's voice calling "'Tina, 'Tina" through the storm,—the sound of a scuffle near the well, and the wheels on the grass as the murderers drove away. At last, overmastered by her fear, she left the house and the town, taking the child with her and going to Canada where her friends were living.

Gradually the tragedy ceased to be talked about, except when revived by stories that the house was haunted. It was rented at first, then sold by Robbie, who, after attaining his majority, came once to Ridgefield and was described as a fine-looking young man, much like his father.

There had been a stone placed at his father's grave, but
none at his mother's, nor did he order one. He was there
to sell his property, and he sold it and went away, while
family after family occupied the house. If they did not
believe in the supernatural they heard nothing. If they
did believe in it they heard a great deal; a struggle by the
well at midnight when the rain was falling heavily and
the sky was inky black; a sound of wheels upon the grass;
a choking call for 'Tina; stealthy footsteps across the
floor, as if in response to that call 'Tina had gone to the
window and looked out; and a child's cry for papa and
mamma, which came at any time, day or night. The
mamma lay in her unmarked sunken grave and the papa
under the shadow of the south wall in Ridgefield cemetery. Robert became a husband, a father and a grandfather, and he, too, died. Years passed and every actor in
that tragic scene was dead, but its memory was kept alive
by the house fast going to decay. For a long time it was
unoccupied, and "For Sale" nailed upon the door, while
the storms and the boys played havoc with it, inside and
out. Then Mark Hilton, the clerk at the Prospect House,
and great-grandson of Mr. Dalton, bought it for a song.
He called it his ancestral hall, and said when he married
he should bring his bride there and quiet 'Tina's ghost,
which still haunted it, clad in a soiled white dress, with
her long curls down her back. He straightened up her
grave and put a plain headstone to it with just her name,
Christina Dalton, upon it. Some people censured him
for this, and twice he found the stone lying upon the
ground face down, where it had been thrown by some
malicious or mischievous person. Without a word of
comment he put it in its place, and whatever pain or humiliation he felt for his ancestor he made no sign, and
held his head as high as if, through the vista of nearly a

hundred years, no dark crime was looming which could in any possible way touch his good name. He had come to Ridgefield as a teacher from Amherst College, where he had been for two years, and had taken his place among the best people of the town. Once or twice, after correcting an unruly boy, he found a chalk picture of a gallows on the blackboard in the morning, and, instead of rubbing it out, he drew a fair likeness of the boy artist dangling by the rope and left it there all day. There were no more insulting pictures upon the board, and his pupils treated him with great respect. But school teaching was not to his taste, and he finally gave it up and hired to Mr. Taylor, who was never tired of eulogizing him, and who finished his story of the Dalton house by saying: "There's no more hereditary in Mark than there is in me. No, sir! His folks lived in New Bedford. Father was a sea captain and drowned; mother died a natural death, and left him a little money; not much, and he's willin' to do anything for an honest livin.' If there's anything in envirymen' he's got it strong. Mari brought up his grandfather Robert and had him go to college. He was here once. The Daltons was high bloods and never took much notice of him on account of his mother. But, bless your soul, he wasn't to blame for her any more than Mark is. Mari, who married in Canada, was a good woman, and great-great-grandmother to Jeff, who acts at times as if possessed with the devil; has some habits I don't like, but he'll git over 'em, for he's a good boy on the whole,—well meanin' and friendly. His name is Jefferson Wilkes. His folks is all dead and he was jest a wafer on the streets in Boston, turnin' somersets for a penny a turn and sleepin' in a big hogshead on the wharf at night when Mark found him. He'd kep' track of Mari's pedigree, tracin' 'em down to the boy and was huntin' for him. He asked Dot to take him, and said if he didn't earn his board he'd pay the rest. He'll get plenty of envirymen' here, for Dot makes him toe the mark, especially Sundays, learnin' the catechism and verses in the Bible, and boxes his ears when he don't behave. Mark laughs and gives him a stick of candy for every box. Pays for it, though. He's honesty itself. I'd trust him with all I own."

"Yes, Dotty. I'll be there," he added, as there came 'round the corner a call to which he always paid attention. "I'll be back in a few minutes and tell you the rest," he said, as he hurried away in the direction of the call.

CHAPTER VI.

EXPECTED GUESTS.

It was fifteen minutes or more before he returned, and taking his seat, began: "Dot is so flurried and upset about them Tracys that she actually consulted me. You know they are comin' to-night?"

"Who is coming?" Craig asked, rather relieved with a change from the Daltons to the Tracys.

"Why, Miss Freeman Tracy, from New York," Uncle Zach replied. "Her grandfather was Gen. Allen, one of our big bugs,—lived in the house with the biggest brass knocker, and has that tall monument in the cemetery. She's comin,' and that's why the west wing is bottom side up, and Dot don't kow whether she's on her head or her feet. It's somethin' to brag about havin' Miss Tracy here. She wrote for a saloon to eat in. We've gin her the west parlor and four bedrooms for herself and daughter and niece and maid. None of 'em can sleep together. Nobody can nowadays. They are comin' to-night, on the eight train."

Craig had been greatly interested in the Dalton story, though a little confused at the last, with so much heredity and environment and so many great-great-grandfathers. Still he managed to get a pretty good idea of it and was deciding in his mind to visit the old house again and go through the rooms where 'Tina's ghost was said to walk on stormy nights. At the mention of Mrs. Tracy, who was coming with two young ladies, his thoughts were directed into a different channel.

"I think I have heard of Mrs. Tracy. Is she very wealthy?" he asked.

"Yes, piles of money, with diamond earrings as big as robins' aigs. I've never seen 'em, but some woman from here was at Saratoga last summer, and said they was the talk of the town, and she never let 'em out of her sight. I hope she'll bring 'em. I never seen such stuns. I wonder what they cost, and what do you s'pose she wants of a maid here, when we cook her victuals and serve it?"

Craig did not reply. He was thinking of Mrs. Tracy and her daughter, who was a great belle and notorious flirt. He had heard of them at Saratoga as occupying the finest suite of rooms at the United States, where the daughter kept around her a crowd of gentlemen, whom she attracted or repelled as the fancy took her. He had only seen her at a distance, when it was impossible to tell just how she looked, nor did he care for a closer acquaintance, and when asked to call upon her had declined to do so. He detested flirts, and was not particularly interested in girls of any kind. Certainly not in Miss Tracy. Still he was glad she was coming. It would be a change, and he was getting tired with no company but Browning. There was no possible danger of his falling a victim to her wiles. He was not a ladies' man, and if he were, a coquette of Miss Tracy's style would be the last woman he should select for a wife. Of the niece he scarcely thought at all, except to ask Uncle Zach her name. Zacheus didn't know. Mrs. Tracy telegraphed that morning that she was coming, and there must be a room for her.

"Probably a poor relation," came into Craig's mind, and the niece was dismissed from it. The daughter, however, occupied a good share of his thoughts as the day wore on, and moving his seat from the north piazza to the south, he watched the settling of the west wing, which the Tracys were to occupy, with a good deal of interest. Once, in passing him, Mark stopped and said: "You would suppose the queen of England was coming instead of a woman with nothing to recommend her but money, or family, which sometimes counts more than money."

He spoke a little bitterly, and Craig wondered if he were thinking of his own tarnished heritage. If it is possible for the future to turn backward and touch those whom its events are to influence, it would seem as if it had done so with Craig and Mark. Both were exceedingly restless that afternoon, and their restlessness manifested itself differently. Mark went to the cemetery, —a very unusual thing for him,—and stood by Tina's grave and looked at the headstone, with only "Christina Dalton" upon it, and for a few moments rebelled against the fate which had linked him with the dead woman at his feet. He had heard the whole story of the tragedy; not one particular had been omitted in the telling of it to him, and now, as he went over it in imagination, he took a different view of it from what he had ever done before. Any thing like heredity had never troubled him, the relationship was so remote. But the possibility came to him now, and he said to himself: "Her blood is in my veins,—strongly diluted,—but it is there, and under provocation might work me harm if I yielded to it. But I will not. I'll be a man for a' that. She was only my great-grandmother, or great-great-grandmother, which was it? Poor 'Tina. Perhaps she was not guilty. She said she was not, except for liking another man better than her husband. Other women have done that."

The year before he had planted a white rose at Mr. Dalton's grave. It was the running species, and one long arm had reached out and twined itself around 'Tina's headstone, on the top of which was a half opened rose nestled among a quantity of leaves. Mark was fond of flowers, and cut the rose carefully from its stalk, intending to put it in the office.

"I guess there's nothing of 'Tina about it," he said, as he picked a few leaves and weeds from the grass on her grave, examined the stone to see if it were secure, and then returned to the hotel.

Craig had been differently employed. He always made some changes in his toilet before supper, and this afternoon he took a little more pains with it than usual, although it was not likely that he would see the ladies that night. As his mother was gone, he took his supper alone, and with his quick eye saw that two or three pieces of china and glass were missing. He might not have given it a second thought if he had not heard Mr. Taylor telling a boarder that the rooms for Miss Tracy were in apple pie order, and the table set for supper in the *saloon*, with the best linen and china and silver. The missing articles were accounted for. They were adorning the table in the *saloon*. Boston had gone down in the scale, and New York was in the ascendant.

"I don't object," he thought, "so long as she leaves us a china tea cup. I should not like those thick things I see on some of the tables."

After his supper he went round to the west piazza, and, walking up and down, glanced into the room where the table was laid for three, and looked very inviting with its snowy linen, china and glass. He recognized the cream jug and sugar bowl which had done duty for his mother and himself, and was glad they were there. It seemed right and proper that the Tracys, as new-comers, should take the precedence. He was getting quite interested in them, and when he saw there were no flowers on the table he asked Sarah, the house-maid, if she had forgotten them.

"We hain't any but flag lilies, and I didn't know as they'd be pretty. I'll pick some if you say so," she said.

He knew she meant the fleurs-de-lis, of which he had seen great clumps from his window. They were blue,—his color,—and he followed Sarah to the garden, where she gathered a large bunch of the lilies together with some young ferns growing near them.

"They do look pretty," she said, admiring the effect, as she placed them in the centre of the table. "Be you acquainted with the ladies?"

"No, I am not, but I know city people like to find fresh flowers in their rooms when they go into the country," Craig replied, and then, as it was nearly time for his mother's train from East Ridgefield, he went to meet her.

As he was walking with her up the long hill from the station he told her of the expected arrivals, and asked if she had ever seen the ladies.

"Once when I called on some friends at the United

States, in Saratoga, the mother and daughter were in the parlors, and were pointed out to me. I remember thinking them very showily dressed, and that Mrs. Tracy's diamond earrings were quite too large for good taste. The daughter had half a dozen young men around her," was Mrs. Mason's reply, and her chin gave a tilt in the air, which Craig knew was indicative of her disapproval of the Tracys.

Craig told her of Mrs. Taylor's elation on account of her distinguished guests, and of the removal of the cream jug and sugar bowl from the table to the salon.

"Boston is nowhere, and we may come down to two-tined forks and plated spoons," he said laughingly, while his mother laughed in return.

She had no anxiety about the forks or the spoons, but she was a little anxious with regard to the young lady, of whose outrageous coquetry she had heard a great deal, and, mother-like, she dropped a word of warning.

"No danger for me," Craig said. "Forewarned is forearmed, but I am glad she is coming. We want something to brighten us up."

Meanwhile Mark Hilton had also made the tour of the west piazza, and glanced in at the table with its centrepiece of fleurs-de-lis and ferns.

"I didn't know you had so much taste," he said to Sarah, who was putting some napkins at the plates.

"'Twasn't me; 'twas Mr. Mason thought of it," Sarah replied, and Mark was conscious of a feeling of not wishing to be outdone by Craig.

"I'll contribute my moiety," he thought, and bringing the rose from the office, he placed it on the table.

It was very fragrant, and filled the room with perfume, and Mark smiled as he thought: "They can't help noticing it, but will not know it came from 'Tina's grave."

EXPECTED GUESTS. 55

It lacked but half an hour of the time for the New York train. The scorching heat of the day had given place to a feeling of rain. In the west great banks of clouds had obscured the setting sun, while growls of thunder, growing louder and nearer, heralded the storm, which came on so fast that by the time the hotel carriage was ready for the station the wind was blowing a gale, and the rain falling in torrents.

"Great guns!" Uncle Zacheus exclaimed as he saw one of the horses rear on his hind feet when a peal of thunder, which shook the house, broke over its head. "If Jake hain't got out the bloods! They are as 'fraid of thunder and lightnin' as they can be. He can't hold 'em a minit. Somebody'll have to go with him and see to the ladies. Mark, do you feel like it?"

"Certainly," Mark answered, and Craig saw him in the hall a few minutes later habited in his mackintosh and wide-rimmed hat, which shed water like an umbrella.

Owing to the storm the train was late, and Mrs. Taylor was greatly worried lest her broiled chicken and coffee should be spoiled. She had put on her second best dress, with a pretty little cap and lavender bow, and with her white apron looked the embodiment of the buxom landlady, as she hovered between the kitchen and the salon and the front door, giving a sharp reproof to Jeff, who came sliding down the banister, nearly upsetting her as, with a summersault, he landed on his feet. Jeff was also interested in the expected guests, and if the future had stretched backward and touched both Mark and Craig, it had grasped him as well, making him seem more possessed than ever as he rolled around the house wherever there was room for his athletics.

"There they be," he exclaimed, as the carriage drove

up with Mark on the box, the water dripping from his hat and coat, for it was still raining heavily.

With a bound he sprang to the ground just as Jeff came darting out with an umbrella and opened the carriage door. On the walk were pools of water, and Mark's feet splashed in them as he stepped to the side of Jeff just as one of the ladies put her head from the door and then, with a cry of dismay, drew back.

"I can never go through all that water; it is actually a pond," she said, and Mrs. Taylor, who was holding a lamp in the door, felt sure that the voice belonged to the matron of the party.

"Let me assist you," Mark said, and, taking her in his arms, he ran up the walk with her and deposited her in the hall.

A second foot was on the carriage step when he went back,—a very small foot,—though to which of the young ladies it belonged he could not tell. He had seen neither distinctly at the station, it was raining so hard, but he felt intuitively that it was Miss Helen whom Jeff was advising to keep still till Mr. Hilton came to fetch her.

"Oh, thanks; don't drop me, please," she said, putting her arms around his neck as if afraid of falling.

He felt her breath through the dampness of the night, and as Mrs. Taylor just then held her lamp higher, he caught sight of two bright, laughing eyes, and if he held her a little closer than he had held the older woman, it was not strange. He was young, and she was young, and would have flirted in her coffin had she life to do it.

"I hope you are not very wet. It is a nasty night," he said, as he put her down by her mother.

"Not wet at all, thanks to your kindness; but please go back for Alice," the lady said, as he showed signs of having forgotten there was another to be cared for.

Alice didn't need him. Jeff was attending to her.

"I don't want to be lifted. I'm not afraid of a little wetting; but hold the umbrella over me. I shouldn't like to spoil my hat," she said, and, gathering up her dress, she ran swiftly into the house, followed by a girl, presumably the maid, as she carried several bags and began to talk to the ladies in what to Jeff was an unknown tongue.

Mrs. Mason's rooms were on the other side of the hotel, but Craig was in the office when the carriage drove up, and saw Mark carrying two of its occupants into the house, and saw a third dashing like a sprite through the rain under the cover of Jeff's umbrella, while the fourth followed more leisurely. Bidding Uncle Zach good-night, he went to his mother's room and said to her: "The Tracys have come."

CHAPTER VII.

THE TRACYS.

On a morning in June, before our story opens, Mrs. Freeman Tracy sat in her breakfast room looking over the papers, hoping to find some advertisement for a pleasant and inexpensive place in which to spend the summer. She had just returned from Europe, and her twelve trunks were not yet all unpacked. So far as real estate, houses and lands were concerned she was rich, but some of the investments on which she depended largely for ready money had failed, and she felt the necessity of retrenching for a time.

"Yes, mamma, but not here; let's wait till we get home

and are tired and glad to go into some poky little hole," her daughter Helen said, when it was suggested to her that they take a less expensive suite of rooms in Paris than they were looking at.

In Florence, where they had spent most of the winter, they had occupied a handsome villa and entertained and been entertained on a grand scale. Horses and carriages and servants in livery had been at their command without stint, and Helen had been the belle of the season. Wherever she went she had taken precedence as the beautiful American to whom both her own countrymen and foreigners paid tribute. If a perfect form and features and brilliant complexion constitute beauty, she was pre-eminently beautiful, with the added charm of a seeming unconsciousness of her beauty. But it was only seeming. She knew her own value perfectly, and had spent much time in cultivating that naturalness and sweetness of manner which seldom failed when its object was to win either attention, admiration or love. Her cousin Alice said of her that a smile or a wink from her eyes would bring any man to her feet, no matter how callous he might be to another lady's charms. To be surrounded by a crowd of young men, each one of whom was struggling for a chance to propose, while she skillfully kept him at bay, was a pastime in which she delighted, and in which she had been tolerably successful. At twenty-two she had received twenty offers, and could count at least twenty more who would have proposed had she given them a chance. She had their names in a blue and gold book which she called her "Blue Book." Those who had proposed were in one column, and those who wanted to in another, with certain marks against them indicative of their standing in her estimation and the possibility of her winking them back if the fancy took her. There was also a third column with a few names of those whom she did not know, and whom she greatly desired to know. Heading this list was "Craig Mason, Boston; old family; woman hater; very aristocratic and reserved, and almost too refined to enjoy himself; does not wish to know me; does not like my style. Should very much like a chance to wink at him, as Alice expresses it."

This entry was made the year before when she was at Saratoga, and nearly every young man from the different hotels had called upon her except Craig. He had been asked to do so by a friend, and had replied: "No, thanks; Miss Tracy is not my style."

This in due time was reported to her, and although she gave no sign, it rankled deeply. She made no effort to meet him after that, and only saw him driving his famous horse, Dido, with his mother, who, she had heard, was very proud of her position as Mrs. Mason, and very watchful lest her son should make a mesalliance, or indeed an alliance of any kind. With her mother she was rather tired of travel. She had had a good deal of dissipation in Florence and Paris and London; had added a few names to her blue book, and had come home heart whole and exceedingly glad to be there.

"If it were the thing to do, and I hadn't so many new dresses to show, I'd rather stay here all summer than go dragging around to the same places, stopping at the same hotels and meeting the same people, who say the same tiresome things," she said to her mother as they were taking their breakfast at home after their return from abroad.

In this state of mind it was easier than it was in Europe for her to fall in with her mother's proposal that they find some quiet place in which to spend a few weeks.

"If it is very dull we can leave at any time, and I may accept Mr. Prescott yet; I haven't quite decided," she said, as she sipped her chocolate, while her mother looked over the papers in quest of advertisements.

Mr. Prescott was the last man Helen had refused, but she had done it in such a way that she felt sure a word from her would bring him back. She always had some one on the leash in this way, marked in her book with a big interrogation, "so as to run no risk of being an old maid," she said to her cousin Alice, who was her confidant in her love affairs, and knew the three sets of men whose names were in her "Blue Book" as possibles and impossibles.

"If you are going to some out of the way place, let it be very much out of the way, where there is no danger of seeing people, or being made love to. I'm so tired of it, and I really begin to think it is wicked. Alice says it is. Dear little chick; I don't suppose any one ever made love to her. Strange, too, when she is so pretty and sweet."

"And poor," Mrs. Tracy added, while Helen continued: "I don't believe that would make any difference with me. I could wink 'em up if I hadn't a dollar. I'd like to pose once as a penniless maiden and see."

"What nonsense," Mrs. Tracy replied, and then suddenly exclaimed: "Here it is at last,—Ridgefield! My grandfather's old home. Strange I've never thought of that place. Listen," and she read aloud Mark Hilton's advertisement of the Prospect House.

Mrs. Tracy, who had been in Ridgefield when a child, had some very pleasant recollections of the town, with its river and ponds and hills, which Mark described so eloquently. The palatial hotel, with its modern improvements, must be something new, she thought, as she had no remembrance of it. But times change, and Ridgefield undoubtedly kept pace with the times, and Mrs. Tracy thought she would like to go there, and said so to her daughter.

"Your grandfather was the leading man in the town, and we should undoubtedly be lionized by the people," she suggested, while Helen shrugged her shoulders and replied: "Oh, mamma, do let me indulge in a bit of slang and say *dry up* on lionizing. I'm tired of it. If you want to go to Ridgefield I am quite willing. I only hope there isn't a newspaper there, nor a reporter, to write up the beautiful Miss Helen Tracy; nor a man to make love to her. Such a state of things would be Heaven for a few weeks; then I should pine for the flesh pots of Egypt. Go to Ridgefield by all means. I'm in love with its scenery as set forth in the paper, especially the haunted house, which makes me feel a little creepy. Did you ever hear of it when you were there?"

Mrs. Tracy replied that she was almost too young to have such things make an impression upon her when she was in Ridgefield, but she believed she did hear of such a house and passed it with her grandfather,—a big old brown house at the end of a lane.

"Delicious! The very place for us. Write at once," Helen urged, and her mother wrote to Mr. Taylor that morning, engaging rooms for herself, daughter and maid, and in two days' time the postman brought her Uncle Zacheus' wonderful production, which Helen read aloud with peals of laughter and running comments on his composition, orthography and honesty. "Perfectly rich," she cried. "Rivers and ponds and meadows and hills and views and graves a hundred years old and a haunted house and a cellar hole where a garrison stood,

I believe I've read about that, haven't I? Alice would know. She's up in history. And then the house; clean sheets,—think of it! All the towels we want! He don't know that I use about a dozen a day. Silver forks, solid, not plated! That is something new for a hotel. Bread that Dotty makes, and washes her hands every time she turns round. Good for the bread; bad for the hands. Big rooms, with a rocking chair in each one. Glad of that. You won't be getting mine. No real suites. He spelled it *sweets*. Dear old man! I shall fall in love with him if he doesn't with me. Only two faucets, and those under the stairs. Can have a *saloon* to eat in. Good! That comes of your confusing him with *salon*. Watched with your grandfather, and helped at the funeral. That must make him related to us. Yes, mother, sweets or no sweets, faucets or no faucets, we'll go, and I'll write and tell him so."

She wrote the letter which Uncle Zach put away in his hair trunk, and after it was gone turned suddenly to her mother and said: "By the way, now is your chance to carry out your promise to Cousin Alice. You have always been going to take her somewhere with us, and have never done it, because it would make our expenses heavier. Ridgefield is cheap. A whole week will not cost much more than one day sometimes did when we had the best rooms in the hotel. Let me invite Alice to go with us. Just think how poky and forlorn her life must be in that stuffy little schoolhouse among the mountains, with those children smelling of the factory and things. Can I write to her? She's such good company and so helpful every way."

After a little hesitancy Mrs. Tracy consented, and Helen was soon dashing off the following letter:

"New York, July — 18—.

"Dear Allie:—

"Here we are home again; landed five days ago, and I have such a love of a gown for you in some of my trunks. Cream colored, china silk, with puffings of lace and ribbons and everything. I had a gloriously good time abroad. Went everywhere,—saw everything,—was told a hundred times how handsome I was and how strange that I didn't seem to know it! 'The one beautiful woman I have met who is not conscious of her beauty,' I heard an Englishman say to mamma. Oh! oh! oh! As if I didn't look in the glass every time I pass it and say to the face I see there 'You are lovely, but never give any sign that you know it, for this innocent baby way succeeds as well as your good looks. Not know it indeed!' I have some new names in the blue book. One with a big interrogation point. 'Walter Prescott, New York?' That is the way it reads. His is the 20th bona fide offer, and mamma was furious when I refused him. Says I'll go through the woods and take up with a crooked stick. Maybe I shall, but I tell you what; I am getting tired of seeing men turn white when I say no, and fencing to keep others from compelling me to say no. I am going to turn over a new leaf, and not wink, nor smile, nor try to get any one to look at me; and after a while marry Mr. Prescott and lead a perfectly domestic life. He neither dances, nor smokes, nor drinks, nor drives fast horses, nor likes society any way. Prefers a quiet home life, with his wife and his books. Is a great reader. I shall have to take up a course of study with you if I am to be Mrs. Prescott. I am a perfect dunce now and hardly know who discovered America, or shouldn't if I hadn't seen Columbus' statue in Genoa.

"But to come to the object of this letter. Did you

ever hear of Ridgefield? No? Well, that shows a lack in your education. It's a lovely town, famous principally because my grandfather, Gen. Allen, lived and died and is buried there, and Zacheus Taylor watched with him the night he died and keeps the Prospect House, a perfectly delicious house, with all the towels you want, and silver forks and two faucets and blooded horses, Paul and Virginia, all of which and more is set forth in the letter I enclose from the dear old man. I don't care much for the country,—the real article I mean,—with its dusty roads and horn bugs and worms and stupid people, aping last year's fashions, but something draws me to Ridgefield, and mamma and I are going there to spend the summer and rest and get back some of the good looks I lost being so gay abroad and so seasick coming home. And *you* are to go with us. Mamma says so, and I am writing to tell you to meet us in Springfield, July —, in the afternoon. No dress needed. I shall not take much, and if there should be a quilting, or sewing society, or church social you'll have that love of a gown I bought for you in Paris and which I shall bring.

"Only think, what a gorgeous time we'll have, just ourselves. You and I, and not a man to bother. There may be a bartender or something, I presume there is, but he don't count. Nobody to dress for, or pose for, or keep myself always with the same angelic expression. No need of the blue book. Guess I shall leave it at home unless you want to see the new names in it. One, a poor insipid lad, who asked me point-blank how much mamma was worth. I told him 500,000, meaning pennies, but he understood it dollars, and at once offered me his title in exchange. I laughed in his face and he looked astonished."

Here Helen was interrupted by her maid bringing her

a letter the postman had just left. It was from a girl friend living in Boston, who had returned from abroad in the same vessel. After the usual chitchat of girls who have seen the same places and know the same people, she wrote, "Boston is like a graveyard. Everybody out of town and some in the most unheard-of places. By the way, you don't know the Masons, so their whereabouts has no interest for you. I can't endure them, they are so stuck up and prim, but they are the Masons for all that, and their doings of importance. Well, they have gone to a little inland town,—Ridgefield is the name,—to spend the summer, and I dare say are very happy there, as no *canaille* can brush against them, and Mrs. Mason will not be shocked by what she calls second-class in young people who are just lively, and she will not be afraid some girl will look at Craig. Pity you never had a chance at him."

Helen did not read any further for joy. She had so longed for a chance at Craig and now she was to have it. Her friend did not say that he was at the Prospect House, but unquestionably he was. At all events he was in the town, which was not like Saratoga, and her good resolutions melted like wax.

Resuming her letter to Alice, she wrote:

"I broke off abruptly to read a letter from Belle Sherman, who was with us in Europe and lives in Boston. And what do you think? Craig Mason is in Ridgefield, presumably at the Prospect House, and I—well, I am going on the war path just once more before I reform, as I intended to do. You remember I wrote you about him last summer when I was in Saratoga. He was the only young man of any account who did not pay me some attention. He ignored me, and, *entre nous*, I mean to pay him off for saying I was not his style. What is his style, I wonder? If I only knew I could soon adapt myself to it. You'll have to find out and coach me. You have a way which makes people show themselves to you as they are, while with me there is always something held back, as if we were playing hide and seek. *Entre nous* again. I don't know about Mr. Prescott. It seems as if fate were leading me to Ridgefield and Craig Mason. He is a most desirable *parti*, and mother would be in a state of beatitude to be allied with the Masons of Boston. Ah, well, *nous verrons*. How Frenchy I am. Bad French, Celine, my maid, would say, with admirable frankness.

"Now, remember, I rely on you to help me in every way with this Sphinx until I can say '*Veni, Vidi, Vici.*' Latin, as well as French. I am rather learned after all. Write at once and say you will meet us in Springfield.

"Lovingly, but on mischief bent,

"Your cousin, Helen."

"P. S. I shall take *some* of my best clothes, and you better put in your trunk a book or two of such literature and poetry as you think adapted to my capacity in case the Sphinx proves bookish like Mr. Prescott.

"Again adieu,

"Helen."

CHAPTER VIII.

ALICE.

THE hot sun of a July afternoon was pouring in at the west windows of a little red schoolhouse among the mountains between Springfield and Albany. It was the last day of the term and as was the custom in district schools in New England the Committee men had been in to see what progress the scholars had made and to pronounce upon it at the close of the exercises. It was examination day and looked forward to with as much interest and anxiety by the teacher and pupils as are the commencements in larger institutions. To the red schoolhouse among the mountains had come this afternoon the minister, the doctor, the lawyer with several other visitors, parents and relatives of the children who had acquitted themselves so creditably that only words of commendation were spoken by the lawyer and doctor and minister when each in turn made remarks.

Rocky Point was to be congratulated upon having secured the services of so competent a teacher as Miss Tracy had proved herself to be, the lawyer said, and the doctor and clergyman acquiesced in his opinion, while the visitors bowed their approbation. Then a prayer was said, "Shall We Meet Beyond the River?" was sung, and school was dismissed. There was a scramble for books and dinner pails and sunbonnets and caps, and the children hurried away, glad that vacation had come, with no more study for many long weeks. The minister and doctor and lawyer and visitors went next after a few complimentary words to the young teacher, and the natural question as to where she intended to pass the summer. She might go to Cooperstown to visit a friend, she said, but more likely she should remain at home and help her Aunt Mary, as usual.

"I saw among the arrivals from abroad the names of your aunt, Mrs. Freeman Tracy, and her daughter, and thought you might possibly visit them," one of the ladies said.

Alice replied, "I have no expectation of visiting them, and I hardly think they will stay in New York all summer."

The ladies bowed and went out, and Alice was alone, tired and hot, and so glad her first term of teaching was over and that she had given satisfaction. Better than all was the fact that she would in a few days have thirty-six dollars of her own. It was the first money she had ever earned, and it seemed like a fortune to her. Sitting down upon one of the hard benches by an open window she began to plan what she should do with it. Give part of it to Aunt Mary to get her a new dress, and with another part buy herself some boots and gloves. Her old ones were so shabby, and she was very fastidious with regard to her hands and feet, if she were only a little country girl, living among the mountains of western Massachusetts, where city fashions did not prevail to a great extent, except as some ambitious factory girl aped them so far as she could. Alice's father, George Tracy, had been half-brother to Helen's father, Freeman Tracy, who had inherited his large fortune from his mother. George, who was ten years older than his brother, was a languid, easygoing, handsome man, with no more talent or inclination for work than a child. Twice Freeman, who was very fond of him, had set him up in business, with the result each time of a complete failure.

"No use, Free. It isn't in me to see to anything. Better give me a small allowance, if you want to do anything for such a shiftless good-for-nothing as I am, and let me shirk for myself," George said to his brother, who took him at his word and gave him not a small, but a liberal allowance, which kept him quite at his ease.

It had been Freeman's intention to make his will and leave George the income of a certain sum, but death came suddenly, before the will was made, and there was no provision for George. The whole of Freeman's large fortune went to his widow and infant daughter a few months old. Between George and his sister-in-law there did not exist the most amicable relations. She looked upon him as a dreaming neer-do-weel, through whom her husband had lost a great deal of money. Of the yearly allowance she knew nothing, and as George was too proud to enlighten her he found himself at his brother's death without money and with no means of support, unless he went to work,—a new state of things for him, as he had never in his life been really fatigued from any physical exercise. But the strain had come, and he met it by hiring as a clerk in a cotton mill in Rocky Point, where he married a beautiful young girl, who died when her baby was four weeks old. Her home had always been with her aunt and uncle, Ephraim and Mary Wood, plain, old-fashioned people, with hearts larger than their means, and hands ready to give help to all who needed it. They were very fond of their niece and very proud of her alliance with George Tracy, whom they looked upon as a prince in disguise. A poor one, it is true, but still a prince, and they gave him a home as soon as he was married, and when his young wife died and left a little girl, whom they called for its mother, they still kept him with them and never lost their high opinion of him as one whom it was an honor to have in their family. Of her father, Alice had some remembrance, as she was nearly five years old when he died suddenly, as his brother had done. Tall, well-dressed, with long, white hands, of which he took a great deal of care; always looking for a seat and always reading when he found one, was the picture she carried of him. Of her mother's personality she knew nothing, except what she heard from others, and what she gathered from an old-time photograph of a young girl with a lovely face and large, beautiful blue eyes, with a laugh in them which the bungling photographer had not been able to spoil, as he had the pose of the head and hands.

When George died Mr. Wood felt it incumbent upon him to notify Mrs. Freeman Tracy, who was at Richfield Springs, having an ideal time, she told Mrs. Wood, rather complainingly, when she came to the funeral with her daughter Helen, who was nearly three years older than Alice. It was Helen's first experience in a country farmhouse like the Woods, and some of her remarks on what she saw were not very complimentary. But Alice was too young to resent them, or understand. She admired her cousin greatly, especially her bronze boots, with their high, French heels.

"I wish I had some like 'em. Do they cost more than a dollar?" she said, with a rueful glance at her own coarser shoes.

"A dollar! I guess they do. Forty or fifty dollars at least!" Helen replied, at random, and without the slightest idea of the real cost of them or anything else.

Stooping down, she unbuttoned her boots in a trice, and, removing Alice's shoes, put her own upon a pair of feet much too short for them, for Alice was small for her years and Helen was large.

"Why, they are too big. Your feet wobble awfully in

them," Helen said, "but I'll tell you what to do. Put some cotton in 'em. Our maid Susan does, and mamma did once for me when my boots were too long. Find some, and I'll show you."

The cotton was found and the boots stuffed and pronounced a splendid fit, as Helen proceeded to button them. Suddenly it occurred to her that she had nothing to wear herself, as she couldn't begin to get her foot into Alice's shoe. With a jerk the boots came off, and, to Alice's wondering looks, she said, "I must not give 'em to you, for I can't go in my stocking feet to New York, but I'll have mamma send you some, if you can't buy 'em. You are real poor, ain't you?"

Alice didn't know whether she were poor or not. She only knew she wanted boots like these being taken from her feet and transferred to Helen's, and two great tears rolled down her cheeks as she resumed her own despised shoes.

"Don't cry," Helen said, brusquely. "I'll send you some boots and a lot of things."

She kept her word, and from time to time boots and other articles of dress,—some new and some second-hand, but quite as good as new, when Mrs. Wood's skillful fingers had made them over,—found their way to the farmhouse, and little Alice Tracy was for years the best-dressed child in Rocky Point. As the children grew older and saw each other on the very rare intervals when Mrs. Tracy stopped for a day at Rocky Point, they became very fond of each other, and Helen, who inherited her father's generous nature, was often troubled because Alice was not wealthy like herself. All that she could make her mother do for her she did, and it was owing to her influence that when Alice was fifteen she was placed in a boarding school in Albany with her cousin, who did not care for books and who managed to elude her teachers and give more spreads and have more larks and still retain her good standing than any pupil in school. At the end of the year she left, a fully fledged young lady, "with more beaux on her string," her companions said, than they all had together.

Alice stayed two years longer, and, at eighteen, went back to Rocky Point, with somewhat different views of the world from what she had when she left it. In one point, however, she was unchanged, and that was her love for the old couple, Uncle Ephraim and Aunt Mary, who had been so kind to her. If the homely ways and duties of the farm grated upon her she kept it to herself, and was the same sweet, lovable, sunny-tempered girl she had always been, putting her young strength to the wheel when the strain of work was hardest, and making the labor easier by half by the way with which she planned and executed it.

"Where does that girl get her vim and go-ahead?" the neighbors used to say, remembering her mother's frail constitution and her indolent and easy-going father.

Alice knew all about him. She had overheard a farm-hand telling another of his laziness, his selfishness and love of ease and pride, which sometimes rebelled against his plain surroundings and the people of the town, the mill-hands, the shoemakers and machinists who constituted a large proportion of the inhabitants of Rocky Point.

"I know now where I got that little mean thread in my nature. I am naturally lazy, and selfish, and proud, and sometimes grind my teeth hard at what seems common and vulgar. But I'll kill it dead," she said, with a stamp of her foot. "I'll do what my hands find to do without shrinking, and not mind the rough men whom Uncle Ephraim has on his farm."

On two or three occasions she had spent a month in New York in Mrs. Tracy's elegant house, and although she did not go a great deal into society, she went enough to get a taste for something different from her life at home. But she resolutely set her face against any repinings which might show on the surface, and was as bright and cheerful and sunny as if the rambling old farmhouse, with its low ceilings, its square beams in the corners of the rooms, and its iron door latches were a palatial residence and she the queen; and, in a way, she was queen of the place, for the old couple loved her as if she had been their own child. Nothing was too good for her, and no sacrifice they could make too great if it made her happier. In return for this she lavished upon them all the love of her ardent nature, and gave to them a helpfulness and thoughtfulness beyond her years.

Just before going to Europe Helen spent a week at the farmhouse, declaring herself ennuied to death with the dulness.

"I like being with you, of course," she said to Alice. "You rest me and bring out the best there is in me, and when I see you washing those dreadful dinner dishes and skimming the milk and pouring tea and coffee for those sweaty men who come to the table in their shirt sleeves, I hate myself for the useless piece of pottery I am, and feel tempted to try the dairy maid business like you. If I had a little *chalet* and a *petit Trianon* like Marie Antoinette I'd do it. Truly, Alice, I don't see how you endure it as you do, with nothing livelier to go to than a church social, where they play kissing games, but won't let you dance, because it is wicked, and not a single man to flirt with. I am positively getting rusty for some male to wink at!"

Alice laughed and replied, "I believe you'd flirt with the undertaker if you could get your eyes on him. Why, you have winked at every sweaty man on the farm, and there isn't one of them who doesn't brighten up the minute you appear in your stunning gowns, with your cheery good-morning. There are men enough to flirt with, but not exactly your kind."

"Nor yours, either," Helen rejoined. "Honestly, how are you ever to be married, unless I send you some of my cast-offs?"

"Which one?" Alice asked, and Helen replied, "I really don't know, there's ——," so and so, repeating their names; "but, I dare say, whichever one I made over to you I should want back again. I wrote you from Saratoga about Craig Mason, who didn't care to call upon me. Do you know, I'm dying to see him. Something tells me *you* would suit him to a dot, but it can't be till I've met him in fair conflict and been defeated."

This conversation took place the day before Helen left Rocky Point, and a week later she sailed for Europe, leaving Alice very lonely with the ocean between her and the cousin to whom she was greatly attached. The next April she was offered the spring term in the district school at three dollars a week and board herself. It was something to do,—something to earn,—and she took the school, and made believe she liked it, although Helen herself could scarcely have rebelled more against it than she did, mentally, or have been more relieved than she was when the last day came and she was released from the daily routine which had been so irksome to her. She was to take it up again in the autumn, it was true, but for ten weeks she was free to do what she liked.

Skimming the milk and washing the dreadful dinner dishes and pouring coffee for sweaty men she preferred to school teaching, if it were not that the latter brought her money of her own. "Thirty-six dollars," she repeated, as she fanned herself with the cover of a spelling book. "What shall I do with it all? Ten shall go to Aunt Mary; five to Uncle Ephraim, and I really think I need ten more for gloves and boots and things. Twenty-five dollars in all—oh my!" and she stopped, appalled at the thought that there were only eleven dollars left for the trip to Cooperstown, she was so anxious to take. It couldn't be done. She must stay at home, as she had the previous summer, and she wanted so much to get in touch with the world as she had known it in Albany, and the glimpses she had had of it in New York, if it were only for a week. It seemed hard, and for a moment her bright spirits were clouded, and there were tears in her eyes, which she wiped away quickly as she heard a step and a whistle by the door. It was a young lad, one of her scholars, who came in without at first seeing her. Then, with a start, he said, "Oh, Miss Tracy, you here? I left my jography and come in to get it. I was goin' out to your house. I've been to the office and they gin me a letter for you, 'cause it says on it 'In Haste.' Here 'tis."

Alice knew before she took the letter that it must be from Helen, who was very apt to put "In Haste," or, "Please forward," on her letters, with a belief that it expedited their delivery, as it had in this instance. The boy found his geography and departed, leaving Alice again alone. Tearing open the letter she read it rapidly, and felt that the aspect of everything had changed. Even the weather was not so oppressive as it had been. She was going somewhere. It was the country, to be sure, but she liked the country and Ridgefield was different from Rocky Point. Then she would be with Helen, of whom she was very fond. She understood her, and knew all about her flirtations and the blue book, and what names were in it. She had written some of them herself at Helen's request, because her handwriting was better than her cousin's. She had heard of Craig Mason, and the fact that he did not care for her cousin's acquaintance had awakened her own interest in him and she was nearly as pleased as Helen herself for a chance to meet him. That she could be preferred to Helen never entered her mind. She was simply glad to be with her and ready to do her any service in her power.

When Mr. and Mrs. Wood heard of Helen's wish for Alice to accompany her to Ridgefield they at once urged her going, and refused to take the money offered them by the generous girl.

"Keep it for yourself," Mrs. Wood said. "Ridgefield may not be a fashionable place, but you will see new people and want new things."

"No one will know what I wear when Helen is with me," Alice said, but she bought herself one or two inexpensive dresses, freshened up others with ribbons and ruches, retrimmed her hat, paid five dollars for a pair of boots, and two for a pair of gloves,—the greatest extravagance she had ever committed, and one which kept her awake for hours as she reflected that cheaper ones would have answered every purpose and left something for Aunt Mary.

The good woman, however, insisted that she did not need it, and, unknown to Alice, slipped a dollar of her egg money into the young girl's purse on the morning when she started for Springfield where she was to meet her aunt and cousin. The New York train was late and when it came in Helen was on the platform motioning frantically to Alice to hurry and come on board.

"Mamma is in the parlor car. We were both there, but as there is no vacant chair I'm coming with you where we can sit together and talk. I've so much to tell you," she said, as she followed Alice into the common car, and as soon as the train started she was under full headway, telling where she had been, what and whom she had seen, and what she proposed to do and expected Alice to do. "You are looking lovely in that grey gown which I know is made over, but is quite up-to-date, and I would not be surprised if you eclipsed me," she said; "but if Craig Mason is there, hands off till I have had my try with his royal highness. Oh, mercy!" and she gave a cry of alarm as a flash of sharp lightning lit up the darkening sky,, followed by a terrific peal of thunder.

The storm had burst upon them in its fury, and between the roar of the thunder and the dashing of the rain against the windows, Alice could hear but little more that Helen said. She caught Craig Mason's name two or three times and knew he was the theme of conversation as the train sped on, and finally drew up at Ridgefield station, where it only stopped when it had New York passengers.

"Oh, what shall we do?" Helen cried, drawing back in dismay from the rain which came driving in at the door.

"Open you umbrella and go on," Alice said.

Helen obeyed, but her flimsy parasol was turned inside out as she sprang from the car, not to the ground, but into somebody's arms, she did not know whose. They were very strong and held her fast while they held her, which was only an instant, for there was her mother uttering cries of dismay at the wetting she was getting. Dropping Helen, Mark took her mother and set her down upon the platform, while Alice helped herself. Her alpaca umbrella did not turn inside out, but protected her and her cousin, while Mark held another over her aunt as they ran to the carriage, into which Mrs. Tracy sank exhausted, blaming somebody, she did not know whom, for the storm and her discomfort generally.

"You are not going to leave us? The horses might start," she cried as she saw Mark turn again toward the station.

"The horses are safe, madam, and there is still another of your party. Had you forgotten her?" he said, as he went after Celine, the maid, who was drenched to the skin and struggling with two or three satchels and wraps.

"Oh, must she come in here? Is there no other carriage?" Mrs. Tracy said, as Mark put the half-drowned girl in beside her and shut the door, saying, "There is no conveyance but this, except the van for the baggage. She surely cannot go in there."

"I feel as if I were taking a bath," the unhappy lady moaned, as they started up the hill, while Helen, true to her nature, said, "That man speaks like a gentleman. I wonder who he is."

CHAPTER IX.

WAITING FOR T'OTHER ONE.

THE morning following the arrival of the Tracys was bright and beautiful as summer mornings are apt to be after a heavy rain. There was no sign of the storm which had swept so fiercely over the hills the previous night except in the delicious coolness of the air, the muddy street and the few pools of water still standing upon the walk. Craig, who was never a very good sleeper, had heard every sound in the usually quiet house. It had been nine o'clock before the Tracys had divested themselves of their wet garments and were ready for their supper, which, in spite of Mrs. Taylor's protestations that every thing was spoiled, they enjoyed immensely.

Helen was in high spirits and knew she was going to enjoy herself, everything was so funny and clean. She had made friends with Mrs. Taylor by praising her supper, and won Uncle Zacheus' heart by looking into his face with her beautiful eyes as she squeezed his hand and said, "My dear good man, you don't know how glad I am to be here."

"He don't know whether he's on foot or on horseback, that girl has so upset him," Mrs. Taylor said, as she hurried from the salon to the kitchen, and the kitchen to the salon, occasionally administering a sharp reproof to Jeff, who was dodging round corners, and again whispering to Sarah, the waitress, to keep her wits about her and be sure and pass things to the left instead of the right.

Craig's room was in the north hall, which communicated with the west at right angles, but he could hear the clatter of feet on the stairs, the sound of talking and laughter in the hall, the running of water in the bathroom, until he began to wonder if they would empty the reservoir and leave nothing for his morning bath. There were calls for Celine to open a trunk, or bring a bag, or a wrap left below, and then at last the final good-nights were said, the doors shut and quiet reigned in the house.

"I can't imagine why I am so restless when I have been in so many noisy hotels and never minded them," Craig thought as he stepped out of bed to see what time it was.

"Only eleven, I thought it must be midnight," he said, going to the window and looking out into the night.

The rain was over, the stars were coming out, and the moon was scudding between the few misty clouds still hovering in the sky. From below he caught the odor of a cigar and heard a man's tread on the piazza. It was Mark walking up and down as if he, too, were restless and could not sleep. The sight of him brought back the story heard from Uncle Zacheus that morning, and while recalling its details Craig, who had gone back to bed, fell asleep and dreamed that 'Tina came to him in her white dress and blue ribbons, with the gold beads around her neck, which Mr. Taylor had said she wore on the morning when she left home for the prison. She had a sweet, innocent face for which many a man would peril his life, Craig thought, as he awoke with a start to hear a robin singing outside his window and to see a sunbeam on the wall above his head. It was nearly six o'clock,—later than he usually slept,—for he was an early riser. Dressing himself, he went to the dining-room and breakfasted alone. Everything was quiet in the west wing and he saw no signs of the Tracys, except a big Saratoga trunk in the hall waiting to be taken upstairs, and a smart-looking maid, in white cap and apron, carrying a tray from the kitchen with dishes upon it. "One of the ladies breakfasts in her room,—Mrs. Tracy, probably," he thought, as he sauntered into the office and turned the leaves of the register, finding the names: "Mrs. Freeman A. Tracy, New York city; Miss Helen A. Tracy, New York city; Miss Alice Tracy, Rocky Point, Mass."

The handwriting was very plain and Craig studied it for a moment, while Uncle Zacheus, who was present and still under the spell of Helen's eyes and smiles, said to him, "Writes a good fist; plain as copper-plate, and she's a daisy, too, but not up to t'other one. Wait till you see her."

"What do you mean?" Craig asked. "Which is 't'other one,' and which is the daisy?"

"Why, t'other one is—t'other one, and the daisy's gone down to the river with Jeff after pond lilies," Uncle Zach replied.

"Gone to the river with Jeff?" Craig repeated, and Uncle Zach answered, "Yes, sir. She was up with the sun. Wrote the names; her's is the last one; and then went off with Jeff, holdin' up her white skirts and showin' her trim boots and ankles just like what Dot's was once when she was slimmer."

Craig did not ask any more about the daisy. He felt sure it was Alice, the cousin, from Rocky Point, of which place he had never heard. He was not as much interested in her as he was in the 't'other one,' who occupied more of his thoughts than he would like to confess. He remembered his prejudice against her as a heartless coquette, and his declining to call upon her when asked to do so in Saratoga. But she was here in the same house with him and it was incumbent upon him as a gentleman to treat her with some attention. She might not be as bad as she was painted; at all events, he would like to see her, and he had found himself taking more pains than usual with his toilet. He was always faultlessly neat in his person and attire, especially in the matter of collars and cuffs, and this morning he had tried and discarded two or three pairs, and as many neckties, before he was satisfied that his *tout-ensemble* was all that could be expected in a country tavern. He had looked for Jeff to give an extra polish to his shoes, but not finding him, had put on a pair of tans, and felt himself quite *au fait* and ready to cope with the young lady who, rumor said, had lured so many men to her feet only to be refused. He had no intention of following their example. He expected to amuse himself and be relieved from the ennui which was beginning to affect him in the quiet place.

As he was leaving the office the maid came in to drop a postal in the box. She was a trim little black-eyed French girl, who, in her bright plaid dress, high-heeled slippers and red stockings, looked very pretty and picturesque.

"Good mornin', Miss—er—What is your name," was Uncle Zacheus' salutation.

"Celine, monsieur," was the girl's reply.

"Oh, yes; to be sure. Mooseer, I think you said. I didn't quite catch it. Uncommon name. Miss Mooseer, this is Mr. Craig Mason from Boston. Mr. Mason, Miss Mooseer, I hope you'll be good friends," and Uncle Zacheus waved his hand in a friendly way from one to the other.

Craig was too much of a gentleman to laugh, but there was a gleam of merriment in his eyes as he bowed to the girl, and an answering gleam in hers as she curtsied and said, "*Bon Jour, monsieur,*" and hurried away.

"What did she say?" Uncle Zacheus asked, and Craig replied, "She wished me good morning, in French."

"Oh, yes; wall, I don't understand French very well. Pretty little filly, but you or'to see t'other one," was Uncle Zach's response, as Craig left the office, thinking, "I've been introduced to the maid, and now I'd like to see her mistress."

As he passed the door of the salon he heard the rattling of dishes and murmur of voices, one very sweet and musical and full of laughter, the other so low he could scarcely distinguish it. Going to the north piazza he sat down in his accustomed chair to wait developments. "They will certainly make the tour of the piazzas and come this way after breakfast," he thought, and by *they* he had no reference to the one Uncle Zacheus had called a daisy. She was scarcely in his mind at all. He was waiting for t'other one.

CHAPTER X.

ALICE AND JEFF.

LIKE Craig Mason, Alice was an early riser. The dewy morning in summer was to her the best part of the day. She had slept well, and before the village clock struck five she was up and dressed. Helen, whose room adjoined hers, heard her moving about and called softly to her.

"What is it?" Alice asked, going to her, and Helen answered, sleepily, "Are you up so soon? It seems to me I've only just got into bed. Open the blind, please, and let in some air and light. How pretty and fresh you look," she continued, as Alice opened the blind and came to the bedside. "That gown is so becoming, and I don't suppose it cost more than fifty cents a yard."

"Twenty-five," Alice interposed, and Helen went on, "Well, it is a heap prettier than my Paris gowns, all fuss and feathers. You are going out?"

"Yes; to see what the place is like, and report."

"That's right. Find out if Craig Mason is here. I am awfully tired and don't believe I shall get up for ever so long. If he is here you will see him and tell me what manner of man he is; what he likes and dislikes, so I can like and dislike the same. I don't know why, but I fancy he may be bookish. Did you bring Tennyson?"

"Yes."

"And English Literature?"

"Yes."

"Whose?"

"Taine's."

"All right. I guess I can master enough of him to talk about. Won't you bring me Tennyson before you go? I may look him over a little. It is well to have a favorite poet, and he'll do as well as any body. I know about that poem, 'Why don't you speak for yourself, John,' and should do just as Priscilla did. Wasn't that her name? and was it Whittier who wrote it, or Longfellow?"

"Longfellow," Alice answered, as she went for Tennyson's poems.

"Find the 'May Queen,' and put the book on the bed," Helen said.

Alice did so, and started to leave the room, when her cousin called her back and whispered very low, as if afraid the walls might hear, "I want to know who that tall man is who carried me in his arms through the rain, and spoke so like a gentleman. I can't get him out of my mind. He held me so delicately, as if it were a pleasure, but one for which he ought to apologize."

Alice did not wait for any more directions, but passed downstairs to the office, where she registered their names, and then stepped out upon the piazza just as Jeff appeared with a large basket on his arm.

"Hallo, Jeff; where you goin'?" Uncle Zach asked, and Jeff replied, "To the river after pond lilies." ,

"Oh," Alice said, "pond lilies and the river. Is it far? Can I go?"

She spoke to Jeff, who replied, "Not very far if we go acrost the lots through the wet grass, but you'll have to hold up your gown."

At this point Uncle Zacheus, who was famous for introducing people, came up and said, "Miss Tracy, this is Jefferson Wilkes, our chore boy. We let him get the lilies and sell 'em for a penny apiece. 'Tain't far to the river, but pretty wet for them boots; bran' new, ain't they?" and he glanced admiringly at Alice's five-dollar boots, worn that morning for the first time.

"Yes; quite new, and I can't afford to spoil them," Alice said. "Wait, Jefferson, till I change them."

She ran up to her room, put on her second-best boots and rubbers and was soon off with Jeff, holding her skirts above her ankles, while Uncle Zacheus looked admiringly after her. Jeff was very proud and attentive, and led her through the driest places and helped her over the stone wall and into the boat, asking if she were at all afraid.

"Not in the least," she said. "I know how to row, and if I didn't I feel sure of you," and she beamed upon him a smile so bright that if he had been on the land he would at once have stood upon his head, his favorite way of showing his delight.

He knew that one of the young ladies was very wealthy, but did not know which one it was sitting with him and helping him with the boat when it got entangled among the lily pads. At last, as his admiration increased, he asked abruptly, "Be you the rich Miss Tracy, with such piles of money?"

Alice laughed and answered him, "Oh, no. I am the poor Miss Tracy and teach school among the mountains."

"Golly! I thought you's the rich one, you're so— kinder—I don't know what," Jeff said.

School-teachers, as a rule, were not great favorites with him, but this one must be different from those he had known. Steering the boat to a shaded place where a birch tree drooped over the water he began to pull in the lilies which were very thick just there, and finally said, "Did you have boys in your school; boys like me, I mean?"

"Oh, yes. Quite a number your size, and some older."

"Did you have to lick 'em?"

"Never," Alice answered, greatly amused with the boy, who continued, "What did you do when they cut up?"

"They didn't cut up much, and when they did I talked to them till they were sorry," Alice replied, while Jeff rejoined, "I wish you was my schoolma'am. I get whaled two or three times a week. Don't hurt me, though."

"What do you do to get punished so often?" Alice asked, and Jeff replied, "Oh, nothin' much. I hide the scholars' books and pails and dinners,—for fun, you know,—but I'm whaled the most for gettin' things out of their pockets when they don't know it."

"A pickpocket!" Alice exclaimed, and Jeff rejoined, "No, I don't do it for keeps, but to see if I can,—and I can, too," he added, with the air of one well pleased with himself. "I'll bet you a cent I can take everything out of your pocket there is in it, and you not know it, as we go back to the hotel. Take the bet?"

Alice looked in a kind of terror at this boy, whose frank, handsome face belied his words, and who, having filled his basket with lilies, was rowing out into the river, preparatory to landing on the other side.

"Oh, Jefferson," she said, "never pick a pocket again, even for fun. It is dangerous business, and will get you into trouble,—prison, maybe."

She spoke with great earnestness, and put one of her

hands on Jeff's arm to emphasize her words. Her face was very close to his and her blue eyes looked at him just as no other eyes had ever rested upon him. Mrs. Taylor had always been angry when reproving the young scamp, and usually rounded her reproof with a box on the ear. His teacher *whaled* him as he said, while Mark, the only one who claimed jurisdiction over him, smiled at his dexterity while scolding him for it. Alice took a different course, appealing to his better nature, and, after listening for a few moments to her, he said, "I never meant no harm. I called it sleight of hand, but I b'lieve I'll quit it. Nobody ever talked to me this way before, makin' me feel ashamed. Miss Taylor cuffs me when she jaws; the teachers thrash me, and Mr. Hilton scolds with one corner of his mouth and laughs with the other. Yes, I'll quit it, if you say so; but what'll you bet I can't stand on my head in the boat and not tip it a bit?"

He seemed resolved upon showing his accomplishments in some way, but Alice declined taking the last bet, as she had the first, and was rather glad to find herself on *terra firma*. The mention of Mr. Hilton reminded her that possibly there was a chance for her to learn something of the inmates of the hotel. A boy like Jeff would be likely to tell the truth. First she asked him of himself,—how old he was, and where he was born. He told her his age as nearly as he could, but did not know where he was born; nowhere, he guessed. His father and mother died in Boston and he lived anywhere, in alleys and streets, turning summersaults in the day time and sleeping at night in a big old hogshead that had drifted ashore on the wharf. He concluded his story by saying, "Mr. Hilton found me and brought me to the hotel."

"Who is Mr. Hilton?" Alice asked, and Jeff replied,

"Why, he's Mark, the clerk, who sees to things and insults with Mrs. Taylor about everything. He put that rose on your table last night. Did you smell it?"

Alice had noticed it, and said so, while Jeff continued, "He got it off of a grave down in the cemetery, where some of his kin is buried. I seen him, for I was in the brook close by, trying to catch some polywogs."

Alice wanted to ask what polywogs were, but would not interrupt the boy, who went on: "He met you last night, don't you know, and carried you into the house."

"Not me; that was my cousin. *You* helped me," Alice said, and asked next, "Are there any other gentlemen in the hotel beside Mr. Hilton?"

"My, yes; I guess there is," and Jeff warmed up at once. "There's Mr. Mason from Boston. Awful swell; takes a bath and has his shoes blacked every morning, and wears a clean shirt and collar and cuffs every day. I only wear one shirt a week. Mr. Hilton wears three."

Alice thought it possible that neither Mr. Hilton nor Craig Mason would care for her to have a more intimate knowledge of their habits, and began to speak of Mr. and Mrs. Taylor. Here, too, Jeff was very communicative. "Mr. Taylor was fust rate, and let a feller alone," he said. Some called him shiffless, but he liked that kind of shiffless that wasn'a allus pitchin' in to a chap. Miss Taylor was boss, and smart as chain lightnin', only she couldn't git round quite so quick, she was so big,—tipped the scale at two hundred. He liked her some and should like her more if she didn't make him go to Sunday-school and learn twenty verses in the Bible beside. He was through with the Sermon on the Mount, and was tackling Nicodemus, which was easier.

They had reached the hotel by this time, and with every step Alice's interest had increased in Jeff, whose admiration for her had kept pace with her interest in him. He offered to go with her to the woods and show her a big hornet's nest and a mud turtle's bed in the pond, of which no one knew but himself, and he made her take half of the lilies, refusing any remuneration at first. Then, suddenly, with a merry twinkle in his eyes, he said, "If you want to pay me so bad give me a dime and we'll call it square."

Alice put her hand in her pocket for her purse, which was gone, with her handkerchief and her gloves, which she had taken off when she helped pull in the lilies. Before she could utter an exclamation of surprise, Jeff, who was watching her, had turned a summersault and was on his feet with her missing articles in his hand.

"Here they be," he said, but the laugh died away when he saw the expression of Alice's face and the tears in her eyes as she said, "Oh, Jefferson, how could you! You promised you wouldn't, and I believed you."

If she had struck him she would not have hurt him as much as did the sight of her tears and the sound of her voice.

"I didn't mean to when I promised, but I wanted to try it just once more," he said. "I'm awfully sorry, and I'll never do it again, never. I don't want to be a bad boy."

"I am sure you don't, and as a beginning, never try that trick again," Alice said, putting her hand on his hair and smoothing it as she talked.

"I won't; I won't," Jeff said, "and you'll go with me to see the hornet's nest and the mud turkles just the same?"

Alice promised, and feeling that he was restored to favor, Jeff ran off with his basket of lilies, while Alice changed her boots and went down to breakfast with her aunt, who asked where she had been and with whom.

Alice told her of Jeff, who had offered to stand on his head in the boat and not rock it, and had picked her pocket as they came up the hill.

"The wretch!" Mrs. Tracy exclaimed. "A pickpocket! A thief! You ought to report him. We are not safe here, and Helen so careless with her money and jewelry."

As well as she could Alice explained, saying it was done for fun,—that there was no harm in the boy,—that she liked him immensely, and would trust him anywhere. While she talked Jeff was crouching under an open window, cutting the long grass with a sickle and hearing all that was said. At first he resented Alice's telling of his prank, but his anger died away as he listened to her defense of him. Mrs. Tracy had called him a thief, and it had a bad sound.

"I ain't a thief," he thought, wiping his eyes where the tears were beginning to gather. "I never kep' a cent's wuth from anybody. I do it because I can't help it, my fingers tingle so to try it. I was mean to lie to her when she spoke so nice to me, and put her hand on my head as if she liked me. I feel it there now," and he put his soiled hand where Alice's white one had lain and where in imagination he would feel it again in after years when temptation and sin had marred the beauty and blighted the innocence of a face which was so frank and open now in its young boyhood.

CHAPTER XI.

ALICE AND CRAIG.

Craig had been sitting on the piazza a long time waiting for somebody to come, but the somebody waited for had not appeared and he was growing rather impatient and wondering what kept her. Twice Mark Hilton had walked the length of the piazza,—an unusual proceeding for him at that hour in the morning when his duties confined him in the office. Once as he was passing Craig he stopped abruptly and asked, "Have you seen her?"

Craig felt intuitively whom he meant and answered, "No, have you?"

"Only very indistinctly in the rain," Mark replied, and walked on wondering at the unrest which possessed him and had made him quite as wakeful the previous night as Craig had been.

He knew it was Helen whom he had carried through the rain, for he heard her mother speak her name. He had not seen her face, but the way her arms had clung around his neck, as if afraid he would let her fall, and the pressure of her hand on his as he put her down, had been like an electric shock which he still felt, calling himself a fool many times to be upset by the touch of a hand and the clasp of a girl's arms around his neck. It was a new experience for him, as he had never paid much attention to the ladies. No one who saw him ever suspected the morbid vein in his nature which made him dwell secretly upon a past in which he had no part and with which few ever connected him. He had felt it to an unusual degree that afternoon when he stood by 'Tina's grave, the shadow of which was always with him when his laugh was the lightest and his manner the proudest. He couldn't forget it, and fancied that other people remembered it, as he did. To the guests at the hotel he was polite and kind and attentive, but never familiar with them, especially if they were ladies, who were sure to hear the story and gossip about it. He had thought a good deal about the Tracys, who represented a different class from those who usually frequented the hotel. They were the extreme fashionables, who would probably think of him as a kind of servant to do their bidding. His attention to them in the rain was what he would have given to any ladies, and he was not prepared for the way in which Helen had received it. She certainly had pressed his hand and clasped his neck as her mother had not done, and she was just as conscious of the act as he was. This he did not know. It was an accident, he believed, and she would never give him another thought, while he should subside into his place as the hotel clerk and watch and admire her at a distance. This was his decision as he left Craig and went to speak to a gentleman who had come from the train and was inquiring the way to a farmhouse among the hills of West Ridgefield.

Left to himself Craig looked at his watch and then picked up Browning, which he usually had with him. He had joined a Browning club in Boston, partly because it was the thing to do, and partly because he really liked the poet and enjoyed trying to find out what he meant, if anything. He had taken up the Story of Sordello for his summer work, resolved to make himself master of its obscurities and astonish the club in the autumn with his knowledge. But reading Sordello alone, with no one to suggest or disagree, was up hill business, and he had only accomplished the first book. This he had read three times and was debating whether to give it a fourth trial, or to attack Book second, when he heard the sound of a footstep and a young girl came round the corner singing softly,

"Oh the glorious summer morning
With its dewy grass and flowers,"

"Only there are no flowers here," she added. Then seeing Craig she stopped suddenly and said, "I beg your pardon; I didn't know any one was here."

She was tall and slender, with a willowy grace in every motion. Her complexion was pale, but betokened perfect health and vitality. Her light brown hair was twisted into a flat knot low in her neck where it was making frantic efforts to escape in little wisps of curls. Her eyes were large and blue and clear as a child's. Her mouth was rather wide, but very sweet in its expression when she smiled. Her dress was a simple muslin of lavender and white, and at her throat and belt she wore a half-opened lily which she had gathered on the river and which seemed to harmonize so well with her pure complexion and general appearance. Some such idea was in Craig's mind as he rose quickly and said to her, "You are not intruding at all. I come here because it is so quiet and I like the outlook across the fields to the woods, but I have no right to monopolize the place. Be seated, won't you?"

He brought her a chair, but took the precaution to put it at a safe distance from his own and where he could see her squarely. He had been thinking only of Helen, expecting her and waiting for her. This was she, of course, and her simple, unaffected manner was her premonitory artillery against which she would find him proof. She was very pretty, but he was not sure that he hadn't seen faces prettier than hers, and on the whole he was a little disappointed to find her less formidable than he had expected. All this passed through his mind while Alice was thanking him for the chair in which she seated herself, with half of her new boots showing under the hem of her dress. Craig saw them and thought them very small and well fitting and that she was displaying them on purpose.

"Do you think you will like it here?" he asked, feeling he must say something.

"Oh, yes," she answered enthusiastically. "I like the country, and it is so delightfully cool after the heat of yesterday. Do you know I have a great desire to roll in that new mown hay which smells so sweet. I believe I am something of a romp."

Craig did not know what to say to this, so he spoke of the lilies which Alice was wearing.

"I see you like them, too; they are my favorites," he said, "and I always buy one of Jeff. He hasn't been round yet. I wonder what keeps him."

"Pray take this. I have more," Alice said, offering him the lily which was in her belt, without a thought that she might seem too familiar, until she saw something like surprise on Craig's face which brought a blush to her own.

She certainly was a little forward, Craig thought, but he took the lily, thinking it quite in keeping with her character to give it to him. He didn't know that in her forgetfulness of self Alice would give away anything another wanted and that she would as soon have given the lily to Uncle Zacheus as to him. He was a bit of a prig she was thinking, and wondering what she should say to him, when Jeff appeared with his basket.

"You are too late. I have one; the young lady gave it to me," Craig said.

"All right. She helped me pull 'em," Jeff answered, as he darted away, while a suspicion of his mistake began to dawn upon Craig.

"You helped him gather him! Aren't you Miss Tracy?" he asked in some confusion.

Alice laughed and replied, "*A* Miss Tracy, yes; but not *the* Miss Tracy you have evidently mistaken me for. That is Helen. I am Alice,—the cousin. I live at Rocky Point, among the mountains between Springfield and Albany, and taught school there the last spring term. My aunt very kindly invited me to spend my vacation with her and Helen, and here I am, and so glad to be here."

She was not Helen, for whom Craig was waiting. She was an unaffected country girl, with the manners of a perfect lady, and he began to admire her greatly and to think Uncle Zach not far out of the way when he called her a daisy. She had given him her confidence and he began at last to give her his, and before he realized it had told her a great deal of himself and what he liked and disliked; had told her about the hotel and the town and the places to visit and had introduced her to Mark, who had joined them for a moment.

When he was gone Craig spoke of him in the highest terms, and then the talk turned upon books, for a part of Alice's duty was to find out what Craig's favorites were.

"Do you have much inclination to read here?" she asked, glancing at the half-open volume beside him.

"Not much," he replied, taking up the book and passing it to her. "I have been trying to master Sordello, but guess I shall have to give it up unless you can help me. Do you like Browning?"

"Mercy, no!" Alice answered quickly, then added, as she saw a shade of disappointment in his face, "Perhaps I should not say no so decidedly when I know so little about him. I might like him if I knew more of him. I have always thought him very obscure. You like him of course?"

"Yes, I like him for his very obscurity. There is a pleasure in finding out what he means just as there is in cracking a hard nut for the rich meat you know there is inside. It is pleasanter, though, studying him with other people. I belong to a Browning Club in Boston and find it rather different here plodding along alone. I suppose you have no clubs in Rocky Point."

He did not think how the last part of his speech sounded, nor mean any disrespect to Rocky Point. But Alice resented it and answered quickly, "No, we haven't. We are nearly all poor working people earning our bread, with no time for clubs. Many of us never heard of Browning; certainly not of Sordello. I think, though, some of us *could* understand him as well as members of clubs, give us a chance. Even *I* might, if I could hear you read and explain. Perhaps you will do me that honor."

She spoke sarcastically, but Craig, who was conscious of no blunder in his speech, did not notice it and was only pleased with her wish to hear him read Browning. He should be delighted, he said, and if her cousin would join them with Mr. Hilton and perhaps his mother and Mrs. Tracy, they would make quite a class. Between them all they ought to master Sordello. Did she think her cousin would like it?

Inwardly Alice shook with laughter as she thought of

Helen, who at that moment was struggling with the May Queen in order to appear learned, posing as a lover of Browning, and expounding the meaning of Sordello. She could, however, say truthfully that she was sure her cousin would be happy to hear Mr. Mason read, whenever he was kind enough to do so.

At this point his mother joined him and was presented to Alice. Mrs. Mason was a woman with some strong opinions, one of which was that no coquette could be a well principled girl. Helen Tracy was a noted coquette, consequently she was not well principled and might lead Craig into all manner of wrong doing. He was not very susceptible, it was true, and for that reason there was more to fear, for if he were once interested he would be in deadly earnest, and she was thinking of proposing that they leave Ridgefield for some other place. Her first thought when she saw Alice talking so familiarly with her son was, "She has lost no time."

Craig's introduction to Miss *Alice* Tracy disarmed her at once. She had seen a great deal of the world and could judge one's character pretty correctly by the face. What she saw in Alice was a frank, open countenance, with eyes which met hers steadily, and a voice so pleasant and winsome that she was drawn to her immediately, and as they talked together her admiration increased. Alice was so artless and frank and so inexpressibly glad to be enjoying herself, with no dread of the dingy school house among the hills, with its closeness and smell of tin pails, and children not always the cleanest.

"Only think," she said, "of two whole months of freedom and how much can be crowded into them. You don't know what this vacation is to me."

She was not in the least affected, and as she talked

there came a faint flush to her cheeks and her eyes sparkled with excitement.

"She is very pretty and very sweet and very real," Mrs. Mason was thinking, when Celine appeared, and told Alice that Mademoiselle Heléne wanted to see her.

With a bow and smile for Mrs. Mason and Craig, Alice said good morning and hurried away.

CHAPTER XII.

A COQUETTE.

ALICE found Helen in her room, seated before a mirror and waiting for Celine to arrange her hair. On the dressing table were combs and brushes and cut glass bottles and all the paraphernalia of a lady's toilet, golden stoppered and silver mounted, showing a luxurious taste and utter disregard of expenditure. She had read Tennyson's May Queen in bed and two or three shorter poems, and had committed a stanza or two here and there in order to seem posted, if Craig proved to be an admirer of Tennyson. If he were not and she found herself in deep waters she trusted to her tact and Alice's help to extricate herself some way. Getting tired of Tennyson and the bed she arose at last and in her dressing gown dawdled about the room, beginning to feel bored and wondering why Alice did not come. She had heard from her mother that Craig was stopping in the hotel, and Celine had told her of being introduced to him by a funny old gentleman as Miss Mooseer, and Helen had laughed till she cried. Celine had also told her that Alice was talking with him on the north piazza.

"Pumping him," she said to herself. "I hope it won't take her long. I am so impatient to hear the result and know if he is worth the trouble."

Sitting down by the window in a chair she began to think of the past and the white faces and sad eyes which had looked at her during the seven years since her first offer when she was only fifteen. Behind these were other faces, some of boys, some of men, whom she had played with and flattered and then thrown aside without regret.

"Doesn't it say somewhere in the Bible 'Vengeance is mine and I will repay,' saith the Lord," she thought. "Surely my payment will be heavy if it equal my indebtedness; but it is my nature, and I cannot help it."

At last as she grew more and more impatient and Alice did not come, she sent Celine for her. Celine, who had been Helen's maid for years and knew her nearly as well as she knew herself, was never in the way, and Helen bade her go on with her hair dressing as soon as she re-entered the room. To Alice who came in with Celine her first word was, "Well?"

"Well!" Alice returned, and Helen continued, "What news from Genoa? You have been gone a long time and must have something to tell."

"Lots! About everything. Shall it be the Sphinx first, or Hercules?" Alice asked, and Helen repeated, "Hercules? Who is he? Oh, yes, I know. I'll take him second, and the Sphinx first. I know he is here; mamma told me. You have been on the river with a dreadful boy who stands on his head and picked your pocket. Skip him, and begin with the Sphinx. What is he like?"

"Very much like any other city bred gentleman," Alice replied. "A little stiff, perhaps, especially in the matter of shirt fronts and collars. Jeff,—that's the dreadful boy,—says he changes them every day, and he does impress you as having just been washed and ironed, he looks so clean from his head to his feet."

"Nonsense! You are comparing him with those sweaty men on your uncle's farm. Seven shirts and collars and fourteen cuffs a week! What a laundry bill! But go on. Is he good looking?"

"Yes; with a rather delicate cast of countenance for a man. He was very polite, and after his stiffness wore off, talked delightfully. He mistook me for *you*."

"Oh," Helen said quickly, as if not quite pleased. "You undeceived him of course."

"Certainly I did. I told him I was only your cousin, a teacher in a district school among the mountains."

"I don't see the need of your dragging that in," Helen said, and Alice rejoined, "Knowing how rich you are he might think me rich, too, and I don't want to sail under false colors."

Helen, to whom deception, or even a lie was nothing, if circumstances warranted it, tossed her head and continued, "What are his tastes? What does he like?"

"He likes the country, especially Ridgefield."

"So do I adore it. Go on."

"He likes rowing."

Helen had a mortal terror of a sail boat and could scarcely ever be persuaded to enter one, but answered quickly: "So do I. Go on."

"He likes driving over the hills and into the woods."

Helen made a grimace, for if there were anything she detested it was driving over the country roads in country vehicles. But if Craig liked it, she liked it, too, and said so.

"What next?" she asked, and Alice replied, "He likes to

sit on the north piazza, where it is cool, and away from the street."

"Now you please me; that is delicious. What does he do? Smoke?"

"I think not, or drink either."

"That's bad. What *does* he do?"

"Reads, I judge, as he had a book with him."

"Reads what? Tennyson, I hope. I went through with the May Queen and one or two other poems."

"I think his preference is Browning."

"Browning!" Helen almost shrieked. "I never read a line of him in my life. Do you mean he likes Browning and will talk to me about *him?*"

"I think so. He belongs to a Browning club, and is trying to master Sordello."

"Sordello! What's that?" Helen asked.

"I am sure I don't know. A man, I imagine," Alice replied. "He said he found it hard work reading alone and suggested that we join him for half an hour, or an hour, every afternoon."

"Oh, horror," Helen cried in dismay. "Join a Browning club, and not know a thing except that I have seen Mrs. Browning's house and grave in Florence, and mamma had to tell me who she was. Do you think there is a library in town?" and Helen began to brighten.

Alice thought there must be. She would inquire.

"No, that would give me away. Take a walk by yourself, and if there is one, get me Browning's Poems. Wretched, that I must wade through them, when I was getting on so nicely with Tennyson."

Alice laughed at her distress, but promised to go for a walk and find the library, if there were one, and get Browning, if she could.

"But suppose there are several volumes? What shall

I do? I can't get them all," she asked, and Helen replied: "Get the one with that man in it, if it is a man. Sorrento, isn't it?"

"Sordello!" Alice answered, beginning to understand Helen's drift.

Her toilet was completed by this time and Alice thought she had never seen her lovelier than she was now in her Paris gown of some soft, creamy stuff, with its frills of lace and knots of ribbon and wide sleeves, which fell away from her white arms every time she raised them, which she often did, for she knew their beauty. Her complexion was of that smooth satiny kind which suggests art in its perfection. But no cosmetic of any description had ever touched her face, which was of rare beauty. Her greatest charm was in her large brown eyes, which she knew so well how to use and could make grave or gay, or even tearful at her will. They were very bright this morning, with an unusual sparkle in them, for she was on the warpath, with a new kingdom to conquer, and felt her blood tingle with excitement and pleasure.

"By the way," she said, after surveying herself in the mirror and walking before it several times, as she always did when dressing, "Mrs. Mason is here,—a kind of dragon, I am afraid. I hear she is very proud.. Did you see her?"

"Yes, and she didn't impress me as proud at all. She was very kind to me. I like her," Alice replied.

"You like everybody, and everybody likes you," was Helen's rejoinder; then she said suddenly: "What about Hercules? I came near forgetting him. Who is he?"

"Mr. Hilton, the hotel clerk," was Alice's reply.

"Oh—h," and Helen's countenance fell a little. "A clerk! A bartender! I was afraid of that."

"He is not a bartender; there is no bar to tend. This

is a strictly temperance house. You couldn't get a drink if you wanted it. Jeff told me so. Mr. and Mrs. Taylor are both good Christian people, and Mr. Hilton seems a gentleman every way. He is splendid looking and Mr. Mason likes him. He came when we were talking and I was introduced to him."

Alice had made quite a long speech in defense of Mark Hilton, while Helen, who was still surveying herself in the glass, smiled and said, "Oh, hit, are you? Well, I wish you success, but to me there is not much difference between a hotel clerk and a bartender. He did carry me beautifully though, and I'd like to see him. Am I all right, and does my dress hang as it should?"

"You couldn't look better," Alice said, and Helen continued, "I wish I had a flower of some kind."

"How would a lily do?" Alice asked, and Helen replied, "No, thanks. You have chosen the lily, and resemble it more than I do. I ought to have a rose."

Here Celine, who had heard all the conversation, said, "There is a beautiful rose on the table in the salon. It was there last night. Shall I bring it for mademoiselle?"

She did not wait for an answer, but hurrying to the salon returned with the rose which, though not quite as fresh as the previous night, was still very fragrant.

"Oh, what a beauty! Did it grow in the garden? If so, there must be more," Helen said, inhaling the perfume, while Celine replied, "It didn't grow here. I asked Sarah and she said Monsieur Hilton put it on the table. She did not know where he got it. Monsieur Mason helped pick and arrange the *fleurs-de-lis* in the centre of the table. There are plenty of those. Shall I gather some for Mademoiselle?"

Helen was radiant. Both young men had put flowers on the table,—for *her*, no doubt. Fond as she was of

Alice, she never thought she could be considered before or with herself. Everything was for Helen Tracy first; then, Alice, if anything were left.

"*Fleurs-de-lis!* Yes, I remember thinking them pretty with the ferns. And Mr. Mason put them there? I ought to feel flattered and to wear one of them. His color, too, as he is a Yale man; but they will not go well with these ribbons. I must wear Mr. Hilton's rose. I hope it won't fall to pieces. It does seem a little droopy."

She fastened it in a knot of delicate pink ribbon near her shoulder where it would be very conspicuous, and declared herself ready for the preparatory skirmish.

"I suppose one can go on the north piazza any time. I wonder if Mr. Mason is there still? Celine, please go and see," she said.

Celine went out, and when they were alone Alice, who had never had quite so clear an insight into Helen's character before, said to her, "Do you care for Mr. Mason?"

"Of course not. How should I, when I don't know him," Helen replied, and Alice continued, "Then why not leave him alone. Will it be any satisfaction to win him just to throw him over as you have so many others? Is it right, or womanly?"

"A second Portia come to judgment," and Helen laughed merrily. "Seriously, though, it isn't right, or womanly. It is wicked and mean, and I know it as well as you do, and I had made up my mind to quit the business, and maybe take Mr. Prescott for fear some terrible judgment would overtake me. But when I heard Mr. Mason was here all the old Satan woke up in me, and I said I'll pay him for his slight of me last summer. Perhaps I shall not throw him over. He may be the twenty-first and last. Who knows? I shall be twenty-three in December,—time I was married. Is he there?" and she turned to Celine who had just entered the room and who reported that he was there with Monsieur Hilton and Monsieur Taylor, too.

"Three men to subjugate. Nothing could suit me better," and Helen clasped her hands in ecstasy. "*Au revoir*, cousin mine. Wish me success, and don't forget the library."

"If it were right I'd pray that she might not succeed. I have prayed for more trivial things than that, and been heard," Alice thought, as she watched her cousin going down the stairs and saw her turn in the direction of the north piazza.

CHAPTER XIII.

ON THE NORTH PIAZZA.

CRAIG had been to the post office after his mail, and taking his mother's letters to her room, had returned to his accustomed place on the north piazza. Here he found a large glass of iced lemonade with a straw in it waiting for him, and Uncle Zacheus, with his coat off, seated in an armchair, mopping his face with a yellow silk handkerchief.

"It's swelterin' hot again to-day. Most 90 in the shade, and I thought mabby some lemonade would taste good after your walk," he said to Craig, who thanked him and began to sip the cool beverage. "That's on old-fashioned toddy tumbler. I told Mark to use it, as I thought you'd want a big drink," Uncle Zacheus said, and Craig thanked him again, and said he was very thoughtful.

At that moment Mark joined them, glad to escape from

the office which at that hour of the day was very warm. There had been a lingering hope in his mind that Miss Helen Tracy might be there. But she wasn't, and taking one of the vacant chairs, he brought it near to the railing on which he put his feet and leaning back with his hands behind his head, gave himself up to a rest which he felt he needed. Craig, too, had hoped to find Helen on his return from the post office. But he did not, and, both young men had seated themselves with a feeling of disappointment and with no suspicion of the preparations making for a raid upon them.

For a time Uncle Zacheus rambled on about the weather and the new fence for the "cemetry" for which "Widder Wilson had only given five dollars."

"I mean to ask Miss Tracy to give sunthin' seein' her gran'father is buried there," he said; then, turning to Craig, he asked, "Have you seen t'other one yet?"

Craig knew whom he meant, but wishing to hear what Uncle Zacheus would say, he asked with an air of some surprise, "Who is t'other one?"

"Why, you know. You've seen the one I call the daisy, though she's more like them lilies she got with Jeff, who has never behaved so well in his life as sense he come up from the river with her. I mean the cousin,—the rich one. I seen her last night, and I tell you she's a dandy. Shorter than the daisy,—plump as a partridge, and such eyes. Old as I am they gave me some such feelin's as Dot's used to when she talked to me over her father's gate. She's the one writ that nice letter I've got put away with Johnny's blanket and the old sign."

Neither of the young men could help laughing at Uncle Zach's comparing Miss Tracy's eyes with Dot's, which, if they were ever bright, were faded now and expressionless.

"That is the kind of love God meant when He said a man shall cleave to his wife and they shall become one flesh," Craig was thinking when Uncle Zach startled him by clutching his arm and whispering, "Wall, I'll be dumbed. I didn't tell you half. There she comes."

Mark's feet came down in a trice from the railing as he straightened himself up, while Craig hastily took his straw from his mouth and dropped it into the big tumbler. Around the corner nearest to Mark Helen came, gracefully holding the train of her dress with one hand and with the other affecting to brush something from the front of her skirt. Apparently she did not see either of the three men and nothing could have been more natural than her start of surprise and pretty blush when she at last looked up.

"Oh, I beg your pardon for intruding. My cousin told me it was cool here and so I came," she said, dropping her train, and half turning to leave.

Instantly Craig and Mark were on their feet, while Uncle Zach, feeling it was incumbent on him to speak, said, "Don't go. The piazzer is free. I'm glad to introduce you to Mark and Craig. Take a chair."

Craig and Mark put their hands on the same chair in their efforts to serve her, and bowed so close together that their heads nearly touched each other. Helen took the offered chair and laughed as she said to Uncle Zach, "Please, Mr. Taylor, which is Mark and which is Craig? You didn't tell me," and her bright eyes met those of the young men who were laughing with her at Uncle Zach's blunder.

"Well, I'll be dumbed if I hain't done a smart thing," he said. "Dot would give me Hail Columby if she knew it, but I was so frustrated I didn't know what I was about. This is Mr. Mason, and this is Mr. Hilton."

Helen knew perfectly well which was which without an introduction, but Uncle Zach's mistake put them at their ease at once. Helen was always at her ease, and seemed so unconscious of herself and so natural that Craig's prejudice began to give way under the charm of her voice and the glance of her beautiful eyes. They were so bright and searching that he winced every time she looked at him, while Mark grew hot and cold with a feeling he could not understand. He saw his rose among the ribbons and wondered if she would keep it there if she knew where it came from, or that he had picked it for her. She was a little reserved toward him at first, for the bartender was in the ascendant, but at last she divided her smiles and blandishments pretty evenly between him and Craig, asking questions in the most *naive* way concerning the town and the people. Uncle Zach answered most of these, and while she managed to bow assent in the right place and pretended to give him her undivided attention she was mentally sizing up Craig and Mark and weighing them by her standard. She had dropped the name of *Hercules* for Mark and substituted *Apollo*, which suited him better. He was the finest looking man she had ever met, she thought, and with the speech and manners of a gentleman. There was nothing about him but the fit of his clothes to indicate that he was not up to date. He might be a hotel clerk, and as such lower in the social scale than Craig Mason, but he was very fascinating, and would do to flirt with if she failed with the Sphinx, as she still designated Craig. That the latter was a gentleman in every respect she decided at once. He was rather too dignified and reserved and was evidently ignorant of small talk as she understood it. But she was sure she could make him unbend; he was unbending under the artillery of her eyes, which never did better execution than they did now, while her rippling laugh at some things Uncle Zach was saying kept pace with them. He was certainly up to date in everything, and she noticed each item of his dress and saw his immaculate shirt-front and collar and cuffs which Jeff had said were clean every day.

"I believe he is just as clean in his character as in his linen," she thought, and a most unbounded respect for him and desire to stand well in his opinion began to take possession of her.

Meantime the young men were summing her up and arriving at nearly the same conclusion. She might be a coquette, but she gave no sign of it, and was the loveliest piece of womanhood they had ever seen. She was charming; she was everything that was feminine and sweet. This was their verdict as they watched her, now leaning back in her chair in a languid kind of way like a child that is tired, now managing to show her white arms under the wide sleeves of her dress, and all the while keeping up a flow of talk as if she had known them always. She had a faculty of making every man in her presence appear at his best, and also of making him conscious if anything were wrong with him, and she exerted that power over Uncle Zach. His shirt sleeves had surprised her, reminding her of the farm hands at Rocky Point and she did not think it quite respectful to herself that he should continue to sit thus after she joined him. He, however, was oblivious to anything out of the way in his toilet until her eyes had travelled over him several times with questioning glances. Then suddenly, as if her thought had communicated itself to him, he started up, exclaiming, "I'll be dumbed if I ain't here in my shirt sleeves, with a lady, too, Mark. Why didn't you tell me, and what would Dot say. Let me get my coat."

He seemed so genuinely distressed that Helen's feelings changed at once. He had recognized the respect due to her and she was satisfied.

"My dear good man," she said. "Sit still and don't mind me. I know you are more comfortable as you are."

"Thank you," Uncle Zach said, resuming his seat. "I had a notion that you thought I or'to put on my coat, and it's so much cooler without it. Dot wouldn't like it though. She tries to keep me a gentleman, but land o' Goshen, what can you do with a tarvern keeper? I slipped it off because she's gone over the river a huntin' aigs. It's time she was back, if she didn't have to go clear to the town farm,—a long ride this hot mornin'."

"Are there many pleasant drives in Ridgefield?" Helen asked, and Uncle Zach replied, "Hundreds of 'em,—round the ponds and over the hills and through stretches of woods half a mile long with saxifax and shoe-makes and blackb'ry bushes growin' by the road."

Helen shivered mentally and smelled the *saxifax*, which she detested, and felt the scratch of the brier bushes which grew by the roadside in the long stretches of wood. But she made no sign, and when Craig said to her, "Are you fond of driving in the country?" she unhesitatingly answered, "Oh, very."

"Then, I tell you what," Uncle Zach began. "You shall have piles of 'em and cost you nothin'. There's the open carry-all, and there's the bloods, Paul and Virginny, doin' nothin'. Splendid critters, too. Have run on the race track, and beat. Mr. Mason, you haven't been there; on the course, I mean. Suppose you and Mark and the girls take a ride this afternoon, when it gits cool. What do you say?"

He looked at Helen, who answered that it would be

delightful if Alice would go and the gentlemen were agreeable.

"Are the horses perfectly safe? I am sometimes a little timid," she asked.

Craig laughed as he recalled the habits of the bloods and wished so much for his fleet Dido, standing idle in her stall in Auburndale, his mother's country residence. He had not taken a sip of his lemonade since Helen joined them, but he did so now, and that diverted Uncle Zach's thoughts into another channel.

"George of Uxbridge!" he said, "what are we thinkin' about, not offerin' Miss Tracy some lemonade. Mark, go this minit and make her a glass."

It grated on Helen to have her Apollo ordered as a servant, and she made a faint protest, begging Mark not to trouble himself for her.

"Yes, he will, too; he's made hundreds on 'em,—tip-top ones, too. No sticks in 'em, though. We are tee-totalers here, we be," Uncle Zach said.

There was nothing Helen enjoyed more than champagne and sherry, and she thought a fashionable dinner very tame without them, and that lemonade was improved with claret, but she was a Roman with the Romans and smiled on Uncle Zach as she said, "And you are quite right, too."

Then she settled herself to wait for her lemonade which was longer in making than Craig's had been. For her the ice was chopped fine, every seed and bit of pulp was removed and the mixture beaten until it had a creamy look on the top. Lemonade spoons had not been invented, but Mark put a fresh straw and teaspoon and napkin on the tray, which he took to the young lady, who declared she had never drank anything more delicious. As she talked some leaves from the rose in her ribbons fell into her lap.

"My poor rose, it's fading, and it was so sweet, and I am so fond of roses. Sarah said you put it on the table for us. Are there more where this came from?"

She turned to Mark with a look which, had he been Jeff, would have sent him on to his head at once. As it was he merely lost it and stammered out that he didn't know,—he'd inquire, and get her more, if possible.

By the time she finished the lemonade so many leaves had fallen that she removed the rose and laid it on the tray which Mark took from her, carefully gathering every leaf which had dropped upon her dress, and then, foolish man that he was, putting them away in his pocketbook. Mark was in love. Hopelessly, of course, and though nothing could ever come of it he made no effort to smother it. He could, at least, enjoy the crumbs and leave the full table to Craig, who was not so far gone as himself, but whose prejudices were rapidly giving way. It was scarcely possible that so much naturalness and graciousness of manner were consummate acting. Public opinion had been mistaken and had vilified the beautiful girl who sat there, so unconscious of herself, and the admiring glances he gave her from time to time. Mr. Taylor nad been called away by Dotty, who had returned with her eggs, and as Mark did not come back Craig was alone with Helen.

This was what she had looked forward to. Uncle Zach was a garrulous, amusing old man, who at times was better out of the way. Mark interested her more than she would have thought it possible, and had he been the equal of Craig, as the world defines equality, she would have given him her attention and left Craig alone. She had never flirted with a hotel clerk,—a bartender,—and she scolded herself for thinking so much about him, and contrasting him with Craig, who was inclined to be silent at first. Evidently she must lead the conversation, and she began by asking if he found it at all dull in the country.

"I shall like it for a while," she said. "It is so different from the places we are in the habit of visiting, Saratoga, for instance. We were there last summer. I suppose you have been there?"

She looked at him as innocently as if she did not know that her question would pique him a little. Craig Mason and his horse, Dido, had been nearly as conspicuous at the Clarendon as Helen Tracy had been at the United States, and that she should not have heard of him was, to say the least, rather humiliating to his pride. He didn't know that she was paying him for his slight and that she felt quite repaid when she saw his look of chagrin, which he covered with a laugh as he replied, "Oh, yes, I was there last summer, but did not have the pleasure of meeting you. I heard of you, though. Indeed, everybody did that. How could they help it?"

He was complimenting her rather stiffly and blushing like a girl as he did it, but Helen knew she was gaining ground, and thanked him with her eyes which were always as expressive as words. After that they grew very social, and at last, although she tried to stave it off, the conversation turned upon books. It was in vain that Helen brought forward Tennyson as a most charming author. Craig brushed him aside for Browning, his favorite, and hers, too, she finally said, suggesting that she believed he was too obscure for most people to enjoy thoroughly without a teacher.

"Yes, that's true," Craig admitted, "but I like him, though I confess it is rather tiresome reading him alone. I have taken up Sordello, and your cousin was kind enough to say that she thought you might like a short reading some afternoon. My mother, I know, will join us; possibly your mother and Mr. Hilton, when he can. He is a very intelligent man,—far above the average. Do you think you would like it?"

"I shall be delighted," Helen answered promptly, wondering which she should find the pleasanter, driving over dusty, stony roads, with sassafras and brier bushes growing beside them, or listening to Sordello, of which she had not the most remote idea.

But she had commited herself, and Craig was pleased, and believed he had found a bright disciple of Browning, and told her he expected much from her opinion and quick appreciation of what was to most people abstruse and dry. Helen thought of the Potted Sprats in Mrs. Opie's White Lies, and concluded she was eating a tremendous one.

"What shall I do if Alice doesn't get me the book?" she asked herself, deciding that a sick headache, whenever Browning was on the carpet would be the only alternative.

As if in answer to her thought Alice appeared at that moment, and in response to an interrogatory glance from Helen nodded an affirmative. She had unquestionably found the book and Helen's fears were given to the winds. With her ready memory she could, if she tried, commit pages of Sordello, or anything else, and her face glowed with satisfaction and confidence. Craig had scarcely given Alice a thought in his absorption with Helen, but when she appeared a reaction came and he wondered why he should suddenly feel so cool and restful. It was because she looked so restful and cool, he concluded, and yet she declared herself very warm, and, declining the chair he offered her, sat down upon the steps and fanned herself with her hat, while Helen, relieved from all anxiety, began what Alice called an outrageous flirtation of jokes and brilliant sallies which poor Craig no more understood than she did Browning, and which so confused and bewildered him that he was glad when at last he saw his stately mother coming toward him with a showily-dressed woman whom he recognized as Mrs. Tracy.

CHAPTER XIV.

THE DIAMONDS.

Mrs. Freeman Tracy was a faded, washed-out woman who had been very pretty in her girlhood and who thought with the aid of dress and cosmetics to retain a remnant at least of her former youth and beauty. Celine, who understood make-ups to perfection, always did her best with her older mistress, and Worth and New York modistes did the rest. On this occasion her dress would have been suitable for Narraganset or Saratoga, though even there it would have been noticed for its elaborate elegance, but in plain Ridgefield it looked, with its sweeping train and flounces and ribbons, as if designed for a ballroom rather than a country tavern. But no such idea troubled her. She was vainer of her looks, if possible, than her daughter, and a great deal more shallow. She was proud of being Mrs. Freeman Tracy and the granddaughter of the tallest monument in Ridgefield cemetery; proud of being the mother of the most beautiful girl in New York, or any other city she had ever visited, and very proud of the famous Tracy diamonds.

They had been brought from India by her husband's uncle on his mother's side and given to her on her wedding day, with the understanding that they were to go to her daughter, if she had one, on her bridal day. There was a cross, with pin and ear-rings,—the whole representing a fortune in itself. The ear-rings especially were of great value and once seen could readily be identified. They were pear shaped, very large, white and clear, and always attracted attention and excited comment when she wore them. The care of these costly gems was the bane of Mrs. Tracy's life, and numberless and curious were their hiding places when not in a downtown safe at her banker's where she kept them during Lent and at such times as she did not wear them. Helen had urged her leaving them there when coming to Ridgefield, but she had refused to do so. The bank might be robbed, or duplicates might be made of them in Paris where the banker went every few months. She had heard of such things, and when she was not in the city and liable to call for them every few days there was no knowing what might be done. She should take them with her, putting the boxes in a strong linen bag which Celine carried, with instructions never to let it out of her possession a moment. At the Prospect House it would be rather awkward for the girl to be walking around with a bag hung on her arm, and during the night it had reposed under Mrs. Tracy's mattress and been forgotten until Sarah, when making the bed, found it and took it to Mrs. Tracy. Evidently some place where the jewels could stay must be found for them.

"I wonder if there is a safe in the house," Mrs. Tracy thought, as she opened one of the boxes and feasted her eyes upon her treasures. Then she wondered where Helen and Alice were, and why everybody was out of the way when she wanted them.

"Miss Tracy is on the north piazza talking with Mr. Mason," Celine said, "and Miss Alice most likely has gone on some errand for her. I saw her going up the street."

Mrs. Tracy nodded, and after a time decided to go herself to the north piazza, or office, and inquire for a safe. She had not met Mrs. Mason and felt rather anxious to do so. Nothing could be bluer or purer in her estimation than the Tracy and Allen blood mixed, but the Mason blood was nearly as blue, and she had a great desire to be allied with it through a marriage of Helen with Craig. Consequently she was prepared to be very gracious to the mother. The gown she wore was selected with some reference to Mrs. Mason, who had been abroad and would recognize Paris workmanship. As she was passing the foot of the stairs she heard the sound of a footstep and saw a tall lady descending whom she knew must be Mrs. Mason from her air of good breeding and the dignity with which she bore herself.

"Good morning," Mrs. Mason said. "We need not stand on ceremony here. I know you are Mrs. Tracy, and I am Mrs. Mason."

Craig, who knew his mother's opinion of fashionable women like Mrs. Tracy, would have been astonished at her cordiality, but Mrs. Mason was a lady, and as such she would treat Mrs. Tracy when associated with her in the same house. Mrs. Tracy was delighted and met her advance effusively and told her where she was going.

"I think we shall find our young people there. Yes, here they are," she said, with a meaning smile as she turned the corner and saw them; Craig in his usual place; Helen, who, on the pretext of getting out of the glare of the noonday light, had moved her seat, sitting near him, and Alice on the steps.

In a moment Craig arose and bowed to Mrs. Tracy, whom his mother presented to him, and who sank into a chair, as if exertion of any kind were too much for her delicate frame.

"Ar'n't you going to introduce me to your mother?" Helen asked, as she saw Craig resuming his seat.

"I beg your pardon for my thoughtlessness," he said. "I must have lost my head. Mother, this is Miss Helen Tracy."

Mrs. Mason bowed to her a little stiffly, but Helen was not be ignored, and talked on in a familiar, chatty way, until she saw from her mother's face that she was growing restless and anxious for a chance to speak.

"What is it, mamma?" she said at last. "Do you want anything?"

"Yes," her mother replied. "I wish to see Mr. Taylor, or some responsible person with regard to my diamonds. Do you know if he is in the office?"

She looked at Craig, who arose at once and said he would inquire. Returning in a moment he brought Mark with him, saying Mr. Taylor was not in, but Mr. Hilton would perhaps do as well, if she were thinking of the safe. Mrs. Tracy's face showed that she would rather deal with the proprietor, and she finally said so, She had opened the boxes and put them upon the table where the jewels shone and flashed in a bit of sunlight which fell across them.

"Jeff said you wanted me. Here I be," came at that moment from Uncle Zach, who was followed by his wife with her big kitchen apron on, her sleeves above her elbows and a patch of flour on her face. "Wall, I'll be dumbed," he began, when he saw the diamonds. "These must be the stones I've hearn tell on," he said, taking one of the ear-rings from its satin bed and turning it in the sun until a hundred sparks of light danced on the wall and on the floor. "I reckon these cost money,—hundreds, maybe."

"Hundreds!" Mrs. Tracy repeated scornfully, "Thousands are nearer the truth."

"You don't say so," and Uncle Zach gasped as he looked at the stones and wondered where the money was in them.

Holding the jewel up to his wife's ear he asked how she would like to wear it.

"Don't be a fool," she said, "and put the ear-ring back before you drop it and break it and have it to pay for."

At this everyone laughed except Mrs. Tracy, who was too intent upon business to think of the absurdity of breaking her diamond.

"They are in a way heir-looms," she said, "brought from India and given to me on my wedding day. They are to be my daughter's when she marries."

She was looking at Craig who did not seem as much impressed as Mark. To him there was a fascination about those diamonds, which seemed like so many eyes confronting him, and he was glad when Mrs. Tracy closed the box and shut them from his sight.

"You want to put 'em in the safe, do you?" Uncle Zacheus said, "Wall, there ain't no better one in the state than mine. Burglar proof unless they blow it up, and Mark would hear 'em before they got very far at that."

"Does he sleep in the office?" Mrs. Tracy asked, and Uncle Zach replied, "No, ma'am; but in the room j'inin'. That linter you may have noticed is his bedroom."

"How many know the combination?" was Mrs. Tracy's next question, and Uncle Zach replied, "Nobody but Mark and me, and—yes, one more,—Dot. She had to know, but Land sakes, she can no more unlock it than a child. I have tough work at it myself. Mark is your man."

Mark had a feeling that Mrs. Tracy distrusted him, and

he suggested that she might feel safer if her diamonds were in the vault of the bank.

"No," she answered quickly. "I prefer to have them where I can assure myself of their safety any moment."

"Forty times a day if you want to. Mark will unlock it for you," Uncle Zach suggested. "Won't you, Mark?"

The young man did not answer. He was standing with his arms folded and a somber look in his eyes, until they rested upon Helen, who was close to him, and who, with a shrug of her shoulders, said in a low tone, "Don't mind mamma. She is so fussy about her diamonds that she will scarcely trust them with any firm in New York. *I* should let them lie around loose."

Wrapping the boxes in several folds of tissue paper Mrs. Tracy handed them to Mark, saying "I hold you responsible for them." She saw them placed in the safe, and decided that if she dared she would some day ask the high and mighty clerk to show her how to unlock it herself. She had taken a dislike to Mark for no reason at all except that he was made too much of, and as a hotel clerk had no business to be so gentlemanly and fine looking and hold himself in so dignified a manner towards her as if he felt himself to be her equal. The dislike was mutual, for Mark had decided that she was a proud, exacting, frivolous woman, whom it would be hard to please.

"Mamma, I think you were very uncivil to Mr. Hilton, and acted as if you were afraid to trust your diamonds with him," Helen said when they were alone in their room.

"To tell you the truth I was," Mrs. Tracy replied. "I really don't know why, but I have a queer feeling with regard to him. Mr. Taylor makes quite too much of him. I trust you will teach him his place if he tries to step out of it. I saw him looking at you with those queer eyes of his in a way I didn't like. They have a singular trick of moving round, and you can't help following them."

"Oh, mamma, a cat may look upon a king, and Mr. Hilton may surely look at me," Helen said, knowing perfectly well what her mother meant by Mark's eyes, which compelled you to meet them, whether you would or not.

She had met them readily,—in fact had rather challenged them to look at her, and then had sent back a glance which made Mark's blood tingle. No woman had ever affected him as she did and after he knew dinner was over in the salon he found himself constantly watching for a sight of her, or the sound of her voice. Two or three times he went round to the north piazza hoping to find her there, but Craig sat alone poring over Browning and listening occasionally for the trail of a skirt round the corner. He still had upon the table the lily Alice had given him, but it was shrivelled and faded and he scarcely knew it was there. The rose had overshadowed the lily and Alice was forgotten.

CHAPTER XV.

THE DRIVE.

At precisely four o'clock Jeff drove the hotel carriage up to the door with a flourish and a feint as if it were hard to hold the horses, who looked like anything but runaways and would have dropped their heads if they had not been checked so high. Jeff had spent two hours in scrubbing the carriage, polishing the harness and rubbing down the horses. His divinity, Miss Alice, was going to drive, and there was nothing too good for her. Helen had not impressed him as favorably as her cousin. "She don't look as real as my girl," he had thought when he first saw her, and he never had cause to change his opinion. At intervals Uncle Zach had superintended the washing and polishing and rubbing of the turnout which he said couldn't be beaten outside of Worcester, and he waited with a good deal of pride for the effect it would have upon the young ladies.

Alice was the first to appear, looking very cool and fresh and pretty in her dark blue serge made over from a last year's dress, and adapted as nearly as possible to the prevailing style. She was a natural dressmaker and had given her costume a few touches of her own ideas. Like Uncle Zach Jeff thought her a daisy, and although Craig and Mark were both there, the former fastening his gloves and the latter holding the reins by the horses' heads, he gallantly helped her to the back seat and smoothed down her dress with the air of a much older person. Then they waited five minutes and ten minutes until the young men began to get impatient. They did not know that Helen was seldom on time. She had taken her after dinner nap and bath and had dawdled in her dressing, notwithstanding Celine's efforts to hurry her. When at last she did appear she was like a picture stepping out of a fashion plate. Her tailor made dress and jacket were without a flaw in style and fit, her gloves harmonized perfectly with her dress, and the soft light veil twisted around her sailor hat and tied in a big bow under her chin was very becoming. In the morning she had worn Mark's rose; this afternoon she had a great clump of the *fleurs-de-lis,* Craig's color, fastened to her dress.

"Have I kept you waiting long? I am very sorry," she said, with such an air of penitence that both Craig and Mark forgave her, assuring her that it was of no consequence. "Alice, I know, thinks me delinquent," she said. "She is always on time; always doing the right thing."

"That's so," came from Jeff, who emphasized his words with a sudden whopover on the grass.

They all laughed, Helen the most of all.

"You see you have an admiring champion," she said to Alice; then to Mark, "You are to drive, I conclude."

"Yes, I go in the capacity of driver and guide, as I know all the points of interest," he replied, and Helen continued, "I suppose you and Mr. Mason should sit on the front seat, and Alice and I on the back, but I want to drive part of the time, and if you do not mind I will sit with you."

"I shall be delighted," Mark said, and in his delight he dropped the reins and almost lifted Helen to her place in front.

"Take care there! take care!" Uncle Zach exclaimed, hopping about like a grasshopper and seizing one of the horses by the bit. "You didn't or'to be so rash droppin' them lines. There's no knowin' what the horses will take it into their heads to do. Virginny is frothin' at her mouth now. She'll be pawin' next."

"I think it's the high check. It makes her neck ache. Won't you please lower it?" Alice said.

She was a lover of animals of all kinds and could not bear to see them needlessly pained. The high checks were Jeff's idea, but if Alice wanted them lowered they should be, and he at once let them out, evidently to the satisfaction of the horses, who shook their heads as if relieved from some disagreeable restraint. Mrs. Tracy, who had slept longer than usual, now came down the walk, with a frown on her face as she saw where her daughter was sitting.

"Helen," she said, "Won't you be more comfortable with Alice? You will get all the wind and sun and dust where you are, and burn your face. Mr. Mason will change with you."

"I don't want him to change. I like where I am. There isn't any wind, and I neither freckle nor burn; besides that I am going to drive," Helen replied.

There was no use arguing with her, and Mrs. Tracy could only look her disapproval, while Uncle Zach, still hopping about and very proud for this fine equipage to be seen before his door by the passers by, said in some alarm, "Better not let her drive till the horses have had some of the wind taken out of their sails. They've et two quarts of oats extra, and may take it into their heads to run away and upset the kerridge."

"Oh, please go on, or we shall not get started till dark," Helen said, and with a chirrup to the horses the carriage started, Uncle Zach taking off his hat to it, and Jeff indulging in two or three summersaults as it went rapidly up the street and past the houses from which many eyes looked curiously at the young ladies of whom every one had heard, although they had not been twenty-four hours in town.

When the carriage disappeared Mrs. Tracy, who evidently had something on her mind, followed Uncle Zacheus into the office and said in her most insinuating, amiable voice, "Dear Mr. Taylor, I don't want to be troublesome, but would you mind opening the safe for me? I mean would you mind showing me how to open it; then when I feel nervous about the diamonds I can see for myself that they are there, and need not trouble any one. I could ask your hired man to show me if he would, but I'd rather you should do it."

"My hired man! Great guns! How does Joel Otis know anything about the safe?" Uncle Zach exclaimed, thinking of his man of all work.

Mrs. Tracy saw her mistake and hastened to explain: "I mean your clerk, Mr. what's his name? He is hired, isn't he?"

"Why, yes; and I pay him a good round sum. He's worth it, too, and runs everything. I never think of callin' him my hired man, and I dunno's he'd like me to show you how to open the safe."

"Surely you are the master here, aren't you?" Mrs. Tracy asked, in a tone which at once piqued the man's pride.

"Of course I am. This is my house. What did you say you wanted?"

"I want to know how to unlock the safe, so I can see my diamonds whenever I choose," Mrs. Tracy replied.

Uncle Zach thought a minute, standing first on one foot, then on the other, and rubbing his bald head and wishing Dot were there. But Dot was at a neighbor's, gossiping about her city boarders and their elegant clothes, even their night dresses trimmed with real Valenciennes and nothing but silk stockings for every day. Dot could not help him. He must act alone, and it would not do to disoblige Mrs. Tracy, so he finally said, "Wall, seein' it's you, I don't care if I do, though I mistrust Mark won't like it."

"I don't see what business it is of Mark's. The safe is yours," Mrs. Tracy replied.

"That's so," Uncle Zach rejoined, and in a minute he was explaining to the lady the intricacies of the lock.

"The word is '*John*,'" he said. "That's our little boy

who died and is down in the cemetry. For J you give four turns *so;* for O three turns *so;* for H two turns *so;* for N a final jerk, and here you be. No you ain't neither! What ails the pesky thing?" he exclaimed, as with all his right and left turns and twists and yanks the safe resisted his efforts to open it.

He tried again with no better result; then yielded his place to Mrs. Tracy, to whom he gave the most minute directions. She, too, failed and after two or three trials called to Celine, whom she heard on the piazza.

"It's strength we need, and Celine has it," she said, explaining to the girl what was wanted and crouching down by her as she tried her skill on the obdurate lock.

Uncle Zach had lost his wits entirely, and went down on his knees to assist with advice and orders.

"Whew!" came through the window in a tone of surprise, and the next moment Jeff came in like a whirlwind, and made the fourth in the group by the safe. "What are you up to?" he asked, and at sight of him Mrs. Tracy, remembering what Alice had told her, rose to her feet.

Celine, however, had no such prejudice, and she explained the matter very volubly.

"Pshaw!" Jeff said contemptuously. "Is that all? I'lll bet I can pick the lock, give me time. Any way, I can open it. I've seen Mark do it a hundred times. Get out of the way."

He spoke to Celine, but Mr. Taylor and Mrs. Tracy both stepped back with Celine, leaving Jeff a fair field. It did not take him long to open the door, and with an "I told you I could," he disappeared, leaving Mrs. Tracy no better off than she was before. She could not open the door after it was shut, for she tried it until she was tired, and scorning to ask Jeff to teach her, gave it up, saying she supposed she was foolish in wishing to look at her diamonds whenever she chose without calling on any one to assist her, but something made her very nervous about them.

"Dot gets nervous spells, too, about nothin'. It's the way of wimmen," Uncle Zacheus said. "I guess we better not let Mark know we tinkered with his safe. He'd be awful mad."

"I think you defer too much to the opinion of an employee. It spoils them," Mrs. Tracy suggested, and Uncle Zach replied, "Can't spile Mark,—the best feller ever born. I'd trust him with my life."

Meanwhile Mark was feeling that he was as near Paradise as he would ever be until he reached its gates. It was a good deal to be sitting side by side with the most beautiful girl he had ever seen, and it was still more to have the beautiful girl as friendly and gracious as she was, treating him as if she had known him for years, and seldom looking back to speak to Craig, whom she left entirely to Alice. She professed to be enchanted with everything, and her face glowed with excitement. The spirit, which in one of her confidences with Alice she had ascribed to his satanic majesty whom she called the *old gentleman* was upon her, and she could no more help flirting with Mark Hilton than she could have helped breathing. Craig's reserve had piqued her, but while ignoring him she didn't forget him at all, or lose a word he was saying to Alice. He was the fish she meant to draw into her net eventually, but she was very happy watching Mark getting more and more entangled in her meshes.

It was a lovely summer afternoon and owing to the heavy rain of the previous night the road was neither dusty nor rough, and for a time Paul and Virginia did credit to Uncle Zach's praise of them and trotted on without a sign of lagging. Mark still held the lines, but when they had crossed the river and the causeway and were out among the hills Helen said to him, "Don't you believe the bloods have digested that two quarts of oats by this time and had the wind taken out of their sails sufficiently for me to drive."

She held out her hands for the lines which Mark gave to her, asking if she had ever driven much.

"No," she said, "but I want to learn, and I like to drive fast and feel the wind on my face. Touch them, please, with the whip."

Mark touched Paul, while woman-like Helen jerked the reins and told them to go on, which they did at a rapid rate, until a long, steep hill was reached, or rather a succession of short hills, with level spaces like plateaus between. Up two of these hills the bloods pulled steadily, but stopped at the third, while Paul looked back expectantly and Virginia laid her head against his neck in a caressing kind of way.

"What have they stopped for? Get up! Get up!" Helen said, but her get ups were unavailing.

Paul still looked back and Virginia finally joined him while Mark and Craig laughed aloud. Craig had been up that hill, which was known as the mile hill and was rough and stony, but had at its summit one of the finest views in the surrounding country. He knew the habits of the horses and wondered that they had not stopped sooner and signified their wish for the load to be lightened, especially as it was more than double now with four people and the carryall to what it had been with himself and Uncle Zach and a light buggy.

"What are they stopping for?" Helen asked again, and Craig replied, "Stopping for us to get out and walk.

Have you never heard that the horses in Norway are brought up to do that? I fancy the bloods may have come from that region."

Alice sprang out in a moment and began to pat Virginia, whose eyes were beginning to have in them a dangerous gleam as she felt the weight of the load behind her and saw the long steep hill in front, with still another and another beyond. Craig alighted, too, and so did Mark, and tried to coax the horses to move on. At first Paul seemed inclined to do so, and turned half way towards Virginia, who, true to her sex, stood her ground and would not budge. She knew there was still one occupant in the carriage and until all were out she would stay where she was.

"Make them go. Give them the whip. I'm not going to walk up that mountain to please any brute," Helen said, beginning to grow impatient.

Mark knew better than to use the whip, much as he wished to do so. Paul might not resent it, but Virginia was of a different make and knew how to use her heels if thwarted in having her way.

"How long do you think she will stand here if I don't get out?" Helen asked, and Mark replied, "All night, I dare say. She is gentle enough except about the hills, which she abominates. She was born on a western ranche. Hadn't you better give in?"

"No, never," Helen said laughingly. "I'll not be beaten by a horse. I can stay here as long as she can, if you'll stay with me."

"Of course I'll stay," Mark said, and folding his arms resigned himself to the situation, wondering which would give in first, the woman or the beast.

Neither showed any signs of it, and he began to think what he should do. Craig and Alice had walked on slowly, sometimes stopping to gather wild flowers and sometimes sitting on a boulder to rest. Evidently they were enjoying themselves, for more than once Alice's merry laugh came down the hill and Helen saw Craig pinning some field flowers on her hat. Suddenly it struck her more forcibly than it had ever done before that Alice was just the one to attract a man like Craig. This would never do, for whatever her relations to Mark might be she looked upon Craig as her property.

"I submit to the inevitable," she said, extending her arms to Mark, who lifted her very carefully and set her down upon the grass with a slight pressure of which he was scarcely conscious, but which Helen felt and knew that her subjugation of him was complete.

He was her slave and she could now give her attention to Craig. She had said she could not walk up the hill, but she did walk very rapidly until she reached the boulder on which Alice and Craig were seated. Then she grew so tired and exhausted and faint that when at last they started up the remainder of the declivity she said to Alice, "I must lean on you or never get there."

This was surprising to Alice, who had heard her cousin boast of her ability to walk miles among the Alps and knew that she had walked up Mt. Washington without apparent fatigue.

"Let me assist you," Craig said, offering her his arm, and finally passing it round her the better to support her when he felt her totter as if about to fall.

He was very kind, and the weaker and fainter she grew the kinder he became and the closer he held her, while he tried to divert her by laughing at the idiosyncrasies of Paul and Virginia, who were rushing up the hill with a rapidity which compelled Mark to run to keep pace with them. Of the two he was more exhausted than Helen when the crest of the hill was reached, for he was white about the lips and the perspiration was standing in great drops on his face. But he gave no thought to himself when he saw how limp and helpless Helen seemed as she sank down upon a broken bit of stone wall and closed her eyes wearily.

"You are not going to faint? You must not faint here where there is no water, and nothing but this hartshorn," Alice said with energy, giving Helen a little shake as her head fell over on Craig's shoulder, the only place where it could rest easily.

She did not look like fainting, for her color was as brilliant as ever, but she kept her eyes shut while Alice held smelling salts to her nose, and Mark and Craig fanned her with their hats, the former envying the latter his position with his arm now entirely round her and her head on his shoulder. Suddenly Mark exclaimed: "There is a spring not far from here where I can get some water in my hat," and he darted off in the direction of a clump of trees. Helen was perfectly quiet until Mark came back with his straw hat half full of water. Then she started up with a laugh and throwing back her head said, "I am all right now. It was a little touch of the heart, climbing the steep hill. I hope I haven't made a lot of trouble."

She looked down at Craig still sitting on the stone wall, then at Mark holding his hat with the water dripping from it. From this she recoiled and held back her dress lest a drop should fall upon it.

"I am awfully sorry about your hat. Do you think you have spoiled it?" she asked, giving him a look which she knew always did its work and which made Mark feel that the price of forty hats would scarcely pay for a look like that.

He and Craig were greatly relieved at her recovery, and assisted her to the carriage, one on either side, while she made a protest against being helped, when she was perfectly able to walk by herself.

"Did you ever have an attack like this before?" Alice asked.

Helen gave her a warning look and answered, "Not exactly like this. My heart has troubled me some. Let us go home, please, before I do anything more that is foolish."

CHAPTER XVI.

THE RETURN HOME.

MARK put her into the carriage on the seat with Alice where she wished to sit. She had accomplished her object. She had made both men dance to her music and was satisfied to take a back seat and to admire the splendid view from the top of the hill. The river, the meadows, the ponds, the wooded hills and several distant villages were spread out before them in a grand panorama.

"It is lovely and I am glad you brought us here," Helen said, leaning from the carriage, more conscious of the admiration she was exciting than of the view for which she really cared but little.

"I came this way to show it to you," Mark said, "but I'll never try it again with these blooded brutes."

They were very quiet and docile now and continued so all the way home, and although there were several hills to go up and down they neither flinched nor stopped. Virginia, who was the ruling spirit, would put her head over against Paul's neck when the hill was steeper than usual, and with a little neigh seemed coaxing him to good behavior; then, squaring her shoulders for the effort, plunged up the ascent at a pace which showed she at least had no heart trouble. Mark took the party round one of the ponds and into the village the opposite way from which they had left it. The road was past the Dalton House which caught Alice's attention at once. The windows had nearly all been broken and the setting sun poured a flood of light through them into the empty rooms. A mass of woodbine had climbed up one of the gables to the top of the chimney, around which it had twined itself with graceful curves, and on one of its branches, which swayed in the wind, a robin was singing his evening song.

"Look, Helen, what a picturesque old ruin. It must have a history," Alice said.

Before Helen could reply Mark rejoined, "That is the haunted house. You'll hear enough about it if you stay here long. It has something to do with *me*."

Helen was interested at once and asked that the horses be stopped while she looked at the ruin.

"The advertisement mamma saw had in it something about a haunted house, put in to attract attention, I suppose. Is this it, and is it really haunted, and what had you to do with it? Was somebody killed here? How dreadful! I dote on haunted houses," she said flippantly.

For a minute Mark made no reply; then he answered in a tone she had never heard before, "My great-grandfather was killed here, and the credulous people say his wife comes back to visit the scene of the tragedy."

"Poor thing! Where is she now?" Helen asked at random.

Mark laughed and thought of the withered rose in his pocket book and the grave from which he picked it; then he said, "Hard telling where she is. She has been dead nearly a hundred years."

"How sad; died of a broken heart, I suppose," was Helen's next remark.

Craig moved uneasily, wondering what Mark would reply, and wholly unprepared for his quick answer, "Died of a broken neck! She was hung!"

Helen gave a little screech and fell back against the cushioned seat, while Alice turned pale with wonder and surprise.

"That's my pedigree,—my heredity," Mark went on, with a certain defiance in his voice. "Mr. Taylor will tell you all about it, if you ask him. It is his crack story; but remember I had nothing to do with it."

He turned and looked at Helen, who met his look with tears in her eyes.

"I am so sorry," she said, very softly, and the words and the tears compensated for the shame Mark had felt when he avowed his ancestry.

"I am glad I was the first to tell it," he thought, as he told the horses to go on.

Not another word was spoken till the hotel was reached; then, as Mark helped Helen out, she said to him again, "I am sorry I gave you pain."

"And I am glad you did," was his answer.

They found Uncle Zach in the depths of humiliation and remorse. He had confessed to Dot the affair with the safe and received so severe a castigation from her tongue that he had crept up to the garret and looked at "Taylor's Tavern" and Johnny's blanket, and the envelope with Zacheus Taylor Esq. on it and had sat a long time on the trunk wondering if he were a fool, with no more judgment than a child, as Dot said he was.

"I guess I be," he said, "but if Johnny had lived I

b'lieve I'd been more of a man;" and a few hot tears fell upon the yellow blanket which was once little Johnny's.

The sight of Taylor's Tavern did not have its usual uplifting effect, for there was still Mark to meet. But Mark did not prove very formidable. Jeff had told him the whole story, blaming Mrs. Tracy most, and saying, "If I's you, I'd let him off easy. The old lady lammed him till he felt so small you could put him in a coffee pot. It hain't done no harm. He'd forgot how to work the combination. Miss Tracy can't open it, nor Celine, neither. Nobody but *me*."

"And if I ever catch you at it I'll break every bone in your body," Mark said, expending his wrath on the boy, who, with a laugh, went rolling off on the grass.

"I didn't or'to do it; no, I didn't or'ter," Uncle Zach said, half an hour later to Mark, who answered, "That's so; but I reckon no harm is done. Jeff is the only one who is any wiser, and we can manage him."

Thus reassured Uncle Zach brightened wonderfully, and inquired if Paul and Virginny had kept up their character.

"Yes, more than kept it up," Craig answered for Mark.

He had come to the office to drop into the letter box a hastily written postal to his coachman in Auburndale, telling him to send up Dido and his new light buggy at once. He had made up his mind to this that afternoon and already anticipated the pleasure it would be to drive over the Ridgefield hills with the young ladies, meaning mostly Helen, who had woven her spell around him when he sat on the broken wall with his arm supporting her and her head on his shoulder. His mother might not approve, but he was old enough to act for himself. To go out with the bloods again was impossible. So Dido was sent for, and Craig told his mother of it before he went to bed.

Mrs. Mason made no comment except to ask how soon he expected his horse. He didn't know,—within three days at the latest, and glad that his mother had taken the matter so quietly, he said good night and went to his room to dream of laughing brown eyes, which had stirred in him feelings he had never believed could be stirred by one whom he had not known twenty-four hours.

Mark, too, had his dreams,—wakeful ones,—which for a long time would not let him sleep. Every pulse was vibrating with the feverish madness which had possessed him since he first looked into Helen Tracy's face and had strengthened with each moment he had been with her.

"I'll win her, too," was his last conscious thought, as he dropped into an uneasy sleep, in which Helen and 'Tina and Paul and Virginia were pretty eagerly blended.

Helen also had her dreams or schemes, which she communicated to Alice, whom she asked into her room before going to bed.

"It is quick to make up my mind when I have only known them a day," she said, "but it seems to me I have known them years, so much happened in that absurd drive with those wretched *bloods*, as Mr. Taylor calls them. I am perfectly fascinated with Apollo, notwithstanding the terrible thing he told us. I was so sorry for him I could have cried. Mrs. Taylor told me some of the story after supper when you were on the piazza. It is very interesting, but too long to repeat tonight. It was a case of a woman loving some man better than her husband and getting that man to kill him. It often happens, you know. The great-grandfather was a Dalton,—a splendid family. Mamma has heard of them. There's a governor and a judge and a good many more things somewhere, but they have always ignored Apollo's branch because of that woman, 'Tina somebody. She was from a good family, too,—but if a woman does not love her husband and does love some one else, what would you have?"

"Not murder, certainly," Alice said, vehemently, and Helen replied, "Of course not. How you startled me, and how funny you look, as if I were defending 'Tina. I am not. I am defending Mr. Hilton, and shall treat him just the same as if his grandmother hadn't killed somebody. If he were only the Sphinx and the Sphinx were Apollo, I should be so glad. There is more warmth, more magnetism about him, but it is not to be thought of. Helen Tracy and a hotel clerk! That would be funny. He must have sense enough to know it, so there will be no harm in enjoying myself with him, and being in earnest with the other one, of whom I really think I can learn to be fond. It came to me when I was sitting on the wall with his arm around me, and you all thinking I was faint."

"And weren't you?" Alice asked, in a voice which made Helen look at her quickly, as she answered, "Not a bit. I was tired walking up that horrid hill in boots a size too small and which hurt me every step I took, but I wasn't faint. I was making believe."

"Why?" Alice asked, sternly, and Helen replied, "Don't be so cross. I always tell you everything, you know, and it was really nothing more than lots of girls do. I was tired and could have screamed with the pain in my feet, and then they seemed so concerned I thought I'd put on a little just to see what they would do. I hope I posed gracefully. My heart did beat faster than usual with the climb, so it wasn't much of a fib, but I wasn't going to have my dress and veil and gloves spoiled with that water which, I dare say, he would have dashed all over me if I hadn't recovered in time to prevent it. It was a jolly lark and pretty good for the first day in Ridgefield."

Alice did not answer. The soul of truthfulness herself, she could scarcely imagine her cousin guilty of so contemptible a ruse for the sake of attention and adimration. She knew she was a flirt, but not of this sort, and her good night was rather constrained and cold when she at last said it and went to her room.

CHAPTER XVII.

PROGRESS.

THREE weeks had passed of glorious summer weather, which the guests at the Prospect House had enjoyed to the full. There had been sails on the river, walks under the Liberty elms, and drives among the hills and through the woods, off into the lanes where solitary farmhouses stood, and where the inmates looked curiously at the stylish turnout and high buggy with its red wheels, and at the young people whom they designated the "swells from town." Paul and Virginia were no longer called into service, but in the pasture north of the hotel fed and drank at their leisure from the running brook and the fresh green grass, and when the sun was hottest stood under the shade of a huge butternut tree, their heads together, but held down as if they knew they had been set aside by a city rival and were rather sorry for it. In the only box stall the hotel boasted Dido, when not on duty, munched her hay and oats, slept on her bed of clean straw and whinnied a welcome whenever her master appeared, although his appearance was the herald of a long and fatiguing drive. She had been sent at once in response to Craig's postal, and the young man had harnessed and driven her with a great deal of pride up the hill and through the village to the door of the hotel, where the entire house had come out to welcome her.

Helen, who had a suspicion that she had been sent for on her account, was very effusive, calling the horse a darling and winding her arms around its neck, when assured there was no danger. Dido liked to be petted, and she had it in full measure, from Helen to Uncle Zach, who, while praising Dido, insisted that if "Virginny had the same trainin' and the same care she'd of been about as good." Naturally Mrs. Mason was the first whom Craig took to drive, then Mrs. Tracy,—and then Mrs. Taylor, who, Uncle Zach said, looked with her two hundred pounds "as if she was squashing Craig to death on that narrer seat." She never went but once; neither did Mrs. Tracy, and the drives were mostly given up to Helen and Alice. Craig had intended to take one as often as the other, but it so happened that Alice went occasionally, and Helen very often. She needed the exercise, her mother said, and was apt to have a headache when she missed it, and she looked so beautiful and happy when she came down the walk to the buggy that Craig always felt glad it was Helen instead of Alice, and always wondered when he returned why he was more tired than when he had driven with Alice. Helen fatigued and intoxicated him, she was so full of spirits and extravagant exclamations of delight and small talk, to which he could not respond, although he tried to do so, and felt that she was laughing at him for his awkwardness. And still he was very happy and proud to have her with him, and, like the foolish fly, was drawn closer and closer into her net.

With Alice it was different. She was never gushing, nor effusive. She never laughed up into his face, nor took off her gloves because her hands were warm and asked him to button them for her when she put them on, as Helen did. She was quiet and enjoyed everything in a quiet way and talked of what interested him most,— books, and art, and his college life. With the one girl he was himself and in his right mind, with the other he was giddy and dazed; bewitched, his mother thought, as she watched the progress of affairs, but wisely kept silent, knowing that interference on her part would be of no avail.

Mark Hilton, too, was a silent and watchful spectator of what seemed a serious flirtation between the two, —the flirtation on Helen's side, the seriousness on Craig's. But Mark was not unhappy, and bided his time. He did not drive with Helen, nor sail with her on the river, nor walk under the Liberty elms, but there were many chance meetings when her eyes shone on him just as brightly as they did on Craig, and her smile was just as sweet. Once, when Mrs. Tracy was asleep and Alice was driving with Craig, he went with her to the cemetery on the pretext of visiting her grandfather's monument, which she had never seen except at a distance. From the monument to the angle in the wall where 'Tina was buried was not very far, and Mark purposely took her that way, and said to her, half mockingly, half sadly, "We have visited the graves of your ancestors, now I want you to visit mine. These are the

Dalton graves; this is my great-grandfather's; that his wife's,—'Tina, people call her. You have probably heard the story since the night we passed the house. Mr. Taylor is rather fond of telling it, and pointing me out as a descendant."

"Mrs. Taylor told me something, but I'd like to hear it from you, who would tell it differently," Helen said.

"I will tell you, certainly," Mark replied, "Sit here;" and he led her to the low wall, the top of which was very wide and covered with large smooth stones.

The thick branches of a willow tree shaded it from the sun and hid it from the highway. Birds were singing among the willows, and the low murmur of a brook falling over a miniature dam the school children had made, could be distinctly heard. Altogether, it was a most romantic place to sit and hear the story, which Mark told, keeping back nothing, nor trying to soften the guilt of the woman who had been dust for many a year. As he talked Helen was very attentive, and once, when he spoke of the child calling for its mother, she put her hand on his arm, "Please don't tell me any more," she said, "I can't bear it, and I am so sorry for you; that is, if you care. I should not, if I were you. It was so long ago."

She was all sympathy. Her face and eyes shone with it, and the latter were full of tears. She could cry almost as easily as she could smile, and she had never looked fairer to Mark than she did now, with the tears on her long lashes and her hand on his arm. She had forgotten to remove it until he put his on it in token that he appreciated her sympathy. Then she withdrew it and said, "Don't you think it time we were going; Mr. Mason and Alice must be coming home soon?"

"Is that any reason why *we* should go?" Mark asked,

with a look she could not mistake and from which she turned her eyes away.

Much as she enjoyed the situation she felt that it was getting rather too personal, and was glad when, as if in answer to her mention of Craig and Alice, the sound of wheels was heard and Dido came dashing through the avenue of willows close to where she was sitting. Mark's impulse was to keep quiet and he made a sign to Helen to do so. But the sight of Craig and Alice together marred the bit of romance and almost love-making in which she was an actor, and springing to her feet she waved her handkerchief and called out loud enough to attract their attention and make Craig rein Dido up suddenly, while he asked what she was doing in the cemetery.

"Seeing the old graves. I've never been here before. Mr. Hilton is with me. We are coming at once."

She was over the wall by this time and Mark felt obliged to follow her, cursing the luck which had sent Craig in his way and transformed Helen from the tearful, sympathetic woman into the gay, coquettish girl, who insisted that Craig should let Dido walk, while she walked beside them, asking where they had been, what they had seen and wholly ignoring Mark, who, at last, when he met some one to whom he wished to speak, asked to be excused, and left her.

"Polite, I must say," was Helen's laughing comment, as she chattered on, evidently oblivious of the man who had held her hand in his and for whom her tears had fallen rather copiously.

Mark did not forget it, and when that evening he saw her on the piazza settee with Craig beside her, his arm across the top of the seat, but not touching her unless she leaned far back, as she occasionally did, he smiled and thought, "It is an even race, and I know her better than he does."

Where Craig trusted he had no suspicion. He had come to believe in Helen, and was pretty far on the road to being in love with her, but his matter-of-fact, quiet liking bore no comparison to the passion which possessed Mark Hilton, who, as he had said, knew the girl better than Craig knew her, and knew how much her tears and sympathy and pretty words were worth, and was still determined to win her. Craig could drive with her and walk with her and sit with her on the piazza where others passed and repassed and feel himself supremely happy. To Mark, Heaven came down into the shadowy corners of the old hotel and into the office when no one was present to hear the low-spoken words, not of love exactly, but merging rapidly toward it with the lingering touch of the hands when accident brought them together,—the conscious look in the eyes,—and the sudden starting apart when a third party appeared. Could Mrs. Tracy have known all this she would have told her daughter she was acting the part of a bar maid with a bartender. But she did not know or suspect how often Helen was with Mark Hilton, not openly, as with Craig, but secretly and alone. Alice watched quietly the march of events, satisfied with the few crumbs which came to her in the form of pleasant words and smiles from Craig, when he was not too much absorbed with Helen.

Jeff was her devoted slave, and had been since he heard her words of commendation when she defended him against her aunt. She had been with him two or three times on the river after lilies, with which he kept her supplied and which he once told her she was like. She had been with him to see the mud-turtle's bed and the hornet's nest, and said to him many things which would sometime come back to him in a paroxysm of remorse and regret for those days, the happiest he would ever know. He no longer tried to pick pockets for fun, and he did not object to Sunday school and the verses in the Bible which Mrs. Taylor required him to learn. He was, however, quite awake to the state of affairs between Mark and Craig and Helen, and knew pretty accurately how much time the young lady spent with each of her lovers and where, and drew his own conclusions.

"A girl can flirt with two fellers at a time, but she can't marry them both, and I'll bet my new jack-knife Mark will come out ahead," he said to himself, but did not communicate his opinion to Alice, lest she should reprove him for eaves-dropping, and he wished to stand well in her estimation in every respect.

CHAPTER XVIII.

BROWNING.

The north piazza, which was the widest and pleasantest around the house because the coolest and most quiet, had assumed quite a cozy, festive air since the Tracys came. Several bits of carpet and rugs had been spread upon the floor,—three or four easy chairs had been brought out, with a settee over which a bright afghan was thrown. A hammock had been put up in which Helen posed, with Mark and Craig standing by and swinging her gently to and fro. Alice said the hammock gave her a headache and left it to Helen, who monopolized it entirely, either sitting or reclining, and doing both naturally and gracefully, as a little child might do. A small round table had been brought out and covered with a dainty tea set, which Mrs. Tracy had found in Worcester, and here Helen dispensed tea nearly every afternoon, and sometimes in the evening when the moon was shining upon them, softening the beauty of her face and making it more like a Madonna than a young girl whose brain was sometimes aching with the feeling of unrest gradually stealing over her and bringing into her eyes a troubled look never seen there before.

Every few mornings she found a fresh bouquet of roses upon her tea table. Taking it for granted they were for herself, she went into ecstasies over them and wondered who sent them.

"Not I. I didn't think of it. I wish I had," Craig said in his honest way, as she buried her face in the roses and then looked inquiringly at him.

If Craig did not send them, Mark did, and whether she thanked him in the office or on the stairs no one knew. He was satisfied and happy, and would have ordered all the roses in the North Ridgefield greenhouse if he had thought she wanted them. Craig still kept his small table for his lemonade, of which he was very fond, and for his papers and books. These last had been sadly neglected. Browning had scarcely been touched, but was not forgotten. He meant to have the readings yet, and spoke of them several times to the young ladies. Alice was always ready, although frankly admitting that she knew nothing and must be a mere listener. Helen was never ready. Nothing would give her greater pleasure than to spend an hour each day with dear old Browning, she said, but there was always some reason why she couldn't give herself that pleasure. At last, as the sultry August days came on and it was too hot and dusty to drive until after supper, Craig, who was not one to give up an idea readily, decided to bring his club together, and on a certain morning gave notice that he should expect its members on the north piazza at 4 o'clock sharp, to hear him read Sordello. He was sure of Helen and Alice, and probably his mother and Mrs. Tracy, with Mark, when he could find time, and Mr. and Mrs. Taylor, if they chose to come.

"Come? In course we shall," Uncle Zacheus said. "I'm rather old to begin to improve my mind and shan't catch on worth a cent; but Dot will. She's quick to see a p'int. Who was Browning, anyway? I used to know a family down east by that name. Any relation?"

Craig explained as well as he could and smiled as he thought of Uncle Zach trying to master, or even listen to the intricacies of Sordello. But he was glad for an audience, if half were Uncle Zach's, and was very much engaged and excited for him. The chairs were arranged in a semi-circle, a little away from the hammock, which would not, of course, be used. Helen, the only one who was really interested, or knew much of the poet, would sit at his right. He had arranged for that by having a chair placed close to the stand on which were the roses which had come fresh that afternoon for the occasion. There were bowls of lilies on the wide railing of the piazza and at 5 o'clock Celine was to bring out biscuits and wafers and preserved ginger to be served with chocolate which Helen was to pour. Nothing could be pleasanter, he thought, as at a quarter before four he took his accustomed seat. Mrs. Tracy was the first to join him. She knew nothing of Browning and cared less, but was glad of any break in her monotonous life which did not require exertion. She did not like to drive, or sail, or walk; she had visited her grandfather's monument, and the house where he used to live, and had been once to church. For the rest of the time she had stayed at home, doing nothing except to watch the progress of affairs between Helen and Craig. She would like to have her daughter settled, and nothing could suit her better than to see her married to Craig Mason. That morning she had broached the subject to Helen, who had replied, "If Mr. Mason proposes to me I shall not refuse him."

This had put Mrs. Tracy into so good a humor that she had forgotten to see if her diamonds were safe. Twice a day,—morning and night,—since her failure to open the safe herself, she had asked Mark to do it for her. This morning she had not made him her usual visit, and when, as she was going to the north piazza, he called to her and asked if she had forgotten her diamonds, she waved her hand patronizingly, and said, "I had; but no matter, I can wait till night."

She took the seat indicated by Craig, and was soon joined by Mrs. Mason and Alice. Then Uncle Zach came, pleased as a child "to be invited to a literature."

"Dot will be here in a minute," he said, as he seated himself in a chair so high that only his toes could touch the floor. "She's seein' to some sass on the stove."

Dotty soon came, heated and perspiring, and more interested in the jelly she had left in Sarah's care than in Browning, of whom she had never heard till invited to attend the reading. Even then she would have declined if it had not been for her husband, who told her they didn't or'to lose a chance to improve their minds.

If she thought he had not much mind to improve she did not say so, and in her best gingham gown and white apron, she took the only chair left except the one near Craig, reserved for Helen. That young lady had been having a rather unenviable time with Browning.

It was now more than three weeks since that first day at the Prospect House when Alice had gone out to find the library, if there was one. She had found it without difficulty and inquired for Browning's Poems.

"Which volume?" the librarian said.

Alice didn't know, and confessed her ignorance.

"What particular poem do you wish to read?" was the next question.

"Sordello," Alice replied, and the librarian brightened at once.

"Oh, yes; Vol. I. We have that, and it is nearly always in, so few care for it; they find it tough reading, they say. You like it, I suppose?" and the librarian looked over his spectacles at Alice, who said, "I don't know; I never read it."

"Wouldn't try, then; hard work and little pay," and the old man shook his head; then added, as he handed the book to her, "if you must read it, better take the encyclopedia, which will help you amazingly. Here 'tis."

Alice took the book and turning the leaves found the story which she knew would be a help and which she might herself like to read.

"Thank you," she said. "I will take both; they don't look as if they were often used."

"Very seldom. Not on an average once a year. There's a chap at the hotel been in twice and looked at the encyclopedia. He's pretty well up in Browning, I guess. You are from the hotel, too, aren't you?"

Alice bowed in the affirmative and left the library. For some days the books reposed quietly on Helen's dressing table. So many things came up to occupy Craig's mind that it took but little tact to put the club out of it for a while. The moment, however, that Helen saw signs of its revival she attacked Sordello in earnest, taking the poem first and reading five or six pages very carefully, over and over again, first to herself and then to Alice, who consented to listen unwillingly, for she knew that Jeff was waiting to take her to the hornet's nest and the turtles, and twice his shrill whistle came in at the window telling her he was ready. For a time she sat very quiet, for Helen was a fine reader, but when she reached the "Progress of a Poet's Soul," and asked what some of the passages meant, Alice sprang up exclaiming, "I don't know any more than the dead, and I doubt if anybody does. I've promised Jeff to go with him to the woods and pond to see a turtle bed and hornet's nest. Good bye, and good luck to you."

She was gone and Helen was alone with Sordello.

"No more soul than to prefer mud turtles and hornets to Browning. I supposed she had a higher grade of mind," Helen said, with a sigh of self-satisfaction, as she thought of her cousin tramping through the fields to the woods in company with Jeff, while she, with her higher grade of mind, was wrestling with Browning.

She didn't find him quite as entertaining or easy to be understood as she had at first. It was not much like Tennyson's "May Queen," or Tennyson's anything, she thought, and at last threw the book down in disgust, half tempted to go after Alice and the hornets, especially as she saw Mark walking down the lane in that direction. Taking up the encyclopedia she turned to the story of Sordello, which pleased her better. Here was something she could understand, and she read it over and made copious notes from it for future reference, and felt herself quite mistress of the narrative in all its different phases. She could not explain why, but Mark Hilton always stood for Sordello, while she was Palma, and with this fancy she finished the story. To wade through the poem was a different matter. Then a happy thought occurred to her. She could commit parts of it, and, if necessary, fire them off at Craig, who would be impressed with her superior knowledge. Just what to commit she didn't know. So she took bits here and there at random, learned them in a short time, with no conception of their meaning, and was ready for the class.

Days and weeks passed. The class was not called and she forgot a good deal she had stored up, and when Craig unexpectedly announced the meeting for that afternoon she was thrown into a state of great consternation and hardly knew whether Sordello had been a troubadour or a hotel clerk,—whether he belonged to a noble family, or was 'Tina's great-grandson,—and whether he was still in Purgatory, where Dante saw him, or at the Prospect House, receiving orders from Mrs. Taylor. Her Browning knowledge was a good deal of a jumble, which she must disentangle. She had made too many admissions of her liking for him to fail when the test came, and all the morning which was one of the hottest and sultriest of the season, she was shut in her room, going over the story again and re-committing the passages which had escaped her memory. Sordello and Mark Hilton were pretty equally mixed in her mind, which for some reason she found more difficult to concentrate on the subject than she did before, and as she spent the morning so she spent the time after dinner alone in her room, letting no one in and saying she had a headache and was resting. She did look a little heavy-eyed when she was at last ready to join the group on the piazza. Tired as she was she had taken a great deal of pains with her toilet, dressing more for Mark than for Craig, who, she had found, was less of a connoisseur in the matter of women's attire than Mark. She would have liked to have worn white that hot day, but Mark did not like white gowns and blue ribbons, because Tina was said to figure in these when she visited the haunted house. So she chose a soft grey chally with elaborate trimmings of pink and white chiffon. Two or three of Mark's roses were her only ornaments except her costly rings. With her smelling salts to keep up the appearance of headache, and a fan which matched her dress, she went languidly toward the group on the piazza, all seated except Mark, who was standing at a little distance with a quizzical expression on his face. He was something of a lover of Browning and had read Sordello two or three times. Since the club had been talked of he had thought to read it again and had inquired for the book at the library. He was told one of the young ladies at the Prospect House had had it for some time, and he readily guessed that Helen was "loading up," as he expressed it. He did not believe she cared a straw for Sordello, or anybody like him, and was anxious to see how she would acquit herself.

"We are waiting for you," Craig said, getting up and putting his hand on the chair reserved for her. "You are to sit here near me, as you are the one who will be most in sympathy with the reading. The others do not like Browning."

"What a pity, and how much they lose," Helen replied, "but if you'll excuse me I'd rather sit in the hammock. My head still aches a little."

She had no idea of being in close proximity to Craig, who might ply her with troublesome questions. She preferred the safety of the hammock, and, with the help of Mark, who at once came forward, put herself into it, half sitting, half reclining on the cushions, with her face away from all the party except Mark, who stood just where he could see her. No one would ever have suspected there was anything of the schoolmaster about Craig, but he assumed that rôle to some extent, and before commencing to read, he said, "I think we shall understand the poem better if we know something of the subject, Sordello. Who was he? Miss Alice will perhaps tell us?"

"Oh, don't ask me! Pass on to Helen. She is posted," Alice said, while Helen raised herself on her elbow,—moved her fan back and forth slowly, and replied, hesitatingly, as if cudgelling her memory for something she had once known and which had become a little indistinct.

"I don't know that I can talk very clearly about him, there were so many fictitious accounts of him. I believe, though, he was a troubadour, who was born in the twelfth or thirteenth century at Goito, near Mantua. Am I right?"

She was looking at Craig, who nodded affirmatively, and smiled upon her as she went on still more slowly

"Wasn't he at first in the family of some count, who was chief of the Guelph faction, and didn't he afterward enter the service of Berenger, of the house of Barcelona?"

Again Craig bowed and Helen continued: "He wrote songs and poems and was distinguished for his pleasing address and grace of manner, although said to be small in stature. The stories told of him are so filled with anachronisms, romances and fictions that it is difficult to decide which are true and which are false."

"That is all encyclopedia. Of herself Helen never mastered such a word as anachronism," Alice thought, while Mark had a similar idea.

Craig had no suspicion, and was delighted to find one

person in so perfect accord with himself. He motioned her to go on, and, pleased with the attention she was receiving, she went on rapidly now and a little incoherently, as her memory was beginning to fail her.

"I think," she said, "that some writers have accused him of eloping with another man's wife. This is doubtful. There is a Palma, who figures very conspicuously with him. I can't tell you all about it, or just how he died. I know Dante met him in Purgatory with those who had died without a chance to repent."

"Served him right, too, for running off with another man's wife. Has he ever got out of Purgatory?" Uncle Zach exclaimed, and Helen blessed him for creating a diversion at a point from which she dared not venture much farther.

Everybody laughed except Mrs. Taylor, who had caught a whiff of burning jelly and arose hastily, saying she must be excused.

"Come back, Dot, as quick as you can; it won't do to lose none of this feast of ——, what do you call it?" Uncle Zach said to her, putting his hand on her chair as if to keep it from some imaginary claimant.

Dot did not answer, nor did she come back.

"I think I've done my part," Helen said, but as Craig urged her to go on she continued, with an air of superior wisdom, "As to the much-abused poem, it was written, I suppose, to show the times in which Sordello lived, and is in some sense the history of the development of a great soul. It is the most obscure of all Mr. Browning's poems, and is like a beautiful palace without a staircase; so if one would reach the rooms on the second floor, he must climb."

"Bravo! Miss Tracy. That is a most original idea,

and you have described it exactly;" Craig cried, enthusiastically.

He evidently had not studied the encyclopedia as she had, and was giving Helen credit for an originality of thought she did not possess. The absence of a staircase had struck her forcibly, and she remembered and repeated it, and, flushed with success, ventured out into waters which proved too deep for her. Why commit portions of Sordello, if she did not use them? she thought. "It is a grand poem, with so many fine passages," she said, and began to repeat portions of it, but became confused, and strung together parts of sentences in two or three different books, making a medley at which even Craig looked perplexed, wondering where such passages occurred, while Mark disappeared around the corner to hide his merriment.

It was his face which told Helen of her blunder, but she was equal to it. With a gay laugh she said, "I've made a horrid mistake, I guess, and jumbled things some, but have done the best I could. Now I'll give place to the master."

She made a graceful gesture with her hands toward Craig, and then lay down among her cushions and prepared to listen. Craig was a fine reader and interested in his subject, but the air was hot and sultry and none of his audience very appreciative except Helen. He was sure of her; he was reading to her, and occasionally casting a look at the hammock and the white hand which lay on her grey dress, and the perfect contour of the side of her face he could see, with the rich coloring on her cheek and the soft curl of hair around her delicate ear. He did not mind if Mrs. Tracy did nod occasionally and his mother yawn and Alice cast glances at the village clock which could be seen up the street, while Uncle Zach was placidly sleeping with his head thrown back and his mouth wide open. He had his Plato and was satisfied. As yet he had asked no one for their ideas of the meaning of anything he had read. He had merely given his own and that of the most approved critics.

At last he came to a sentence rather obsure to himself. He asked for an opinion, looking first at Mrs. Tracy, whose eyes were closed,—then at his mother who shook her head,—then at Alice, who was convulsed with laughter, although what there was to laugh about he could not guess.

"Miss Tracy will have to help me out," he said, turning to the hammock, and dropping his silver paper cutter at the same time so that he only caught a faint sound of what he had not observed before, or which his voice had drowned.

"What did you say, please? I didn't quite catch it," he asked, bending towards the hammock from which the sound came again and very decided this time; not an explanation of Sordello, but an unmistakable snore!

Helen was fast asleep. Mark, who had returned to his post and had been watching her for a few moments, gave a loud laugh, in which Craig, after a moment's discomfiture, joined.

"I think it time to stop," he said, "as I have read part of my audience to sleep."

Helen was awake by this time, greatly distressed and a little ashamed as she guessed why they were all laughing.

"I am so sorry and mortified," she said, getting out of the hammock and stretching up her white arms like one rousing from sleep, "but my head aches and the day is so hot that I cannot help it. Did I,—did I really—?"

She looked at Alice, who answered, "Yes, you did; but

it was a very ladylike snore, and not at all like Mr. Taylor's; he has been off for some time."

He was awake now, and rubbing his eyes, looked round bewildered, "What's that? What's that?" he said. "Is the meetin' over? I must have fell off a minit. Great chap, that Sour fellow; mighty queer name! Where'd you say he was? In Purgatory? Let him stay there! Honest, though," he continued, as his truthfulness came to the rescue, "I couldn't get head nor tail to it, if there was any. I s'pose though to you who see through it 'twas a feast of —, what do you call it? Hello, there comes the chocklet. I guess we are all ready for that kind of feast," he exclaimed, as Sarah appeared with the chocolate mug and the basket of biscuits and wafers.

Helen was certainly ready for it, and took her seat at the table, and poured the chocolate, which Craig handed round, while Sarah passed the wafers and biscuits. It was a very merry party which gathered near the table and Helen was the merriest of all, and was so graceful and fascinating that Craig would have forgiven a much graver offence than falling asleep while he was reading. Having no sisters, and a mother who was almost painfully matter of fact and frank, he had no knowledge of girls and their ways, and could not understand that nothing about Helen was genuine except her beauty; everything else was studied for effect,—from the intonation of her voice to the droop of her long eyelashes and the tears she could summon when she wished to be particularly pathetic and interesting. Mark knew her much better than Craig, but her deceptions, which would have filled Craig with disgust had he known of them, did not touch his moral sense of what was right and wrong. He did not look beyond the beauty of her person, which he coveted and meant to possess. He knew she did not care for Browning, or books of any kind, and was not at all surprised at her falling asleep. The flippancy with which she repeated Sordello was easily accounted for. He knew she had the encyclopædia, and Jeff, who was everywhere and saw and heard everything, had heard her reciting passages from Sordello, and when he was under the window waiting for Alice to go with him to the woods he had caught snatches of the conversation and had heard Helen say "I hate it all, but must keep up my reputation as a Browningite."

This he had reported to Mark, and had asked, "Is she going to speak a piece, and can I hear her?" Jeff was obedient to every known wish of Mark, whose will dominated him, and, actuated by a desire that the latter should be a winner in the race he saw was running between the two men, he frequently gave information to his master as to where Helen could be found alone, and sometimes stood guard at a little distance, ready to whistle, or turn a summersault when any one was approaching.

"Both of 'em after her," he thought, "and it's a toss up which will win. Time will tell. I can't."

CHAPTER XIX.

WHAT TIME TOLD.

FOUR weeks more passed much as the preceding ones had done, and it was the middle of September when as a rule city people return to their homes, and the summer hotels are closed. Mrs. Mason and Mrs. Tracy were anxious to leave but as neither Helen nor Craig were willing to go, they felt obliged to remain, one to watch her son and prevent him from committing himself to what she knew he would regret, and the other to bring about, if possible, what Mrs. Mason so much dreaded. In the second week in September Alice went back to her mountain home and the red schoolhouse which one of her scholars wrote her had been "mopped real clean and had a new blackboard and a new water pail and dipper." There was a letter also from Aunt Mary, telling of a room refurnished with fresh paper and paint and a single white iron bedstead, with muslin hangings; a pretty bureau, with a long glass and a silver backed brush and handmirror,—these last the gift of the school children, who had picked berries on the mountains and sold lilies from the pond to buy them for their teacher, whose return they were anticipating with so much pleasure.

Alice cried over this letter so full of love and thoughtfulness and wondered why she should shrink from a return to the farmhouse and the homely duties awaiting her there. With the sound of Craig Mason's voice saying to her, "I hope you have no bad news," she knew why the thought of leaving Ridgefield gave her pain, and scolded herself for it. Craig could never again form any part of her life and she resolutely set herself to work to put from her all thought of him and made her preparations for leaving quickly and quietly, saying to every one that she had had a delightful summer and should not soon forget it. Quite a crowd accompanied her to the station, Craig and his mother, Mrs. Tracy and Helen, Mark and Uncle Zach, and Jeff, who was inconsolable.

"I'll go to the bad. I know I shall. I feel as if I wanted to pick forty pockets," he said to Alice, as he bade her good-bye, and then went into the meadows behind some alders and cried.

Helen was very sorry to part with Alice. "I have lost my ballast, and, like Jeff, shall go to destruction sure," she said, and for days she seemed so sad and depressed that Craig tried every effort to comfort her, taking her for a long drive around the chain of ponds and talking to her of what he thought would interest her most. There had been no Browning readings after that first attempt. "As no one cares for them except ourselves, we may as well give them up, but whenever you feel like it I shall be glad to read for *you*," he had said to her, and Helen, while lamenting the non-appreciation of the others, had acquiesced in his decision, and on two or three different occasions, after Alice left, she sat on a low ottoman very close to him and listened patiently for half an hour while he read to her, once from Sordello, once from poems easier to be understood, and last from Pauline, whose opening stanza thrilled them both with as much of real love as either could ever feel for the other. In a voice, full of feeling, Craig read:

"Pauline, mine own, bend o'er me,—thy sweet eyes,
And loosened hair and breathing lips and arms
Drawing me to thee,—these build up a screen
To shut me in with thee, and from all fear;"

And again:

"Thou art so good,
So calm—"

And again; in a lower voice, which was almost a whisper:

"Thou lovest me;
And thou art to receive not love but faith,
For which thou wilt be mine—" etc.

He did not ask her what she thought was meant by this outburst of passion. He only looked at her once as she sat beside him, with her hands working together nervously on her lap, her "sweet eyes" upon him with a coy expression in them, and her "breathing lips" a little apart as she drank in the words and felt that something more was meant for her than a repetition of an imaginary love-sick boy's declaration of love to his mistress. She was very quiet all through the reading, and when it was over left Craig without a word except, "Thanks for the pleasure you have given me."

Had he been making love to her, she asked herself many times in her own room, and would he follow it up with words plainer to be understood than those spoken to Pauline. And if he did, what answer should she give.

"There is only one I can give him, and he is too good a man for that, but mamma, position, society lie that way. To take the other road would be folly," she thought, and for an hour or more fought a fierce battle with herself and her inclination.

For two days she avoided both Craig and Mark as much as possible, and scarcely spoke when she met them. She was missing Alice, and wanted to go home.

"Before anything has been accomplished?" her mother said, "Have we spent the summer in this dull place for nothing? Remember you will soon be *passée*. People now say you are older than you are, you have been before the public so long. You cannot expect twenty more offers. If you get *one,* and it is the right one, I shall be glad. You once told me you would accept Mr. Mason is he proposed;—can you not bring him to do so or have you lost your skill?"

This decided Helen. Craig and his mother were going to Boston the next morning on the early train, his mother to stay and Craig to return, and when that afternoon Craig suggested a drive she assented readily.

"I shall not be back for a few days," he said, "and by that time it may be cold and rainy. We ought to improve this fine weather. I have scarcely seen you for a week."

It was a glorious September day, with that stillness in the air and that haze upon the hills which early autumn brings, and Helen wondered at the feeling which oppressed her.

"I used to like such days, but this one makes me homesick and shivery," she said, as she arranged her hat and buttoned her jacket and gloves.

On the terrace below she heard Mark giving some orders to Jeff and for a moment she held fast to the dressing bureau to steady herself. She had not reached the stage of young ladyhood which requires stimulants every day, but she knew the use of them and going to a bottle labeled brandy she poured out more than she had ever taken before at one time and drank it.

"That will steady my nerves;" she thought, but her step was not as elastic as usual when she went out to where Craig was waiting for her, with Mark standing beside him.

She did not look at the latter as she took her seat in the buggy. She had made up her mind and there was no going back. She had often boasted that she could make a man propose to her if she wished him to do so. In this instance she did wish it and every art of which she was mistress was brought to bear upon the unsuspecting Craig, who would have been less than a man had he been insensible to her charms. Either the rapid motion or the excitement, or the brandy gave an additional brilliancy to her complexion, and her eyes had never been more beautiful than they were when she told Craig how much she had enjoyed the summer, thanks to him and his kindness, and said this was probably their last drive together, as she and her mother might be gone before he returned, but she should never forget Ridgefield,—never. Perhaps it was the wind which blew a little chilly down the hill they were descending, and perhaps it was real grief which brought a tear to her eyes as she lifted them to Craig's face and then dropped them quickly, as if ashamed of her emotion. Craig had fully made up his mind to ask her to be his wife, but was going to wait till he had decided upon words suited to so delicate a subject. Perhaps it would be better to write when he was in Boston, he thought. Yes, on the whole it would be better, as he could arrange and re-arrange what he wanted to say, so as not to shock her in any way. But all his pre-arranged plans were set aside by Helen's methods, and before he knew what he was doing he had asked her to be his wife and she had accepted him, with a protest that she was not worthy of him,—that if he knew her as she knew herself he would not wish for her, but if he were prepared to take her with all her faults, she was his, and would try to make him a good wife.

He did not know that she had any faults, except that she might be something of a flirt, and this she could not help. He was willing to take her as she was and felt himself very happy, while she tried to believe herself as happy as a girl ought to be when engaged to a man like Craig Mason. She had been wooed by many suitors, but never in this quiet, tame fashion, and she laughed to herself as she thought of the contrast. Some had knelt at her feet with passionate words of love, and two hotheaded, brainless ones had threatened suicide if she refused them, and then had been married within six months. All this was very exciting and exhilirating to one of her temperament, and very different from Craig's style. He had not even touched her hand,—possibly because at the moment her final yes was spoken a baby-cart came suddenly through a gate and both his hands were occupied in managing Dido, whose one fault was fear of a baby-cart, and who started to run furiously. When she had become quiet and they were ascending a hill he said abruptly, but laughingly, "If rumor is correct, I am not the first who has proposed to you?"

There was a world of mirth in Helen's eyes, as she replied, "You are the twenty-first!"

Craig gasped, as if the honor were a questionable one. Helen saw it and hastened to add, "I could not help it if a lot of senseless men and boys chose to think they were in love with me. I never cared for one of them,—never!"

She made the last never very emphatic, and thus reassured the shadow lifted from Craig's face, and during the remainder of the drive he talked of their future which should be as bright and happy as it was in his power to make it. They would have a home of their own in Boston, for he believed in the saying that no house was large enough for two families,—a sentiment in which Helen fully concurred when she thought of his stately mother, who, she felt sure, was not anxious to have her for a daughter-in-law. They would go to Europe, if she liked, when they were married, and it would please him to have the marriage take place as soon as possible, say, at Christmas time.

"No, oh, no! Not so soon as that!" Helen exclaimed. "You do not care for society, and I do. Let me have one more winter of it before I settle down into the domestic wife I mean to be."

She was very earnest, and Craig consented to wait until spring.

"And, please," she said, "don't let us talk of the engagement at once. I mean, not to-night, and you going away to-morrow. Wait till you return."

"But suppose you are not here? You said you might not be," Craig suggested, and Helen replied, "We shall be here. I can persuade mamma to stay, if she still thinks of going. I shall tell her, of course, and shall write to Alice to-night. She will be interested, and, oh, Mr. Mason—"

"Craig, please," he interrupted her.

"Well, then, Craig. I think it such a pretty name," Helen continued. "If we go to Europe,—and I should like that so much,—would you mind having Alice go with us? I am always better when she is with me. Did you ever notice what clear, honest eyes she has,—eyes which keep you from being bad when they are on you. She is so helpful, too, and sees what to do and does it. I should be happier if Alice were with us."

It was a novel thing for a newly-engaged young lady to be asking her *fiancée* to take another young lady with them on their bridal trip because it would make her happier. But Helen was in earnest. She was always at her best with Alice, and much as she might love Craig Mason, if she did love him, she knew there was very little that was congenial between them, and there had already come over her something like homesickness as she thought of months abroad, with only him for company and no one to whom to show herself as she really was,— to let herself out, as she expressed it. Craig was in a mood to promise anything. He could be very happy alone with Helen, but Alice would not be in his way. She was restful and helpful and sunny, and, as Jeff had once said of her to him, "Cool and good to look at, with her blue eyes and lily complexion." He was quite willing she should be the third in his party, for he had an impression that she was a kind of ballast for Helen. That she should go with them was settled by the time they reached the hotel, and Helen's "Thank you, Craig," was very genuine as she arose for him to lift her from the buggy.

Just for an instant he held her in his arms before he put her down. Her face was very near his and he might have kissed her if Jeff, who seemed to be omnipresent, had not rolled up in time to prevent it. Releasing her he said, "You are now mine. God bless you and make me worthy of you."

Helen did not answer, but went at once to her room and, throwing herself upon the bed, burst into a paroxysm of tears. Glad, happy tears she tried to think they were, for had she not secured what she came to Ridgefield to secure in case she found it worth the trouble. And he was worth it, she told herself, over and over again. He was a man of whom any woman might be proud and fond.

"I shall disappoint him every day," she said. "He is far better suited to Alice."

The mention of her cousin reminded her of the letter she was going to write, and, after a hurried supper, during which she said but little to her mother, she commenced it. On the first line in immense letters were the words: "WE ARE ENGAGED; the prize is mine!" Then she went on to describe the drive and the means she took to bring Craig to the point.

"You know I am an experienced hand in love-making, and its different phases," she wrote, "while he is a mere baby;—actually stammered annd blushed when he asked the important question, the *twenty-first* put to me. I told him that, and I could see it staggered him a little, but he soon recovered and I do believe he is happy, while I respect him because he didn't get down on his knees; he couldn't very well in that narrow buggy, with Dido running away from a baby-cart. That was what happened, and maybe is the reason that he was so cold in his wooing. Didn't even touch my hand, and it was lying where it would have been very convenient for him to take if he wanted to. He really acted as if I were a choice piece of pottery, not to be meddled with. On the whole it was a very matter-of-fact affair, something like this: *He,* after two or three coughs, and getting very red in the face, 'Will you be my wife? Behave, Dido, what ails you?' *She,* very much surprised, so much so in fact that without stopping to think, she replied, 'Yes, if you wish it. I think it was the baby-cart that frightened Dido.'

"That's about as it was, and we were engaged, and went at once to talking of the future,—or he did. Wished to be married by Christmas. But I said no. I must have one more winter in dear old New York before settling down as a model wife in stupid Boston. Of course I didn't talk that way about Boston. But he is to wait until spring, when we are going to Europe, and *you* are going with us! I settled that at once. I could not stand a year's travel alone with any man, with no right to look at another or let him look at me, and nobody to talk things over with. I began to feel lonesome until I thought of you, who always do me good. You know I am tricky and false and all that is mean that way. You found out more of it here than you knew before, and your great, pure, white soul rebelled against it, but I know you like me and I like you better than anybody in the world, except, of course, mother and Craig. He wants me to call him that, and—— well, I'll not enumerate my likes and dislikes. I want you to go with us, and Craig wants you, and you are going. So make your arrangements to give up that schoolhouse in the spring and see the old world, and help me through the British Museum, where I have never spent more than two hours, but shall have to spend days with Craig, who thinks me rather intellectual. I have arranged how to manage. I shall have a headache and be tired, and wait while you and Craig examine every coin and piece of old yellow parchment, and all the broken-nosed and broken-legged statuary. Ugh! I shudder to thing of it, and the many more tiresome places, in which Craig will revel. We shall stand by Mrs. Browning's grave in Florence and stare at the house where she lived, and sail past the Browning palace on the Grand Canal in Venice, and I shall be expected to go into raptures over Sordello and that other queer name, Paracelsus, about which I know nothing and care less.

"Poor Craig! He is getting awfully cheated. There is nothing real about me, except my face. I am fairly good-looking and I mean to make him a good wife. He is easily gulled; shy men always are, or he would see through me. Mr. Hilton does, I am sure. I wish Craig had as much fun and fire in him. But comparisons are odious, and sometimes injurious to one's peace of mind. It is something to be Mrs. Craig Mason of Boston, with a fine establishment on Commonwealth Avenue, and one can't have the world. Did I tell you Craig was going to Boston with his mother to-morrow to be gone some days, and I am wicked enough to feel relieved. I know exactly what to say to a man to whom I am *not* engaged, but what to say to one to whom I *am* engaged is a different thing. The excitement is over and only a dull surface of things left. I shall have time to think and get myself well in hand before he comes back. He is to bring several engagement rings for me to choose from, and will look at a house on the Avenue which is for sale and which he thinks will suit me.

"And *you* are to live with us! I have settled that in my own mind. I cannot live alone with a man and that man my husband, and know I am roped in,—done for,—finished; no more need of any little harmless tricks and deceptions, which are my very life. I believe I am growing wicked, so I'll stop. Burn this letter as soon as you read it. It sounds heartless, and as if I didn't care for Craig, when I do; but, oh, Alice, I wish I could turn myself inside out in the lap of some good woman and tell her all I feel. But I can't. Mother would be horrified and so would you, and each for a different reason. I know you pray, and so do I, in a stupid, mechanical way, but I can't to-night, nor ever again, perhaps, but you, who never did a mean act in your life, can pray for me.

Your wicked

"Cousin Helen."

Once Helen thought to tear this letter up, then decided to send it; and bade Celine take it down to the table in the lower hall where letters designed for the early mail were left. For a long time that night she tossed upon her pillow, unable to sleep, and, as a consequence, did not waken until after Craig and his mother had left for the 8 o'clock train.

CHAPTER XX.

IN THE HAUNTED HOUSE.

THE morning was long and lonely to Helen, who wondered what there was for a girl to do when all was over and settled. She felt that she ought to have been up and spoken with Craig before he left. He expected it, she knew, for he had asked Celine if she were awake, and when told she was still sleeping, had given the girl a note for her.

"Darling," it said, "I hoped I might have seen you this morning for a moment, but as I cannot I send you a line to tell you how happy I am, and that I shall count the days before I can return. God bless you, and keep you in safety. Craig."

Helen had received scores of love letters, but none which affected her like these few words, which wrung the hot tears from her eyes as she read them.

"I am not half good enough for him, and when he comes back I shall tell him so, and make him believe it. I don't like to be engaged!" she said, as she dressed herself leisurely, dispensing with the services of Celine, as she would rather be alone.

Her mother, who had waited breakfast till she came down, noticed her languor and depression, and asked if she were ill.

"No," Helen answered, "I am not ill. I am engaged; that's all. Mr. Mason asked me to be his wife when we were driving yesterday, and I told him I would. You are glad, I know."

Mrs. Tracy was delighted. What she so much desired had come to pass, and she began at once to plan a grand wedding and an elaborate trousseau.

"You know the diamonds are to be yours when you are married," she said, "and they must have modern settings. I'll ask Mr. Hilton for them, and we will look them over together."

"But you'll not tell him why you wish to see them. No one is to know that till Craig comes back," Helen said, in some alarm.

"Of course not," her mother replied, as she left the room for the office.

Mark, who knew her errand, unlocked the safe at once and bade her look in.

"I wish to take them to my room," Mrs. Tracy said, and with the boxes she returned to her salon, where the stones were examined and admired, and the change in their setting discussed. "I shall rather hate to part with them," Mrs. Tracy said, "especially the pin and cross. I do not care so much for the ear-rings, they are so heavy."

"And they are all I do care for, so you can have the pin and cross," Helen replied, as she fitted the rings in her ears and turned in the sunlight to see them sparkle. "I think I shall keep them just as they are. I like their hanging, instead of clinging close to my ears. I'll take them back," she continued, and gathering up the boxes she went to the office, where she found Mark alone. "Aren't they beautiful?" she said, turning her head coquettishly from side to side.

"Are you going to wear them?" he asked.

"Oh, no; I am just showing you how much they add to me," she replied.

Mark said they were very fine, and began to unlock the safe to put them away, while Helen took one of them from her ear. The clasp to the other was bent, and after trying in vain to unclasp it, she gave a cry of pain.

"Oh-h! it's cutting my flesh. What shall I do?"

"Can I help you?" Mark said.

"Perhaps so," and she turned her small pink ear to him and stood very still while he loosened the refractory ring, his hands touching her hair and cheek and making her blush as she thanked him and stepped back.

He did not speak of Craig, but he asked how she was going to pass the day without her usual drive.

"I shall not miss it," she said; "there is such a thing as being driven too much," and she looked at him in a way which made it hard for him to keep back the words he was intending to say before Craig Mason returned.

But not in the office. He had the time and place arranged, and he said, "As you cannot drive suppose you take a walk after tea. The evening will be fine. There is a full moon, you know."

Helen assented readily. Here was something to think of; something to do,—and all the ennui of the morning was gone. That afternoon there came a telegram from Craig, who said, "We reached home safely. Shall return on Saturday, instead of Monday, as I first proposed."

"How like him,—making love by telegraph. We shall probably exchange postals for good mornings when we are married," Helen said with a laugh Craig would not have been pleased to hear.

"He was very thoughtful to let you know he would be back sooner than you expected him, and shows his kind heart," her mother suggested.

"I suppose it was," Helen replied, as she tore up the telegram, and tossing the pieces into the waste basket went to dress herself for the anticipated walk.

"Where are you going?" her mother asked, when after tea she saw her putting on her hat and jacket.

"Just to the post office and round the square," Helen replied.

"Alone? Without Celine?" Mrs. Tracy said in some surprise.

"Yes, without Celine, but not alone. Mr. Hilton is

going with me," Helen answered, a little defiantly, in anticipation of her mother's next remark.

"Do you think it proper to be walking in the evening with a comparative stranger? Do you think Mr. Mason would like it?"

"Oh, bother, mamma! Don't be so prudish. I am to be trusted, and so is Mr. Hilton. As for Craig he will not object. I am not going to tie myself up in a bag because I am engaged. By-by, don't worry about me."

She kissed her hand and went out to the piazza, where Mark was waiting for her, with a light in his eyes and a ring in his voice she had never heard or seen before, and which put her on her guard. They went first to the post office where the evening mail was being distributed and where Helen found a letter from Craig, mailed in Boston at 4 o'clock and written after the telegram had been sent. Mark, who was standing apart from her, only saw that she had a letter and crushed it hastily into her pocket. Leaving the office they walked slowly around the square until they came to the turn in the road which led past the old ruin. The sun had been down for half an hour or more, and the full moon was pouring a flood of light upon it, making it look rather ghostly and weird, with the woodbine dropping from the chimney and a lilac tree brushing against one of the broken windows.

"Have you ever been in my ancestral hall?" Mark asked.

"No, and I don't believe I care to visit it," Helen replied.

"Oh, yes, you do. All the young people in town come here. It is quite a rendezvous for lovers," Mark urged.

"But we are not lovers," Helen said, and he replied,

"Very true, but we can go in for all that. Perhaps we may see the ghost, if there is one. She comes in the moonlight, they say, as well as in the rain. You surely are not afraid?"

Helen was not afraid, and only held back from a feeling that it was not quite the thing to do. At last her love of adventure overcame her sense of propriety, and she followed Mark to the rear of the house where a door had fallen from its hinges, giving them free access to the building. Through the lane to this door a path had been worn by many feet, and Helen could well believe that it was a rendezvous for lovers, who either had no fear of 'Tina, or came hoping to see her. "It would have been a great deal more romantic for Craig to have told his love here than while holding Dido in to keep her from running and screaming at he top of his voice to make me hear, the wheels made such a clatter over the stones and ruts," she thought, as she followed Mark in to what had been the family room where 'Tina sat when the tragedy outside went on and where the baby boy called so often for his mother. Through the paneless window the moonlight was shining, making the room almost as light as day, except in the corners where dark shadows lay. Something was stirring in one of them and with a cry of fear Helen pressed close to Mark, who took her hand and led her to an old settee which stood by the wide fire place.

"It is only a rat; the house is full of them," he explained, as he sat down beside her.

"Oh-h! I have a mortal terror of rats and mice, too. Let's go," Helen cried as she drew her feet up from the floor.

"No, not yet," Mark said. "There's a chair somewhere in which you can put your feet and be safe from the marauders."

He found the chair and brought it to her; then resuming his seat he continued: "I am afraid you are not pleased with my ancestral halls."

Now that she was in no danger from the rats, Helen was less nervous and began to look around her with some curiosity.

"It is a creepy kind of place and the last I should choose for a rendezvous," she said. "Why did you bring me here?"

"Because there is something I must say to you which I can say better here than where we would be liable to interruptions," Mark replied, putting his arm on the back of the settee where it would be very convenient for it to drop across her shoulders. "I told you the story of this house in the cemetery, by 'Tina's grave, and only the fact that I had known you so short a time prevented me from telling you another story which I have brought you here to listen to. You have heard it many times, for I know your reputation, and I believe that when you came to Ridgefield Craig Mason was your object."

Helen did not speak, and Mark continued: "I have watched events closely. Craig is interested in you. How could it be otherwise, but I do not believe he will ever have the courage to declare himself. He is not a ladies' man,—is not your style. He is a student, self-absorbed and quiet, caring nothing for the things which make your world. He is the soul of honor, and a splendid fellow, with no fault or bad habit, such as most men have. He neither smokes, nor drinks, nor swears, and is as pure in thought and speech as a woman,—purer than many."

"Then why are you running him down?" Helen asked, and Mark replied, "I am not running him down, and I hardly know why I am speaking of him at all, except that it seems as if he were near us, or that I was taking an unfair advantage of his absence."

Helen's hand was in her pocket clutching Craig's letter, with a view to bring it out and declare what he was to her. But she didn't. Years after, when so much was said of hypnotism, she recalled that night and said she was hypnotized, but she did not think so then. She only knew that the man beside her talking of the man to whom she was engaged had a power over her which she did not try to analyze, nor resist. His arm had dropped from the settee and was lying across her shoulders and she did not shake it off, as he went on:

"I respect Mr. Mason highly, but he is not the one to make you happy. Domesticity is his idea of married life. Yours is different. He has hobbys. The present one is Browning, for whom you do not care a rap."

"How do you know that?" Helen asked sharply, and Mark replied, "I know it as I know you, and Craig does not. You cannot help making believe, and with him it passes for the real coin. If you were his wife there would come an awakening which he would find it hard to forget."

"You are complimentary, I must say, and if you brought me here to lecture me and tell me how unfit I am to be anybody's wife, I think it time we were going," Helen said, making an effort to rise.

Mark held her back, his arm encircling her now so tightly that she was close against his side.

"I know I have not been very complimentary thus far, and I dare say no man has ever talked to you as I am talking in order to show you that I know you thoroughly, and that with all your faults I love you, and have since the night you came and I carried you in my arms through the rain. Something then in the touch of your hands as I put you down gave me an inkling of your responsive nature and I have watched you closely since; have seen every little coquettish air and grace, and known, when you dazzled me with your smile and eyes, that it meant nothing except as a pastime for you; and yet, I have gone on loving you and sworn to win you. Nor am I without hope. You have given me every reason to think I was not indifferent to you and that is why I am telling you of my love and I warn you not to trifle with me. Uncle Zacheus does not believe in heredity, but I know there is enough of my great-grandmother's nature in me to send me to the devil, or make me one, if circumstances were favorable. If the woman I loved and who I had reason to believe loved me thwarted and scorned me, I should not murder her, but there is in me a fire which would burn out all the good and deliver me over to the evil one."

His voice was almost a whisper as he poured out the full measure of his love, while Helen sat still, knowing that his arm was drawing her to him and that his face was close to hers. He made no allusion to the difference in their positions. He put himself on an equality with herself and she respected him for it and knew that she loved him if it were possible for her to love any one. She had no intention to be false to Craig, on whose letter she still kept her hand, meaning to bring it out and show it at the last. She told herself that she had expected something like this and knew that she was very happy and wished it might go on forever.

Mark was waiting for her to speak, and she must bring out the letter. She did not dare let go her hold on it, for it seemed to her as if she were holding on to Craig as long as she felt the touch of the paper he had handled. Tears, which came to her so easily, were pouring down her cheeks. She must wipe them away; as Mark had taken one of her hands she had no alternative but to withdraw the other from her pocket and in so doing lost her grip in more ways than one.

"You do love me a little?" Mark pleaded and lifting her tear drenched face to his she answered, "Yes, a little. I can't help it, but—"

She did not finish the sentence for the kisses pressed upon her lips brought her to her senses.

"Mark! Mr. Hilton! How dare you take such a liberty. No man has ever kissed me since my father died,—not even Mr. Mason, and I am engaged to him! It happened yesterday, when we were driving. This letter is from him."

She took it from her pocket as she sprang to her feet and held it as a barrier between herself and Mark, who had also risen and whose face was white as the moonlight falling over it.

"Engaged to Craig Mason!" he said, seizing her arm with a grasp which made her wince with pain. "You are engaged to Craig Mason, and have sat here and listened to me without a word! Are you woman, or a demon?"

"Don't speak to me like that, and let go my arm! You hurt! I tried to tell you, but couldn't, you influence me so, and——" Helen said, putting her hands over her face and crying out loud.

In a moment Mark's anger left him, and his great love came surging back.

"Forgive me," he said. "I was a brute, but you took

me by surprise. Sit down until you are more composed."

He felt for a moment as if the earth were slipping from him, leaving him utterly stranded; then his indomitable will came to the rescue and he was himself again, quiet, tender, earnest, with his magnetic powers in full swing. She had said, "You influence me so," and this gave him courage. Taking her hands from her face he held them in his and said to her jestingly, "You say no man has ever kissed you since your father died, and you are engaged to Mr. Mason. I am afraid he did not claim his privileges."

"He couldn't; he had all he could do to keep Dido from running away, and the wheels made such a racket I couldn't hear half he was saying," Helen replied between a sob and a laugh as she recalled Craig's love making, so different from the one she had just experienced.

Her spirits were returning and with them her blunted sense of right and wrong, and when the moon looked into the room at a different angle from what it was looking then, there were no tears on her face and her head was on Mark Hilton's shoulder, as if that were its rightful resting place. Love was triumphant. Conscience had been smothered, or if it pricked at all it was quieted with the thought, "I could not help it, and Craig will soon get over it."

Everything was settled as to what to do and how to do it, Mark suggesting and Helen yielding to whatever he proposed. She knew her mother would be hard to meet and Craig would be harder.

"We must be quick," she said, "or I shall change my mind. I don't believe I could endure the look on Craig's face when he knows how false I am."

Mark was fully aware of this. He knew the girl better than she knew herself. Opposition from her mother and reproach from Craig would upset her and he did not mean her to come in contact with either. Fortunately for him it had been arranged that morning that he should go to New York the next night on business for Mr. Taylor. If Helen could be there at the same time all would go well. Could she manage it?

"I think so. Yes, I am sure I can," she said, as they went back to the hotel, where they found Mrs. Tracy very anxious to know what had kept her daughter so long."

"The night is so fine that I wanted to enjoy it and see if it would help my head which aches awfully. I must go to bed at once," Helen said.

She was longing to be alone and think what she was doing. It seemed to her that she was in a vise from which she could not escape, and Mark held her even in her room.

"I cannot go back now," she said, "and I would not if I could. I do not love Craig Mason and I do love Mark Hilton. The world will call it a mesalliance and I suppose it is, but love laughs at such things. It would be more honorable to stay and meet Craig face to face and ask for a release. But I can't do it. With mother going into hysterics, as she certainly would, I might yield."

She was removing her jacket and felt Craig's letter in the pocket. It was crumpled and tear stained, for she had kept it in her hands before her face when she was crying. She studied the address,—"Miss Helen Tracy, Prospect House, Ridgefield, Mass.," carefully, and with a little choking in her throat.

"It is like him," she thought. "Every letter precise and square and plain as print."

Then she wondered what was inside. How had he addressed her? Was it a genuine love letter or not? She could easily ascertain by opening it, but something in the better part of her nature made her shrink from doing this. She had separated herself from Craig and the letter did not belong to her.

"I'll return it unopened in the one I must write him," she finally decided, and putting it away she tried to sleep, but could not.

Her conscience was not at rest, although she told herself she was very happy, or should be when it was over and people had ceased to talk.

"It will cause a great commotion in this quiet town and give them something to gossip about for a month," she said, "and I can almost hear Mr. Taylor's 'I'll be dumbed,' when it comes to his ears."

She laughed when she thought of that, and burying her face in her pillow tried, by counting a hundred backwards and every other device she had ever heard of, to sleep, but in vain, and morning found her just as wakeful as she had been when she first sought her bed.

CHAPTER XXI.

THE DENOUEMENT.

It was not a feigned headache of which she complained when she went down to breakfast. Her temples were throbbing with pain and there were dark circles around her eyes.

"Mother," she said, "I am going to New York on the noon train to see Dr. Allen. I believe I am malarious,

I am having so much headache and feel so languid. Charlotte, you know, is in our house. I can stay there to-night and come back to-morrow."

Mrs. Tracy was at once concerned and anxious and unwilling to have her go alone, or to have her go at all.

"Why not consult some physician in town?"

"Yes, and have tons of quinine prescribed, with a little morphine, perhaps, to make me sleep!" Helen answered impatiently. "No country quacks for me. I want my good old Dr. Allen or nobody."

"Then I shall go with you, and for that matter we might as well pack up and leave altogether. I am quite ready," Mrs. Tracy said.

Here was a dilemma which Helen had anticipated and which she met promptly.

"Of course not," she said, in the tone which usually subdued her mother. "Have you forgotten that Craig is coming back on Saturday? What would he say to find us gone, and what use for you to fatigue yourself with a journey to New York just to chaperone me? No, mamma; make yourself comfortable with Celine and don't worry about me. If there are any errands I can do for you I may perhaps have the time. I can at least see the fashions."

Mrs. Tracy was not convinced and to the last insisted that if Helen must go she or Celine ought to go with her.

"I tell you I prefer to go alone, and if I can't do that I'll not go at all," Helen said, and that decided it.

When Uncle Zach was told of the arrangement and asked to have Paul and Virginia ready to take her to the station for the noon train, he was at once on the alert for the reputation of his house.

"Got malary here! That can't be. There ain't no sweeter **drain** in the state. Dot never pours bean water in it and keeps it stuffed with copperas all the time. No, sir! 'Tain't malary. It's bile, and boneset tea is good for that. Dot'll steep you some."

Helen declined the boneset and insisted upon New York.

"Wall, then, why not wait till night? Mark is goin' on the eight train, and will see to you," was Mr. Taylor's next suggestion, and when Helen declined Mark's company, as she had the boneset, saying she preferred to go at noon, he continued: "Of course we'll send you down; and what do you say to Mark's tacklin' up Dido? She or'to be used before she knocks the stable to pieces. She's kicked off two boards already."

From this proposition Helen recoiled. To have Mark drive her to the station after Dido would be the acme of cruelty and insult to Craig.

"No, no," she said. "I don't want Dido. Let Sam take me when he goes to the train."

"Mebby that will be best, as Mark is kinder busy lookin' over papers and castin' up accounts," was Uncle Zach's reply, as he went to order Sam to have the carriage and Paul and Virginny ready for the noon train.

Helen felt like a guilty thing as she made her preparations, and once resolved to give it up. Going to the office where she found Mark alone, she said to him, "I can't do it. I'd rather stay and brave mother and Craig than sneak off this way."

"Very well," Mark said, looking at her with an expression before which her eyes fell. "Suit yourself," and he turned to his papers again.

"Do you wish to give it up?" she asked timidly, and he replied, "Certainly not for myself. But I know you, and that between your mother and Mr. Mason I should get the worst of it and lose you, while you might lose us both."

This was a catastrophe which Helen did not care to contemplate. She had staked everything and could not lose.

"I'll go," she said.

Mark put out his hand and taking one of hers pressed it warmly as he said, "My darling, you shall never regret it."

After this there was no wavering on Helen's part. She ate, or tried to eat, her early lunch; was very loving to her mother when she said good-bye, and went so far as to kiss Mrs. Taylor, who wondered at her effusiveness, when she was to be gone so short a time. As she passed the office Mark sauntered to the door and said, "Off so soon? Is it time?"

"Yes, good-bye," she answered gayly, while he returned to the papers and accounts he was putting in order for his successor, and feeling pangs of remorse as he thought how Mr. Taylor would miss and mourn for him.

Uncle Zacheus went to the station with Helen, and at the last moment when the train was in sight he said to her, "Wall, good-bye. You'll be comin' back tomorrer, or I should be sorry, you seem so like our folks."

She grasped his pudgy hand and said, "I can't begin to tell you how kind you have been to me, or how much I have enjoyed myself at your house. Good-bye."

She pressed his hand to her lips and stepped upon the train, which was soon bearing her away across the meadow lands between the river and the cemetery, where her grandfather's tall monument was the last thing on which her eyes rested. It was many years before she saw it again.

On the platform where she had left him Uncle Zacheus stood, looking at the back of his hand as earnestly as if he could see the kiss Helen had imprinted there.

"Wall, I'll be dumbed," he soliloquized. "Yes, I will, if this ain't droll. A young gal like her kissin' an old codger like me! I wonder what Dot would think of it? I guess I won't tell her. She mightn't like it. She hain't kissed me since I can remember."

If the kiss had been in a tangible form Uncle Zach would have put it away in the hair trunk with Taylor's Tavern and little Johnny's blanket. As it was he kept one hand carefully over the spot which Helen's lips had touched and smoothed it occasionally as he was driven back to the hotel.

"Fust rate girl," he said to Mark, to whom he began to talk of what he was to do in New York. "When you git your business done stay a day or two, if you want to," he said. "It's some time sense you was there, and if I's you I'd call at Miss Tracy's. They say her home is grand. You know where 'tis?"

"Yes," Mark answered.

He could say no more for the lump which was choking him as he kept on with his work. It was harder leaving the old place than he had anticipated, and had Helen been there then and said, "Let's give it up," he might have listened to her. Helen was gone. He would not be less courageous than she, and he kept on until every paper and account was labeled and in its place, easy to find and examine. Then he went through the rooms of the hotel one by one, saying good-bye to them, and always with that lump in his throat, making him swallow hard to keep it down.

"I am as weak as a woman," he said to himself, when he went to the stables to say good-bye to the horses.

He was fond of animals, and both Paul and Virginia turned their heads towards him and whinnied as he came in. In her box stall Dido was corvetting round as well as she could in that small space, pawing with her fore feet and kicking occasionally with her hind ones as the spirit moved her. She, too, whinnied when she saw Mark and looked beyond him toward the door.

"I believe she is looking for her master, or Helen," Mark thought, as he remembered that the latter had frequently brought her apples and tufts of fresh grass. "Dido," he said, stroking her glossy coat, "are you expecting Helen? She's gone. She will never come back, or drive behind you again. Are you sorry?"

There was almost a human look in the dumb creature's eyes, as Mark talked to her, and he half felt that he was understood.

"Good-bye, Dido, and Paul and Virginia," he said, as he left the stable and closed the door.

Just outside he met Jeff. Next to Helen Jeff was dearer to Mark than any other living creature. He had rescued him from the street; there was a kind of link between them connecting them with the tragedy of the Dalton house, and the man's heart yearned towards the boy.

"Jeff," he said," when I am in New York I may look around for some place different from this. If I find one and go there later, would you like to live with me?"

"In New York? You bet!" was Jeff's reply, as he darted away.

Mark did not dare to be very demonstrative in his adieus to the family lest they should wonder at it. Mrs. Tracy, who always treated him as an inferior had seen the safe opened that morning and knew her diamonds were there, and it was not necessary to speak to her at all.

He found Mrs. Taylor, with whom he shook hands, feeling glad that it was dusky in the hall so she could not see his face.

"Yes, I *am* weaker than a woman and weaker than water," he thought, as he felt his knees shake under him, for the hardest was yet to come, the saying good-bye to Uncle Zach, who was standing on the walk, bareheaded in a misty rain which was beginning to fall.

"Good-bye, Mark, my boy," he said cheerily. "Have a good time, and don't hurry back. It's lonesome without you, but I can stan' it and git along a day or two, and if you see that gal give her Uncle Zach's love."

Mark could not reply, and opening his umbrella and taking up his gripsack he walked rapidly away, stopping once at the corner to look back at the house, at the lights in the kitchen and office and Mrs. Tracy's salon and at Dot standing in the door and calling to her husband to come in out of the rain before he took his death cold.

"There'll be an awful hubbub there in two or three days," he said, as he hurried away in the darkness to catch the train whose faint rumble he heard in the distance.

This was Wednesday night and neither Mark nor Helen came back the next day, nor the next, nor was anything heard from them, and Mrs. Tracy began to feel anxious about her daughter.

"I told Mark to stay if he wanted to, and I don't expect him till to-morrow. Mabby they'll come together. I b'lieve he was goin' to call on her," Uncle Zach said to her on Friday afternoon, when she suggested telegraphing to Helen, and questioned him with regard to the safe, which troubled him so to open that she had not been near it since Wednesday, when her diamonds were there as usual.

She was getting accustomed to finding them all right, and did not worry about them now as at first. Still they were on her mind and she said to Mr. Taylor, "If Mr. Hilton does not come back to-morrow, you must open the safe somehow."

"I will, I will; yes marm, I will; yes marm," Uncle Zach replied.

He was in the habit of "yes-marm-ing" Mrs. Tracy, when talking with her, and he was quite profuse with his "yes-marms" as he assured her that Mark would be back and the safe opened by the next day at the farthest. She had tossed her head proudly when he spoke of Mark's calling at her house and of Helen coming back with him. Mark was *scum* in her estimation, as were all the people outside her set, and thus she was poorly prepared for the shock which awaited her Saturday morning, when the New York mail was in. Mark did not come, nor Helen, but there was a letter from the latter, which Mrs. Tracy opened eagerly and read with her eyes staring wildly at what the letter contained. It was as follows:

"New York, Friday afternoon.
"Dear Mother:

"I was married to Mark Hilton yesterday morning, and to-night we start for Chicago. Don't faint and make a scene. It will help nothing. I love my husband and he loves me, and we shall be happy together. As to his position that don't count. He is my husband, and whoever receives me will receive him.

"I am sorry about Mr. Mason. It was a mean thing to do, and he is too good a man to be served such a trick. Still it is better for him to be rid of me. We are not at all alike, and it would hurt him more to be deceived in his wife than in his *fiancée*.

"When I know where we are to live I will write you again. Perhaps you will cut me off entirely, but that won't pay; and if you do you know I have quite a fortune of my own. Mark says, tell Mr. Taylor the business he was to transact for him in New York is satisfactorily arranged for 200 dollars more than he expected. The ledger and papers of the hotel are perfectly straight. Mark saw to that.

"If the safe has been opened you will probably find one box of diamonds gone,—the pin and ear-rings. They were to be mine on my wedding day. It was no theft to take them and I had Mark bring them with him. I do not care for the pin and shall leave it for you with Charlotte, who is dazed with what has happened, but says Mr. Hilton is the handsomest man she ever saw. I think so, too. When we are settled you can send my clothes which are in Ridgefield to me, if you choose. If not, all right. I am sorry I was obliged to tell you so many fibs. I had to do something, and I did have a great deal of headache, and I have been to see the doctor. Tell Mr. and Mrs. Taylor I shall never forget their kindness, and sometime I may visit them again when they have forgotten how bad I was to Mr. Mason.

"I must go now and help Charlotte with my trunks. Good-bye, mother. You said I'd take up with a crooked stick; but I haven't. Mark is straight as an arrow, and I am very happy.

"Your naughty, but loving daughter,
"HELEN TRACY HILTON."

CHAPTER XXII.

WHAT FOLLOWED.

Mrs. Tracy went into violent hysterics, which brought Celine and Mrs. Taylor and Sarah, and at last Mr. Taylor and Jeff, to her room, her sobs were so loud, amounting almost to screams.

"What has happened? Is mademoiselle dead?" Celine asked, and her mistress replied, "Worse than dead! She is married to Mark Hilton! Going to New York was a trick to deceive us. And your precious clerk, whom you trusted so implicitly, has taken my diamonds. Open the safe."

The last part of the remark was addressed to Mrs. Taylor, who hurried to the office, followed by the entire party.

"Well, I'll be dumbed if I thought that of Mark," he gasped. "There must be some hereditary in him after all, and I'd of swore there wasn't. Eloped! Run away, did you say, and took them diamonds with him? I'll be dumbed! Yes, marm, I will."

He could scarcely stand as he began fumbling at the safe, trying to unlock it, but it baffled all his efforts.

"I ain't used to the pesky thing. Mark always attended to it, and I'll be dumbed if I can budge it."

The sweat was pouring off his face as he got up from his knees and looked helplessly round.

"Let me try. You know I opened it once," Jeff said.

No one objected, and the door was soon open. Uncle Zach and Jeff bumping their heads together to look in.

"Jerusalem crickets! They are gone!" Jeff said.

"So they be. That is,—one of the boxes; here's t'other,"

Uncle Zach rejoined in a choking voice, as he took out the box which contained the cross. "I feel like a thief myself. Yes, marm, I do. Can they arrest me as an—— I dunno what you call it,—knowin' to it is what it means? Where's Dot? Seems 'sif the bottom had fell out; Mark gone off and got married and took the diamonds, too!"

The little man felt the need of some one to lean on in the calamity which had overtaken him and naturally turned to his wife. She was attending to Mrs. Tracy, who, when sure the diamonds were gone, went into a fit of hysterics worse than the first, and was taken to her room, where Mrs. Taylor, Celine and Sarah were busy fanning her, holding salts to her nose, bathing her face in alcohol and cologne and loosening her dress which was in danger of being ruined with all the liquids spilled upon it. Only Jeff was left to comfort Uncle Zach.

"'Rest you? No. I'd laugh. You've done nothin'. Sarah took up the letter when Miss Tracy was at the worst and read a few lines, and I heard her say Miss Helen told Mark to bring 'em 'cause they were hern. Nobody's stole 'em, and if I'se you, or anybody, I wouldn't talk about 'em. Who's to be your clerk, sir, now Mark is gone?"

"Oh, land if I know. I can't think of nothin' but the trick Mark has served me, and I liked him as I would of liked Johnny if he had lived," Mr. Taylor replied, while the tears rolled down his face.

"Don't cry. Take my handkerchief and wipe up. We'll get along. How would *I* do to help you till somebody turns up? I know what Mark did, and I'll do my best," Jeff said.

The boy had grown old within an hour, and Mr. Taylor felt the comfort of his helpful nature. He took the handkerchief offered him,—a rather soiled one, with a bit of gum sticking to it,—but it was better than none to wipe away his tears, which he said he didn't want the women folks to see. There was no danger, as they were still with Mrs. Tracy, who had gone into a chill and whom they were putting to bed with hot water bottles and hot drinks and whatever else they thought would warm her. Uncle Zach was glad of Jeff's companionship and clung to him as if he had been a man instead of a boy of twelve.

"It's a good idea your helpin' me till I find somebody," he said. "Better lock up the safe and shut them blinds. The sun hurts my eyes. If anybody comes you know what to charge for meals and feedin' horses and stayin' all night."

"Yes, sir, and I can make change most as quick as Mark and add up, too," Jeff said, whistling cheerily as he shut the blinds and brought out the register and the account books as he had seen Mark do.

He was not greatly surprised at what had happened. He had seen it coming and had felt a pleasurable excitement in watching its progress. But why run away, as in one sense they had? This puzzled him, as he went about his work. Stopping suddenly he turned to Mr. Taylor and said, "There's a letter here for Miss Tracy. It came yesterday. I b'lieve it is from Mr. Mason, and there's one from her, I guess, to him. It is the same handwriting as the one to her mother. Do you think there was anythig between them? You know he rode with her a good deal, but she sparked the most with Mark. I seen 'em."

"Oh-h, I did think so one spell, but it can't be; that would be wust of all," Mr. Taylor groaned.

He had no suspicion of the real truth, nor had any

one except Mrs. Tracy, who kept the knowledge to herself. If possible she would spare her daughter, and Craig, too, that notoriety and talk. She knew he had telegraphed to Helen that he would return that day, but she did not know on what train, nor did she speak of him to any one. She was in too collapsed a state to talk and kept her bed, crying continually and occasionally going off into a hysterical spasm as the remembrance of her trouble came over her afresh. No one thought of Craig, who at four that afternoon took his seat in the express train for Worcester where he was to change for the accommodation to Ridgefield. He had in his satchel several costly rings of different shapes and sizes for Helen to choose from. He had a Harper and Scribner for her and a daintily bound volume of Browning's Poems, containing Pauline, Paracelsus and Sordello, the poems which were associated intimately with her, because he believed she cared so much for them. He had also a box of beautiful hothouse roses, and he thought many times as the train sped swiftly on how Helen's eyes would brighten when he gave them to her and how glad she would be to see him. He was very happy and his happiness had been increasing ever since he left Ridgefield and had talked with his mother.

He was sure she did not quite approve of Helen, and believed it was because she did not understand her as he did. When he told her of his engagement she was taken by surprise, for although she had seen the growing intimacy she had tried to think that nothing would come of it, and had hoped that on Helen's side it was only a flirtation, which would end as many others had done.

"Are you sorry?" Craig asked, as she did not speak at once.

She could not tell him she was sorry when he seemed

so happy, and she replied evasively, "Mothers are always sorry to give their sons to another woman. But I shall try and love your wife whoever she may be. I shall not be a disagreeable mother-in-law. Helen is the most beautiful girl I have ever seen, and I hope you will be very happy with her. When is it to be?"

She was talking easily and naturally, and a load was lifted from Craig, who told her of his plans and asked her advice with regard to the rings which she helped him select, and then went with him to look at a house on Commonwealth Avenue which was for sale and of which he secured the refusal. He wanted Helen to see it before he decided, and proposed to his mother to invite Mrs. Tracy and her daughter to Boston for a few days after they left Ridgefield. He had spoken of this in his last letter to Helen, which she was never to see. It had occurred to him that it would be a proper thing to telegraph her of his safe arrival, and then it occurred to him after the telegram had gone that a letter would be still better. He could write what he had not put into words. He had written twice,—once on Monday, and again on Thursday. He felt that he had been rather cold in his love-making, and he told her so in both letters and said that he meant to make up for it in the future. Had Helen read the letter she received she might not have sat so still in the Haunted House and listened to Mark Hilton. But she did not read it, and she was now Mark's wife, and Craig was standing on the steps of the rear car in Ridgefield, ready to jump off the moment it stopped. He had his satchel in one hand and his box of roses in the other, and both were taken from him before he was aware who the boy was thus relieving him. It was Jeff, the *soi disant* head clerk of the Prospect House.

When it was decided that he was to stay in the office

until some older person was found he had scrubbed his face and hands, put on his Sunday clothes, combed and brushed and parted his hair, as Mark wore his, and felt himself quite equal to the emergency. Knowing that Craig was expected that day he had looked for him on the noon train, and when he didn't come, was sure he would arrive on the six.

"Can I go down in the 'bus with the mail and meet Mr. Mason, or anybody else who happens to be stopping off? You know there's a little hotel opened on Elm Street, and they are trying to git your custom," he said to Mr. Taylor, who, pleased to find him with such an eye to business, assented readily.

The 'bus started from the post office, and Jeff went there to take it, and climbing to the box with the driver lighted a cigarette, when sure he was out of sight of the Prospect House. He had been sent supperless to bed twice when bits of cigarettes had been found in his pocket, and it would never do for a similar indignity to be offered to him now. He was a hotel clerk and he smoked on serenely till the station was reached and Mr. Mason alighted from the train.

"I'll take your bag and box. Will you walk or ride?" he said to Craig, who, realizing who it was that had taken possession of him, said pleasantly, "Hallo, Jeff, is it you? How are you?"

"First rate, but there's high old Jinx at the hotel, and I'm the clerk now!" Jeff replied, with quite an air of importance.

"You the clerk! And high old Jinx? What do you mean?" Craig asked, and Jeff, who was bursting to tell the news, began: "Mr. Hilton has gone off,—run away, —eloped with Miss Helen, and took the diamonds. They was married Thursday in New York and started last night for Chicago, and Miss Tracy screeched so you could hear her across the street. She's in bed now with water bags and flat irons and things, and I'm the clerk *pro tem*. That's what Sarah said. What does *pro tem* mean?"

Jeff had told his story in a breath, but was not prepared for the effect it had on Craig, who turned as white as the paper box which held the roses, and grasped Jeff's shoulder to steady himself and keep from tottering, if not falling outright. It was as if a heavy blow had been dealt him in his stomach, nauseating and making him faint and dizzy, and for a moment he hardly knew where he was.

"Going to ride?" the 'bus driver called to him.

Craig looked up and saw in the 'bus a woman who he knew lived in the town. He could not face her with that terrible trouble on his mind.

"I'll walk," he said, and the 'bus drove off, leaving him alone with Jeff, who was looking curiously at him.

"Are you sick?" he asked; and Craig replied, "I think so. Isn't there a short cut across the fields to the hotel?"

"Yes, I'll show you the way. You or'to have rode. You look awful white and queer," Jeff said, starting up the path he always took when going to the river from the hotel.

Craig followed slowly, scarcely seeing where he was going, or realizing anything except that something had happened to him, taking away his strength and sense. When half way up the hill they came to a stone wall where there was a gap with some big boulders for steps, making a kind of stile. Here Craig sat down to rest, while Jeff stood before him puzzled to know what had effected him so suddenly.

"He seemed chipper as could be when he jumped off

the train. Mabby he broke something inside," he thought, just as Craig said to him, "Sit down here, boy, and tell me exactly how it was. Don't add nor subtract. I want the whole truth; all you know about it from first to last. The marriage, I mean. It was not gotten up in a day."

Jeff had no suspicion of Craig's real interest in the matter. He meant to be loyal to Mark, but did not care for Helen, or how much blame he put on her. He liked to talk, and if Craig wanted the truth he should have it. Crossing one foot over the other, he began:

"Well, sir, you shall have the truth. Would you mind my smoking a cigarette?"

Craig looked up in some surprise, knowing that such things were tabooed by the Taylors.

"I don't mind the odor, if that is what you mean," he replied. "But I would not do it if I were you. It is a bad habit, and Mrs. Taylor would not like it."

"All right," Jeff replied, and threw the cigarette away. "Now then," he continued, "I'm going to tell you how it was. I've had my eyes open, and I thought for a spell 'twas *you*, as you and Miss Helen rode together so much and sat so much on the north piazza, and talked about them books she didn't care a cent for, only pretended she did to please you."

"What do you mean?" Craig asked a little sharply, and Jeff replied, "Them books you used to read out loud sometimes. I was waiting for Miss Alice once, and I heard Miss Helen say she hated it like pisen, but she'd got to make b'lieve, you was so *daft* on him. What does *daft* mean?"

Craig did not answer, but closed his eyes and leaned his head against a projecting stone in the wall. Jeff was lifting the veil and letting in the light, and it hurt him cruelly.

"Do you feel worse?" he asked, and Craig replied, "Yes,—no. No matter how I feel. Go on, and never mind the reading."

"I's only tellin' you to show how things was, and that if there was any seducin' it was Miss Helen who did it. Mark was some to blame, of course, but she was most. She is not an atom like t'other one,—Miss Alice. Oh, but she is a dandy, and true as steel. Miss Helen is the handsomest, and when she turns her eyes on you and smiles, you are a goner. And she rolled her eyes at Mark until he didn't know what he was about, and when she was talkin' to him in the office, as she did by the half hour when nobody was there, I've called him two or three times before he heard me. She used to sit on the piazzer with him after you'd gone to bed, and once she staid there so late her mother called her and asked what she was doin'.

"'Been talkin' to Mr. Mason,' she said, and she spoke the *been* low so her mother couldn't hear it, and the 'talkin' to Mr. Mason' high, so she could hear. I was lyin' in the grass and heard her say, laughin' like, 'Tain't a fib. I have been talking to Mr. Mason.' I tell you, she's a clipper."

Craig felt he ought to stop the boy, whose every word was a stab, and he opened his lips to do so, then closed them with the thought, "I may as well hear the whole," and Jeff went on: "The day you went away she talked ever so long with Mark, and right after supper they started for a walk. Miss Taylor sent me over on the North Ridgefield road on an errant to Miss Nichols, and I staid a while to play hide and coop with the boys, and then started home. As I got near the haunted house the moon was shinin' so bright that I said to myself, 'I mean to go in and mabby I'll see the woman who, they say, walks there wringin' her hands.' I ain't a bit afraid, and I went along the lane on the grass till I got near a window, or where one used to be. Then I heard voices very low, almost a whisper. I knew it wasn't the ghost, and I crept up still as I could and looked in, and who do you s'pose was there?"

Craig's eyes were riveted on Jeff, who continued: "Mr. Hilton and Miss Helen, settin' close together with his arm round her, and she a cryin', while he talked so low I couldn't understand, but I could *see*, for the moon fell full on both of 'em. First, I thought I'd give a whoop and scare 'em; then concluded to let 'em alone, and tiptoed away without seeing Mark's grandmother at all. That was Tuesday, and the next day Miss Helen took the noon train for New York. Had malary, she said, and must see her doctor. That night Mark went to New York on some business for Mr. Taylor. He didn't come back the next day, nor she neither; nor the next day, nor she neither, and this morning there came a letter from her, sayin' she was married to Mark Thursday, and was goin' to Chicago last night, and Mark had brought her the diamonds. That's why Miss Tracy screeched so and went into fits. Half the town know it now, and are talkin' about it. A lot have been in the office askin' me questions, but Miss Taylor told me to shet up, and I shet and said I didn't know nothin', but I've told you because you made me, and you'd hear it when you got to the hotel. You are not going to faint?" he exclaimed, as Craig leaned forward with his elbows on his knees and his hands on his face.

"No, no," and Craig straightened up, but his pallid face frightened Jeff, who continued: "You *are* awful sick, and you look bad. What can I do for you?"

"Nothing," Craig answered; then asked suddenly:

"Has any one mentioned *me* in connection with this affair?"

"Why, no. Not in particular," Jeff replied. "Some who come into the office said: "I thought by the looks of things 'twas the Boston chap, and Sarah said: 'I guess the one who was with her last had the inside track.' That's before Miss Taylor told me to shet up. I said I knew all the time it was Mark."

"Thank you, Jeff. There's a newspaper in my coat pocket. Fan me with it, please. I am very warm," Craig said, taking off his hat and wiping the drops of sweat from his forehead.

Jeff took the paper and fanned him, while a suspicion of something like the truth began to dawn upon him. Then, with the bluntness which characterized him, he asked: "Did you care for her, and is that what ails you?"

Twilight was coming on, but Craig could see Jeff's sympathizing face, and, with a sudden impulse, he replied: "She had promised to be my wife."

Jeff gave a prolonged whistle and dropped the paper with which he was fanning Craig. Then, feeling that he must give some vent to his surprise, he had recourse to his usual custom, and turned three very rapid somersaults and landed on his feet in front of Craig. Jeff's mind had worked almost as fast as his body, and, resuming the newspaper and fanning Craig furiously, he said, "I knew Mark liked her, and I liked Mark and used to tell him where she was waitin' for him in corners and places sly like so folks wouldn't see her. I thought you cared for her some, but didn't s'pose you was in so deep, and I'm sorry I've told you about her, but you said tell everything."

What Jeff had told Craig, although heroic treatment, was having its effect. Still he was very sore with the suddenness of the blow, and it would take him a little time to rally. He was humiliated, too, but there was comfort in thinking that possibly no one knew of his engagement except Mrs. Tracy. 'I was foolish to tell Jeff, although I believe I can trust him," he thought.

"Jeff," he began, "if no one knows what I have told you, will you keep it to yourself?"

"You bet!" Jeff answered, feeling that he was of more importance now that he had a secret in common with Craig than he did when he was made clerk *pro tem.*

It was time the clerk was getting home, if he would attend to his business, and he said to Craig at last: "Do you think you can go on now? Mr. Taylor may be wanting me."

"Yes, I am better," Craig answered.

He tried to walk steadily, but his knees shook under him, and it seemed as if his feet were each weighing a ton. Once in the steepest part of the hill he felt Jeff put his arm across his back to help him up the incline. The action touched him deeply, and there was a mist in his eyes as he said, "Thank you, Jeff; but I think I can walk alone. I am feeling better and shall be all right when I reach the hotel."

With a great effort he tried to seem natural when he entered the house and was greeted by Uncle Zach, who plunged at once into the heart of his trouble, bewailing his disappointment in Mark and wondering where he could find one to fill his place. Craig consoled him as well as he could and kept himself in the shade, both in the office and at the supper table, where he ate very little and shrank from the eyes which he fancied were directed towards him by his fellow boarders. He had still a hard task before him,—that of meeting Mrs. Tracy, who, the moment she heard he had come, sent for him. Her hysterics had subsided, but, when she saw Craig, she came near giving way again. Controlling herself with an effort, she gave him her hand and said: "I know your pain is as great, or greater, than mine, and I am sorry for you. I assure you I had no suspicion. It came like a thunderbolt, and to think my daughter should take up with a hotel clerk, whose great grand-mother was hung, is terrible!"

She was getting excited and began a tirade against Mr. Hilton, while Craig put in now and then a word in his defense, saying he hoped the young people would be happy. He was not as crushed as Mrs. Tracy had expected him to be, and she grew a little cool towards him at the last and told him she should leave on Monday for New York and seclude herself from the society she would be ashamed to meet after Helen's disgraceful conduct.

"Here is a letter you sent to Helen on Thursday," she said. "Mr. Taylor brought it to me this afternoon. It is, of course, no use to her now. I shall not forward it. Take it and burn it, if you like."

Craig took the letter, and, bidding her good night, went to his room, where he found on his dressing bureau another letter which had come for him that morning from New York, and was from Helen. Jeff had brought it up while he was with Mrs. Tracy, and was hovering near the door to speak to him.

"Do you want anything?" he asked. "A hot flat iron for your feet, perhaps? I can bring you one, if you do."

Jeff knew that Mrs. Tracy had required water bags and flat irons, and thought it possible Craig might like something of the kind. Craig declined the offer, and Jeff went away, leaving him alone with his trouble and Helen's letter. On opening the envelope a second letter fell out, soiled and crumpled, with tear stains upon it, but with the seal unbroken. It was the first he had sent to her, and she had returned it unread. She had written rather incoherently, as if greatly excited. She did not expect him to forgive her, she said, and she could not help doing what she had done. When Craig asked her to be his wife she had no thought of deceiving him, but she did not then know how much she loved Mr. Hilton, or that he cared for her as he did.

"I am better suited to him than to you," she wrote. "He knows me, and you do not. I return your letter unread. I found it at the office when I started for the walk with Mark, which resulted in my throwing you over. I could not read it after that. Don't think that what I have done has not cost me pain, for it has, but I am very happy with Mark, who knows all my faults. I have nothing to conceal from him, while with you I should have been always trying to seem what I was not and to like what I hated, and you would have found me out and been disappointed and shocked. It is better as it is,—a great deal better, and so you will think when the first wrench is over."

"I believe she is right, but it is very hard now," Craig said, tearing her letter in bits as he did the other and burning them in the stove in his room.

How happy he had been writing to her,— how happy all the week with thoughts of the girl who had deceived him so cruelly.

"But I will not let it wreck my life," he said. "She is not worth it."

Laying his head upon the table, he recalled the past as connected with Helen,—all Jeff had told him of her, all she had said herself, and his mother's opinion, which weighed more now than it did a week ago. He was beginning to see things more clearly than when the glamour of love was over him, and he writhed for a time in bitter pain for his loss, not only of Helen, but for his loss of faith in her. Then he began to wonder why he felt so faint. The window was open, and it was not so very warm, but something oppressed him like a sweet, powerful odor. Suddenly he remembered the roses. The lid had come off as Jeff put the box on the table, and the room was full of the perfume.

"What shall I do with them?" he said, taking them in his hand and thinking how much they were like Helen, beautiful but frail, for they were already beginning to droop. I can't keep them in my room, and I can't throw them from the window to be found and commented upon. I'll burn them, as I have the letters."

Drawing his chair to the stove, he kindled a fire with some light wood there was in a box, and, when it was well started, he burned the roses one by one, feeling a kind of satisfaction as he saw them blacken and turn to ashes. There was still the little white and gold book of poems, and over this he hesitated. He was so fond of Browning that it seemed sacrilege to burn up Sordello and Pauline. They were intimately connected with Helen, who had professed to like them so much. But her liking was all pretence, and leaf after leaf went into the stove, until the whole was consumed. There was nothing now but the rings, and these he would return. With the burning of the roses and book, Craig felt a good deal better, and, quite to his surprise, slept so soundly that he did not waken until Jeff knocked twice on his door and told him it was after eight o'clock.

CHAPTER XXIII.

THE CLOSE OF THE SEASON.

Early on Monday morning Mrs. Tracy began her preparations for leaving the Prospect House. Helen's wardrobe was to be packed as well as her own, and, although Celine did her best, it was impossible to get off on the noon train.

"'Pears to me I'd wait till I was feelin' better. You look pretty white and pimpin'," Uncle Zach said to her.

Mrs. Tracy answered curtly that nothing could induce her to stay another day in Ridgefield, where she had suffered so much. She wished she had never come there, she said, and conducted herself as if somebody in the house was to blame for her trouble. Just who it was she didn't know, but finally decided that it was Craig! If he had been more demonstrative it would never have happened, and she believed he did not care very much now that it had happened. It irritated her to see him appear so natural when he came to call upon her after his breakfast was over. There was a tired, heavy look in his eyes, and his face was pale, but otherwise he was the same dignified, faultlessly attired young man, speaking in his usual manner, and even laughing at something Jeff said when he brought one of her trunks into the room. If he had seemed downcast and sorry, and his cuffs and collar and necktie and dress generally had shown some neglect, and he had spoken low and not laughed, she would have liked it better. She did not guess the effort he was making in order that no one should suspect how deeply he had been wounded. He was very polite to her, and when she took the evening train for New York he went with her to the station, and attended to her wants as carefully as if she had really been his mother-in-law in prospect.

"Did you read Helen's letter?" she asked, as they were waiting for the train.

"Yes," he replied; "I read it and burned it."

"Shall you answer it?" was her next question, put at random, as she wished to draw some expression from him.

"Certainly not. Why should I? That page in both our lives is turned," he said, while she looked curiously at him.

"He will get over it easily," she thought, and she was rather formal and stiff when she bade him good-bye and took the car which was to carry her to the close seclusion she contemplated, where none of her dear friends could witness her humiliation, or inquire for her daughter.

For a few moments Craig stood watching the train, and when it finally disappeared in the darkness he was conscious of being glad that Mrs. Tracy was gone. The burden was beginning to lighten, although there was still a feeling as if he were stunned and that what had made his future seem bright had been swept from under him.

"Nobody shall know it, if Jeff keeps his counsel, and I think he will," he said to himself, as he went back to the hotel.

Contrary to his usual custom, he staid for a time in the office where Jeff was still head clerk, doing his duty well for a boy, and skillfully parrying remarks and questions put to him concerning the elopement, as it was called. For a time Craig sat pretending to read a paper, but not losing a word of what was said. He had no intimates in town. The young men thought him proud and cold and had made no advances, with but one exception. A young M. D. had been called by Mrs. Mason to see him when he first came, and had prescribed for him occcasionally since. He had also driven with him once after Dido, and now, proud of his acquaintance and anxious to show his intimacy, he said to Craig: "By the way, Mason, how is it? I thought one time you were going to carry off the heiress?"

"You see you were mistaken," Craig answered quietly, without looking up from his paper, while Jeff chimed in: "Pho! I guess you wouldn't have thought so if you'd seen all I did. Nobody had the ghost of a chance but Mr. Hilton."

Craig blessed the boy in his heart for having helped him over a rough place, and after sitting a few minutes longer, bade a courteous good night to the men in the office and went to his room.

"Proud as Lucifer and stiff as a ram-rod. I don't blame any girl for preferring Hilton to him," some one remarked, and there the conversation dropped so far as Craig was concerned, but the gossip did not at once subside in town.

There was a half column account of the marriage in the Ridgefield Weekly on Wednesday, and another in the Boston Herald. The bride's beauty and wealth and position were dwelt upon at length, and Mark was pronounced on the whole a good fellow, eligible for any one except for his lack of fortune. Craig read every word and found himself wondering if it was the girl he had hoped to marry whose name was being bandied about. He staid in Ridgefield two weeks and drove Dido nearly every day over the same roads he had been with Helen, and up and down the hill where he had asked her to be his wife, and where Dido usually tried to run from some imaginary baby cart. Sometimes Jeff was with him: sometimes Uncle Zach, but oftener he went alone, thinking over the past, and finding at last that he could think of it without a pang such as had hurt him at first. He had loved Helen Tracy and believed that she loved him, and was a true, womanly woman. He had found his mistake. She did not love him. She was false in every particular; her whole life was a lie, and he would blot her from his heart.

In this state of mind he went home to his mother some time in October, and the season for city boarders at the Prospect House was over. The best china and linen were packed away. The silver forks and spoons were wrapped in the old shawl and hidden on the top shelf in Mrs. Taylar's closet. The rooms in the west wing were scrubbed and aired and fumigated, and then shut up for the winter, and life at the Prospect House went on as usual, except in the office, where Jeff still was clerk, and where Uncle Zach missed Mark more and more every day.

"I wonder that he don't write. I'm owin' him some wages and I want to hear from the boy," he said.

At last there came a letter, and, when Uncle Zacheus read it, he wished it had never come. A portion of it was as follows:

"I was sorry to take French leave, as I did, but there was no alternative. Mrs. Tracy would never have given her consent, and we had to marry without it. Nor have we repented yet, and are as happy as two young people madly in love can be. I have some things in my room which I'd like you to send to the Sherman House, Chicago, where we are boarding at present, but we expect soon to go to housekeeping on Michigan Avenue.

"And now I come to the real object of my letter. I want Jeff. I suppose I can claim him lawfully, but I'll leave the decision to the boy himself. If you wish to keep him let him take his choice between you and me,—Ridgefield and Chicago. If he decides for me, send him on and pay the expense out of what you owe me. The rest you are to keep. I have no use for it.

"With kindest regards to yourself and Mrs. Taylor, in which my wife joins,

"Yours most sincerely,
"Mark Hilton."

"Dot," Uncle Zach called in a shaky voice, when he finished reading the letter; "Mark wants Jeff; read what he says."

She read it twice, and then sat very still, with her hands clasped hard on the arms of her chair. With all his faults she liked the boy, who of late had seemed so much improved and been so useful to them. Her liking was slight compared to that of her husband, whose face looked pinched and grey as they discussed the matter.

"I s'pose we must let him choose," Uncle Zach said, at last, and, calling Jeff to him, he told him what Mark had written.

Jeff's eyes were like saucers as he listened. He was greatly attached to Mark, and any dislike he had for Helen for the trick she had served Craig was overbalanced by Chicago. To live in a big city would be delightful.

"I s'pose I'll have to go, shan't I?" he asked.

"Oh, Jeff, and leave us alone!" Uncle Zach said, with so much genuine sorrow in his voice that Jeff began to waver.

"I'd like to stay here first rate," he said, "and I'd like Chicago, too. I'll tell you what we'll do, you and I. We'll toss up a cent five times. I first, you second, and so on,

If heads win, I go to Chicago; if tails win, I stay here. Do you agree?"

He drew a big, old-fashioned penny from his pocket and gave it a smart twirl with his thumb and second finger.

"Heads!" he said; "but this don't count. We haven't begun yet. Do you agree?"

"I hain't tossed a cent since I was a boy." Uncle Zach replied.

"Let me show you," Jeff said, fixing the copper in place on Uncle Zach's fingers. "You hold it so; give it a snap, so; that's right; off she goes; heads again. But we hain't commenced. You are not quite up to the trick yet, and I want it fair."

Three or four more trials were made and then the game began which was to decide Jeff's fate in more ways than one. Mrs. Taylor was as much interested as either her husband or Jeff and looked on breathlessly at the fall of the penny from Jeff's hand.

"Heads!" he said, as he picked it up and handed it to Mr. Taylor, who threw it up with some trepidation and anxiety.

"Tails!" Jeff cried, examining the coin. "Even so far. Here goes the third toss. Heads again! Your turn now. Let me fix it for you," he continued, adjusting the coin to Mr. Taylor's hand, which shook so he could scarcely hold it. "Let 'er slide!" he said, and the penny went rattling to the floor at some distance from them both.

Jeff was there as soon as the penny. "Tails! we are even still. The next will decide." he exclaimed, pushing back his hair and straightening himself for the final throw.

Mr. and Mrs. Taylor scarcely moved, and Jeff was greatly excited as if he felt that more than Chicago was trembling in the scale.

"Git!" he said, and the copper went spinning in the air and then rolled to Mrs. Taylor's feet. "Heads! Hurrah! Chicago has won!" was Jeff's joyful cry as he picked up the coin and showed it to Mr. Taylor, who said, "Yes, it's heads plain enough. Queer you should throw that all the time, and I tails. Accordin' to the bargain I s'pose you'll go."

The sight of Mr. Taylor's face clouded Jeff's a little, and he offered to throw again. But Mr. Taylor said, "No. You belong to Mark. He took you from the street. You are in a way connected with him far back. You must go."

"When you are real old I'll come and take care of you," Jeff said by way of comfort, and then went hurrying to the kitchen to tell of his good luck.

"What must be done may as well be done at once," was Mrs. Taylor's theory, and in less than a week the Chicago express from Boston carried with it a boy whose eyes were full of tears and whose face was close to the window as long as a spire or treetop of Ridgefield was in sight.

Jeff was gone; a new clerk took his place, and the house seemed lonelier than ever as the dark November days came on, and they missed the active boy everywhere. Mark had telegraphed his safe arrival and three weeks later there came a short letter from him.

"Dear and reverend friends," it began. "I am well. How are you yourselves? How is Sarah and Martha and Sam, and the rest of the folks? My eye! isn't Chicago a buster! Beats Boston all holler, and ain't our house on Michigan avenue a grand one! You never seen such furniture in all your life, nor nobody else. We moved in a week ago, and we've got seven servants to wait on us three, for I ain't a servant. I guess Mr. and Miss Hilton disagreed about me a little, for I overheard 'em talkin' before we left the Sherman House. She wanted to dress me up in livery with brass buttons. What for I don't know. He said I was to go to school in the same voice he used to say to me, 'Jeff, behave yourself.' So I'm goin', and the servants call me Master Jefferson. Ain't that funny?

"I hain't forgot you, and once in a while I feel homesick for the old place and snivel a little. I can't turn summersets here and I can't do a lot of things, but couldn't I pick a pile of pockets on the street. I shan't though. I promised Miss Alice I wouldn't, and I won't. When you hear from her give her my best respects and the same to yourselves.

"Yours to command,

"Jefferson Wilkes.

"Postscript. I forgot to tell you that Miss Hilton is handsome as ever and dresses right up to the handle. Went to the opera the other night with nothin' on her neck and arms but a little puff at the shoulder. We were in a box and everybody looked at us. As we were comin' out I heard somebody say 'That beautiful woman with the big diamonds is Miss Hilton, who ran away with a—' I couldn't understand what, but thought they said 'barber.' I told Miss Hilton, and she looked mad as fury, and Mr. Hilton,—I have to call him that now,—said 'Never repeat anything of that kind, and whatever you know keep to yourself.' He looked mad, too. Strange, how things get from Ridgefield to Chicago, but they do. The servants have heard something about the runaway and things and have pumped me, but I'm tighter than a drum. Mr. and Miss Hilton are very happy and lovin' like right before me. How are Paul and Virginny? You or' to see the horses we drive, and Miss Hilton's coopay. All lined with satin. Good-bye."

This glimpse of the domestic life of Mark and Helen was all that was known at the Prospect House for a long time, and as the winter wore away, the elopement, if it could be called that, ceased to be talked about as other interests occupied the public mind.

CHAPTER XXIV.

CRAIG'S VISIT.

MARCH was nearly gone when Craig Mason arrived at the Prospect House unexpectedly on the noon train, and Mrs. Taylor was greatly upset and flurried in her wish to do him honor. Her silver forks and best china were brought out and Uncle Zach offered him "Miss Tracy's saloon" to sit in, if he wanted it. Craig declined the saloon, saying he was only going to spend the night and preferred to sit with his host and hostess, if they would allow it. He was looking in excellent health, and told them he weighed twenty pounds more than when he came to Ridgefield in the summer. He talked freely of Mark and Helen, and laughed heartily over Jeff's novel way of deciding between Chicago and Ridgefield.

"There is a good deal in that boy to be made or marred, and I am curious to know which it will be."

"Made, I think, for he had good envyrimen' here," Uncle Zach replied, and then branched off into *hereditary* as exemplified by Mark, if he did run off with an heiress. "None of it there, I tell you. No, sir," he said. "A pretty woman will make a man do a lot of things. Adam had no idea of eatin' that apple till Eve tempted him. He hadn't any hereditary. No more has Mark. No, sir! That gal tetered up to him and purred round him like a kitten. I can remember now findin' her time and agin in the office when she'd no call to be there, and she was so all fired handsome he couldn't help it. Why, I liked her myself. Yes, sir, I did!"

He said the last rather low, with a furtive look at Dot, who was picking up the ball of yarn from which she was knitting and with which her kitten had been playing. Uncle Zach had never told her, nor any one, of the kiss Helen had given him the day she went away. But he had not forgotten it, and he stroked the place on his hand as he wandered on about *hereditary* and *enzyrimen'*, till Craig was tired, and seizing the opportunity of a pause, said abruptly, "Can you tell me where Miss Alice Tracy lives. I know it is among the mountains, but have forgotten the place. I am going to Albany, and thought a——, I told mother, perhaps I'd call. Do you remember the town?"

"Why, yes,—Rocky Point," Uncle Zach replied, without the slightest suspicion. "Goin' to call on her, are you? Wall, I'm glad on't. A nice little girl,—not so handsome as t'other one, but mighty pretty, with takin' ways. She's keepin' school up there, and Christmas she sent Dot and me a drawin' made by herself of the north piazza. Did you know she could draw?"

Craig did not, and Uncle Zach continued: "Wall, she can,—nateral, too, as life. It's a picter of that afternoon when we sot on the piazza and you read from that man Brown. We are all there, some plainer than others, and I'll be dumbed if she didn't draw me a noddin', as Dot says I was, but I'd know myself in the dark, though I didn't know I was quite so dumpy. I'll get it and show it to you. We've had it framed and keep it hung up with Dot's ancestors and the Boston tea-party; seems appropriate seein' 'twas a kind of party we was havin'. Here 'tis."

He handed Craig a sketch of a group on the north piazza, each one of which could be recognized. There was Helen gracefully reclining in the hammock, with her arm and hand hanging down as Craig remembered it,—Mark, with a quizzical expression on his face, standing by the corner,—Uncle Zach unmistakably nodding in his chair, and next to him, himself, with a collar which nearly cut his ears and so interested in the book he was reading that his interest showed on his face, and he could almost hear the sentence at which he stopped to find Helen asleep. Alice was the least conspicuous of the group. She was sitting on the steps with folded hands and looking off under the trees where there was a faint outline of a boy balancing himself on his head. Craig looked at her the longest, knowing she had not done herself justice, but seeing distinctly in his mind's eye the graceful figure, the sweet face, the clearly cut features and blue eyes, which, apart from Helen's more brilliant beauty, would be called very attractive.

"Good, ain't it? I wouldn't take a dollar for it without the frame," Uncle Zacheus said.

Craig made no reply, but thought he wouldn't take many dollars for it, if it were his. Giving it back to Mr. Taylor he asked if he knew what trains stopped at Rocky Point, and the name of Alice's uncle. Uncle Zach said only the accommodations stopped there, and he didn't know the name of the uncle.

"Easy to find, though,—or she is, as she's keepin' school. Ask for the schoolmarm, but what are you goin' off tomorrer for? Stay, and if the roads ain't too bad, we'll have a spin on the race track with Paul and Virginny. By the way, how is Dido?"

"I don't know. I've sold her," Craig replied.

"What under the canopy you sold Dido for? The nicest hoss I ever seen unless it was Virginny when she was young," Uncle Zacheus exclaimed.

Craig could not explain that the principal reason for selling Dido was that she was connected with a part of his life he would gladly forget, and he gave another reason.

"I don't know as you know that once when I was driving her she was frightened at a baby cart and ran away with me. I have heard that horses when once they have run are apt to do so again, and I found it true with Dido. She seemed to be always looking for that cart till mother was afraid to ride after her. So I sold her where I knew she would be kindly treated."

The clock was striking ten, and Craig, who knew it was past Uncle Zach's bed time, signified his wish to retire. He was given his old room, where he had burned the roses and the white and gold book, and as he recalled the pain and humiliation of that night it scarcely seemed possible that he could be as happy and light hearted as he was now.

"Thank God, that dream is over," he said, as he lay down to sleep and dream of what might possibly be on the morrow.

The next day he left the hotel, to the great regret of Uncle Zach, who urged him to stay longer and who refused any remuneration.

"I'd laugh to see me take anything. No, sir! I ain't so mean as that. I'm glad to have you here. It does me good to have refined folks round like you. Come again. Give my regards and Dot's to Miss Alice. Tell her to come here next summer. Shan't cost her a cent. I don't s'pose she's got a great many to spend. I liked her build. I b'lieve she's a truer one than t'other one, though I liked her amazingly."

Craig nodded and shook hands with his host and hostess and was gone.

"It seems funny,—his stoppin' to see Miss Alice," Uncle Zach said as he looked after him. He never seemed to take to her much when she was here. What do you s'pose it's for?"

He turned inquiringly to his wife, who, quicker of comprehension, replied, "I don't s'pose; I know, and so would you, if you had half an eye."

Rather slowly it dawned upon Uncle Zach, together with the fitness of the arrangement. No two could be better suited to each other than Craig and Alice, and he gave it his sanction at once, with his characteristic, "Wall, I'll be dumbed! I b'lieve you are right, and I'm glad on't."

CHAPTER XXV.

IN THE RED SCHOOL HOUSE.

CRAIG was entirely cured of his infatuation. Jeff's revelations had commenced the cure, and time and his own good sense had completed it. A girl who would engage herself to him one night and transfer her vows to another the next was not a wife to be desired, were she ten times as beautiful as Helen Tracy. "Fair and false," he often said to himself when thinking of her and the summer in Ridgefield, while over and over again there came to him a thought of Alice, with whom he had always felt rested and at his best. In the early stage of his disappointments he had said to himself, "I shall never try love making again." But he had changed his mind.

Most men would have written to Alice before going to see her, but Craig was not like most men, and some subtle intuition told him that he would succeed. Arrived at Rocky Point he had no difficulty in ascertaining where Miss Alice Tracy lived, and was soon knocking at the door of the farm-house, which stood a little way from the village. It was opened by Mrs. Wood, Alice's Aunt Mary, who felt somewhat abashed at the sight of a strange gentleman asking for her niece. Glancing over her shoulder at the clock, she said, "It's after four. She should be home pretty soon, though she sometimes stays to tidy up and make copies for the children. Maybe you'll find her there, and maybe you'll meet her. The road is straight from here to the school house. You can't miss it."

"Thanks," and Craig turned to go, when Mrs. Wood said to him, "If you don't find her who shall I say called?"

"Craig Mason, from Boston," was the reply, and Craig walked rapidly away towards the village and the school house.

"Craig Mason; that's the man Helen Tracy jilted, and now he's come to see Alice." Mrs. Wood said to her husband, who had just come in from the barn.

"Well, what is there to flutter you so?" the more phlegmatic Uncle Ephraim asked, putting down the eggs he had been gathering and counting them one by one.

"I ain't in a flutter," she replied, "but if Alice brings him home to supper, and she will of course, I mean to have things decent, and do you make a fire in the settin' room the first thing, and I'll make some soda biscuits,

Lucky I baked yesterday. I've cake enough, and a custard pie, and I'll brile a steak. He must be hungry after travellin' from Boston."

She had settled the bill of fare, and while her husband made the fire in the sitting room she proceeded to carry out her hospitable plans.

Meanwhile Craig was making his way along the street, meeting several children with dinner pails and baskets, whom he guessed to be scholars. School must be out and he hurried on, while those he met looked curiously after him, wondering who he was and wondering still more when they saw him pass up the walk to the school house. When Alice received Helen's letter announcing her engagement to Craig she was not surprised, as she had expected it. The tone of the letter struck her unpleasantly, but it was like Helen to write in that vein and she thought there might be more heart in the matter than appeared on the surface. The proposition that she should accompany her cousin to Europe made her pulse throb with delight for a moment, and then her spirits fell. She knew Helen would be kind and considerate, and Craig too, but——; and then she came to a stand, and as many others have done yielded finally to the inexorable *but*, and gave up what had been the dream of her life. She had commenced a letter to Helen, congratulating her on her engagement and thanking her for her kind offer, which she must decline.

Before the letter was finished she received a second mailed in Chicago, and announcing her cousin's marriage with Mark Hilton. "I know you will be shocked," Helen wrote. "I am, myself, when I think seriously about it. I am not sorry, though, that I did it. I am only sorry for the part where Craig is concerned. I treated him shamefully, but he will get over it. His love for me was not as deep as that of Mark, who took me knowing what I am, while Craig would have turned from me with loathing when he found that I detested Browning, which is among the least of my deceptions."

There was more in the same strain, with protestations of perfect happiness and the intention again expressed of having Alice live with her. From this proposal Alice turned as from the other, though for a different reason. There was nothing left her now but school teaching, which she disliked more than she cared to own. "It is such drudgery and I am so glad when 4 o'clock comes," she often said and was saying it that March afternoon when Craig Mason was on his way to change the whole tenor of her life. She had staid after school to look over some essays and copy-books and was preparing to go home when she heard a step on the walk. It was a scholar returning for something, she thought. A knock on the door, however, indicated a stranger, and hastening to open it she stood face to face with Craig Mason.

"Oh!" she cried, with a ring of joy in her voice as she gave him both her hands.

Then, remembering that this was rather a forward greeting she tried to release them, but Craig held them fast. He had heard the joy in her voice and seen the gladness in her eyes and felt nearly sure of his answer before the question was asked. She had put on her blue hood which was very becoming to her and she had her cloak on her arm preparatory to going home, but she allowed Craig to lead her back into the room where they sat down together by the stove before either spoke a word.

"Where did you come from and when?" she asked, and he replied, "From Boston yesterday,—from Ridgefield this morning. I spent the night at the Prospect House."

"Oh, Ridgefield," Alice exclaimed, clasping her hands which she had withdrawn from Craig's. "I was thinking of Ridgefield and the happy summer I spent there and wondering if I should ever see it again. I'm afraid not."

"Why not?" Craig asked, and she replied, "I don't know except that my life is here, teaching school. Tell me about them,—Mr. and Mr. Taylor, I mean. I know that Mr. Hilton and Jeff are gone."

He told her all there was to tell of Uncle Zach and his wife; of their kind remembrances of her and of the drawing in which he was greatly interested. And while he talked he was trying to decide how to say what he had come to say. She had thrown off her hood and a ray of sunlight fell on her hair and across her face, where the blushes were coming and going as she talked with or listened to him, occasionally turning her eyes upon him and then letting them fall as her woman's instinct began to tell her why he was there. He had been in love with Helen, but it was a different kind of love from that which he now felt and which led him at last to taking one of Alice's hands which lay in her lap. She looked at him in some surprise, and said inquiringly, "Mr. Mason?"

"I wish you would call me Craig," he began. "We surely have known each other long enough to dispense with formalities. To me you are Alice, and you know I was engaged to your cousin, Mrs. Hilton."

"Yes, she wrote me so," Alice replied, and Craig went on: "You know, too, the rest of the story: engaged to me one night, to Mark Hilton the next. There is no need to go over with it. I loved her, and in the first days of bitter pain I thought I could never be happy again. I was mistaken. I *am* very happy and would not have the past changed if I could. I think I am a bungler at love making, but I am in earnest and I am here to ask if you think you could in time care for me who once made a fool of himself, but is sane now."

He had made his speech and waited for Alice to answer. "Are you sure you are making no mistake?" she said. "I am not like Helen,—not like your world. I am a plain country girl, who, if she did not teach school for a living, would have to work in the shoe shop or factory. I know but little of fashionable life such as your wife ought to know. I am not very good looking,—and——"

"What else?" Craig asked, with a comical smile of which she caught the infection, and replied, "I do not like Browning, and don't believe I could understand Sordello if I lived to be a hundred."

Craig laughed immoderately, and drew her closely to him. He did not ask her to take time before she answered him. He wanted an answer then, and had it, and they were plighted to each other for all time to come. They had talked over the past and present. Craig had been the one who planned everything, while Alice listened with a feeling that this great happiness which had come to her must be a dream from which she should awaken. But Craig's voice and manner had reassured her. There was no Dido there running away from a baby cart. He had his hands and arms and lips free and had used them in a way which would have astonished Helen could she have seen him. He was not willing to give up the trip to Europe which had been planned under different auspices. He was going in May and Alice and his mother were going with him. There was no more teaching for her after the first of April, when her term expired. If he could have done so he would have had her give up her school at once. But Alice said no; a bargain was a bargain, and she should keep to it.

"Thank Heaven it is only two weeks more," Craig said, as he locked the door for her, and then the two walked slowly down the street towards the farmhouse.

CHAPTER XXVI.

THE LAST ACT OF PART ONE.

Mrs. Wood's supper, prepared with so much care, was near being spoiled, it waited so long for Craig and Alice, who did not reach the house until after six o'clock. To Craig it did not matter what he ate. Nothing mattered except Alice, with whom he grew more and more in love each moment he spent with her. Of the farmhouse and its appointments he scarcely thought at all except as a kind of Elysium which held his divinity. Uncle Ephraim and Aunt Mary he knew were plain country people, but they belonged to Alice and so belonged to him and he once caught himself about to address Mrs. Wood as Aunt Mary in the familiar conversation which ensued after supper was over and he had made his errand known. Neither Mr. nor Mrs. Wood were insensible to the good fortune which had come to Alice, and though it would be hard parting with her they did not withhold their consent and accepted Craig readily as their future nephew.

All preliminaries were settled as far as they could be until Craig saw his mother, and the next morning he left Rocky Point, promising to come again within a few days and saying he should stop in Ridgefield with the news.

Mr. and Mrs. Taylor were just sitting down to their tea when Craig walked in upon them and unceremoniously drew up to the table in spite of Mrs. Taylor's protestations that he must not till she brought down the silver forks and got him a china plate. At the farm house he had not thought whether he was eating from the choicest Dresden or the coarsest of delft, and it made no difference here. The light of a great happiness was in his heart and after supper was over and he was alone with his host and hostess he said to them laughingly, "Guess what I have done."

"I know. You let me tell," Uncle Zach exclaimed, waving his hand towards his wife, who was about to speak. "You have offered yourself to Miss Alice. Ain't I right?"

"Yes, and she has accepted," Craig replied.

"My boy, I congratulate you. Yes, sir, I do, and I'm most as pleased as I should be if it was I instead of you," Uncle Zach exclaimed.

"Zacheus, I'm ashamed of you,—putting yourself in Mr. Mason's place, and you an old married man," Mrs. Taylor said reprovingly, but her husband did not see the point, and answered her, "There's nothin' to be ashamed of, if I be a married man. I've been through the mill and know all about it and I am glad for 'em. When is it to be?"

"Some time in May," Craig said, "and you and Mrs. Taylor are to attend the wedding."

This diverted Zacheus's thoughts into another channel, and after Craig left the next morning he began to wonder if he ought not to have a dress coat for the occasion and if the tailor in town could make it, or should he buy it in Worcester. He finally decided upon the tailor in town and drove him wild with his directions and suggestions and fears that it would not be right.

"I want it O. K., the finest of broadcloth and made up to snuff," he said, and he went every day to see how it was progressing.

Uncle Zacheus in a dress suit was something of a novelty and the tailor could not repress a smile when it was finished and tried on for the last time, with a cutaway vest to show the shirt front in which there was to be a breast pin at the wedding.

"I look kinder droll and I don't feel nateral," Uncle Zacheus said, examining himself in the long glass. "Why, I ain't much bigger than Tom Thumb. Funny that a swaller tail makes you look so little. I wonder what Dot will think. She's havin' a gown made in Worcester,—plum colored satin, with lace."

Dot, who had never taken kindly to the dress suit, told him he looked like a fool and advised him to wear the coat he was accustomed to wear to church.

"Not by a long shot. I guess I know what is what, and I ain't goin' to mortify Craig and Miss Alice," he said, and his suit was put carefully away in a dressing case, ready for the wedding, which occurred the first of May.

Craig would not wait any longer, and when Alice urged her lack of outfit as one reason for delay he argued that a dress to be married in was all she needed. They were going directly to Paris, where she could shop to her heart's content with his mother to assist her. No day in early spring could be finer than the day when Craig and Alice were married very quietly, with only a few of the neighbors present. Mrs. Mason and Mr. and Mrs. Taylor had come the day before, as the wedding was to take place at 12 b'clock. Mrs. Mason stopped at the hotel with Craig, while Mr. and Mrs. Taylor were entertained at the farm house, where Uncle Zach made himself perfectly at home and almost master of ceremonies. He had brought his dress suit and long before the hour for the ceremony appeared in it, greatly to the amusement of Craig and Alice, who were glad he wore it he was so proud and so happy that he had beaten the crowd in their Prince Alberts and cutaways. There were a few presents from some of Alice's scholars and immediate friends; a costly bracelet from Helen, whose letter of congratulations rang true and hearty, and from Mrs. Tracy the diamond pin which had belonged with the ear-rings and which Helen had left at home, as she did not care for it.

"I am pleased to be rid of it," Mrs. Tracy wrote. "It is a constant reminder of my disgrace, from which I have not recovered and never shall. I am glad for you to have it and glad for you to have Craig, too."

She had invited the party to stop with her during the few days they were to stay in the city before the Celtic sailed, and had urged her invitation so warmly that they accepted and left for New York on the afternoon train. Mr. and Mrs. Taylor spent another night in Rocky Point and then returned to the Prospect House, where Uncle Zach was never tired talking of the wedding and showing his dress suit,——"the only one there, if you'll believe it; even Craig wore a common coat. Curis, wasn't it," he said to an acquaintance, who prided himself on being frank and outspoken, no matter how much the frankness hurt.

"Not curious at all," he said. "People don't wear swallow tails to morning weddings. They are reserved for evening. You were quite out of style."

"You don't say so," Uncle Zach replied, his countenance falling as it began to dawn upon him that he might have made a mistake. "Dot will know," he thought, and after a while he went to her and said, "John Dickson says they don't wear swallers to mornin' weddin's. Did I make a fool of myself?"

Mrs. Taylor was out of sorts with some kitchen trouble and answered sharply: "Of course you did. I knew it all the time, when nobody else, not even Craig, wore one."

This hurt worse than John Dickson's words had done.

"I felt so fine and looked so foolish. What must Craig and Alice and Miss Mason have thought of me?" he said to himself. "Yes, I was a fool,—a dum fool, and I looked like a fool in 'em. Dot said so, she knows, and I'll never wear 'em again. I'll put 'em out of sight, where nobody can see the old man's folly, and mabby, bimeby, when they send a box to the heathen, I'll put 'em in. Pity to have 'em et with moths when they cost so much, and only wore once."

He carried them to the attic,—gave one long regretful look at them and packed them away in the hair trunk with Taylor's Tavern and Johnny's blanket.

A few days later there came a line from Alice written on board the ship. The next day there was a letter from Helen, telling of her house and the dinners and lunches and receptions she was attending and giving. She spoke also of Jeff, who was doing well in school, and of Mark, the best husband in the world.

"I'm glad on't," Uncle Zach said, as Dot read the letter to him. "It seems as if they was my children, Alice and Craig, Mark and Helen, and Jeff. I'm glad they are so happy."

Mrs. Taylor had not her husband's hopeful nature. If the sun shone bright in the morning she wanted to see what the weather was at noon before admitting that it was fine, and now she answered, "Wait a few years and see what happens."

"I shan't wait. I'm glad they are happy now," Uncle Zach replied, resolutely keeping his eyes on the present, and never dreaming of the drama which the future was to unroll and in which his so called children were to take an active part.

END OF PART I.

PART II.

CHAPTER I.

FANNY AND ROY.

The October sun was shining brightly into the windows of a handsome drawing room in New York, where two young people were talking earnestly together. The girl was scarcely twenty and looked younger. She was short and slight and dainty and sweet, with beautiful blue eyes which laughed when she laughed and gave a wonderful brightness to her face. There was something peculiar in their expression which was rapid and searching and made the young man beside her wonder if what they saw in him boded good or ill to his suit. He was twenty-two, tall and straight and broad shouldered, with something in his voice and features and manner which reminded one of the July morning twenty-three years before when Craig Mason sat on the north piazza of the Prospect House and talked to Alice Tracy. To one who had been in Ridgefield that summer there would have come back the scent of the new mown hay and the perfume of the white pond lilies Alice wore in her belt, and in the young man's eyes he would have seen a likeness to Alice's eyes, with thicker lashes and heavier brows.

After this the reader scarcely need be told that the young man was the son of Craig and Alice, born abroad where his parents had spent much of their time since their marriage, with occasional visits to America. Alice had been delighted with the old world, and as Craig's health was better there they had staid on and on,—sometimes in Paris where their son Roy was born, sometimes in Switzerland, sometimes in Italy, and once for a winter in Cairo., and again in London, where Craig's mother died. They had brought her back to Boston, and tired of wandering with no particular home, had decided to settle down quietly for a time at least. But not in the house Craig had looked at for himself and Helen. Nothing could have induced him to take that at any price. He preferred his mother's old home, which, if not in so fashionable a part of the city, was dear to him for its associations with his boyhood and manhood and mother. Here they had lived for three years, two of which Roy had spent at Harvard, where he had entered as a Junior, studying hard in order to be graduated with honor, and still managing to join in a good many athletic sports and to fall in love with his pretty half cousin, Fanny Prescott, a pupil in a private school. She had thought him a boy at first and played with and teased him unmercifully, now sending him from her in a rage and then luring him back with a trick of her eyes which we have seen before. She had not inherited all her mother's dazzling beauty and but little of her nature. In her frankness and perfect truthfulness she resembled Alice. Her Sundays when at school had been spent with the Masons, and thus Roy had every facility for falling in love with her. But while she kept him at fever heat with her innocent coquetries she gave him no encouragement. Once, when he said, "I must and will speak seriously to you," she called him a big boy and told him to wait till he had his diploma and a mustache. He had them both now; the mustache was a very small one, which some might think did not add to his face. The diploma, received in June, was *en regle*, and he had come for the serious talk.

He had not seen her since May, at which time she had been called home by the sudden illness and death of her father, Judge Prescott. As it was so near the close of the term she had not returned to school, but had spent the summer with her mother at a quiet place among the Adirondacks. She did not know that he was coming but was glad to see him, and led him to a sofa on which they both sat down. Then her manner changed suddenly to one of shyness and almost shamefacedness as she moved away from him and put a sofa cushion between them. She was in mourning for her father and the black brought out the purity of her complexion and the brightness of her eyes which filled with tears when Roy spoke of her father and his grief when he heard he was dead.

"Don't talk of him. I can't bear it yet. Talk of something else, please," she said, and Roy plunged at once into the object of his visit, reminding her that he had his diploma and his mustache, and now he wanted her love.

"Oh, Roy, it's too bad in you to spoil our good times as friends. As lovers we might quarrel, and then we are cousins," she said.

"Only seconds, which does not count," Roy answered, moving nearer to her, while she put another cushion between them so that only her shoulders and head were visible.

Roy was of a more ardent nature than his father, and there was no stiffness or hesitancy in his wooing when once he was fairly under way.

"You can pile up the cushions till I can't see you at all," he said, "but it will not prevent you from hearing me tell you that I love you and have ever since I saw you in short dresses, with your hair down your back."

For a time Fanny listened with her face bent down, and when she turned it to him there was a troubled look upon it and her lips quivered as she said, "I do care for you, Roy, and always have; but I must not any more. You will not want me to either when you know what I do."

"What do you know?" he asked, beginning to slide his hand under the cushions.

"Have you never heard anything bad about me or mother?" she asked, and Roy answered, with so sudden a movement that one of the cushions fell to the floor.

"Bad about you, or your mother? Never. I would have thrashed any one who insinuated anything against you. What do you mean?"

"I am not Fanny Prescott," the girl said with a sob in her voice.

"The deuce you are not! Who are you, then, if you are not your father's daughter?" Roy asked, and Fanny replied, "I am my father's daughter, but my father was not Judge Prescott, as I thought. I never knew it till he died last May. Mother had to tell me then on account of some business matters and it almost broke my heart, I was so fond of him and so proud of being his daughter and he was so kind to me. I held his hand when he died and kissed him and called him father and didn't suspect the truth. I don't think you will care for me when you know all. I have always heard the Masons were very proud."

"And I have always heard the Tracys were very proud. Greek meeting Greek, you see, Roy rejoined. "But go ahead. Let's hear the story. Nothing can ever change my love for you. Who are you? Who was your father?"

"Have you ever heard of the Prospect House in Ridgefield, Mass.?" Fanny asked, and Roy answered briskly, "I guess I have. It was there father met my mother, twenty-three years ago. I had heard piles about it and the funny little landlord before I went there this last summer with father and mother. We had a fancy to drive through the country, stopping where night overtook us, and the second day we reached the Prospect House, which looks rather old fashioned beside the fine hotel which has been built on the Common. I wanted to stop there but nothing could keep father from the Prospect House, and I was glad we went there. I wish you could see the landlord, Uncle Zach they call him. He is an old man with such a fat body and short legs and round good natured face, and what do you think he called his wife?"

Fanny could not guess, and Roy continued, "Dot, and Dotty, and I'll bet she weighs two hundred, and is nearer eighty than seventy. Think of calling her Dotty! There is love of the right sort, isn't it? But I shall love you just as well when you weigh three hundred and are ninety, as I do now."

His hand had gotten quite under the cushion and had one of Fanny's.

"You hurt," she said, as he gave it a hard squeeze. "And you must not hold it either. You don't know at all who I am. Did they mention Mark Hilton at the Prospect House?"

"Why, yes, I think they did," Roy said slowly, as if trying to recall something which had slipped his memory. "Father and mother and Mr. and Mrs. Taylor were talking and I heard that name I am sure. When I joined them they stopped suddenly, as if they did not care to continue the conversation. Who was he, anyway? Some scamp?"

"He was my father," Fanny said defiantly.

"Your father! Great Scott, why didn't you say so?" Roy exclaimed.

"You needn't swear if he was my father," Fanny answered, beginning to cry.

The second cushion had followed the first to the floor by this time and Roy had his arm around Fanny, to whom he said, "Don't cry. Great Scott isn't a swear. I only said it because I must say something. What of Mark Hilton?"

"He was clerk at the Prospect House, and none the worse for that. The Vanderbilts and Astors and a lot more people did not have as good a beginning." Fanny said, and Roy replied, "Of course not. Very few of us can boast of high-toned beginnings. My great-grandfather was a carpenter."

"Pho!" Fanny said, with a laugh which had not much mirth in it. "I can beat that on a grandmother when I get to her. I don't think a carpenter at all bad."

"Neither do I," Roy said, "and I don't care if your father was a tinker. Tell me about him."

"You see, it was this way," Fanny began. "My mother was at the hotel the same summer with your father and mother. Mr. Hilton was very handsome and very tall and very nice. I know he was nice," and she emphasized her words with sundry nods of her head as a warning that she was not to be disputed.

"Of course he was nice, or he couldn't have been your father," Roy said, and Fanny continued, "Mother, you know, is very handsome now. She was beautiful then,—a belle and an heiress and a great catch. She'd had I don't know how many offers, fifty maybe, and she has a book with all their names in it. I tried to have her show it to me once and she wouldn't. She keeps it to remind her of other days when she feels depressed. Grandma Tracy thought she ought to marry the President, or somebody like him, but she loved my father and the same as eloped with him. She came to New York in the morning on an errand. He came in the evening and they were married the next day. Grandma wouldn't forgive them, or see my mother until after she was divorced. I think that word has a bad sound, and I am ashamed of it, but I am telling you everything just as I made mother tell me. I was ill for weeks after it, and thought everybody who looked at me was thinking about it."

"What a foolish little girl," Roy said, trying to pull her head down upon his shoulder. "Lots of people are divorced and nothing is thought of it. It is quite the fashion."

"I don't care if they are," Fanny replied. "I think it is wicked, and told mother so. Don't hold my head down. I am going to keep it up as long as I can. By and by I shall want to hang it so low,—oh, so low!"

"Not on account of a divorce," Roy said, and Fanny rejoined, "That isn't all; there is something a great deal worse. Father and mother went to Chicago and were very happy for a while,—then not so happy, and then not happy at all. Mother says she was more to blame than he. She liked attention and had it, and that made him jealous, and she used to tell him that she stooped when she married him, and taunted him with what I'm going to tell you about by and by. I was six months old and don't remember it of course,—their quarrelling, I mean. He loved me, I know."

"I am sure he did," Roy interrupted her, giving her at

the same time a squeeze which she did not seem to notice, she was so absorbed in her story.

"Once mother told him she wished he would go away and never come back, and he did go, and never came back. There was a boy living with them,—Jefferson Wilkes, in whom my father was interested and who had come to them from the Prospect House. Jeff, they called him, and he went with my father. After a while mother instituted proceedings for a divorce on the ground of desertion and incompatibility and phychological repulsion. Do you know what that is?"

"I know what it isn't," Roy said, kissing the face which began to look very pitiful as the story progressed.

"Mother knew where father was for a time and sent him a copy of the divorce. He replied, 'I congratulate you on your freedom. You will not have any trouble in filling my place. You are young enough and handsome enough to have twenty-two more offers. Jeff and I are off for the mines in Montana. Tell the baby, when she is old enough to understand, that, bad as I was, I loved her. Mark Hilton.'

"I was ill with diphtheria when mother received the note,—so ill that the papers, when commenting on the divorce, said that I was dead. Six months later mother saw an account of a terrible accident in some mines in Montana. In the list of killed was my father's name, but there was no mention of Jeff. Mother tried to learn the particulars, but could not, and after a while she came back to New York deserted, divorced and widowed, but still very beautiful. We lived with grandma, a proud old lady, who had never received my father. She is dead now and I do not remember her. Among mother's friends was Judge Prescott, whom she used to know, and who, I think, wanted her before she married my father. When I was two and a half years old she married him and at his request I took his name. I was christened Frances, but he did not like that name and I was called Fanny to please him. I like it better than Frances, don't you?"

Roy would have liked any name which belonged to her and said so, while she continued: "You were in Europe when all this happened and knew nothing about it as you are not much older than I am."

"Two years," Roy said, kissing her again, while she tried to disengage herself from him, but could not, for a lock of her hair had become frightfully entangled in a button of his coat.

It took some time to disentangle it and Fanny was obliged to lie quietly upon Roy's arm, with her face upturned to him so temptingly that not to kiss it occasionally was impossible for one of his temperament.

"Roy Mason!" she exclaimed, "You must not kiss and squeeze me the way you are doing, and I not able to get away, with my hair all snarled up in your buttons. It is mean in you, and I'll call mother if you don't stop. I believe she is in the next room, listening, perhaps."

"Let her listen. She was young once," Roy said, going on very deliberately, while Fanny, from necessity, lay passive on his arm.

When the hair business was settled she moved away from him, and picking up a cushion put it between them again.

"I was telling you about Judge Prescott, whom I called my father, although now I have a faint recollection of a time when there was no gentleman in our house," she said. "When he died mother told me everything. I don't think she meant to tell me the whole dreadful story, but she gave some hints and I would not let her stop. I said I'd go to Ridgefield and inquire, and so she had to tell me, and if there is more to know I do not care to hear it. I feel now as if my life had been all a lie. Fanny Prescott, indeed! When I am really Fanny Hilton, and that is not the worst of it. Stop, Roy! You shall *not* touch me again till I'm through," she said, as Roy's arm came over the cushion toward her hand.

"Did you ever hear of a haunted house in Ridgefield, where a woman in a white gown and blue ribbons walks at night and a drowning man calls for 'Tina. That's the woman's name, and she sat still and let him drown, and a baby cries at all hours for its mother? That is 'Tina, too,—who—who—was hung!"

"By Jove, that's a corker for a story!" Roy replied. "I never heard of it before, but I like haunted houses, with women in white and blue ribbons and cries for 'Tina, who was hung! Tell me about it, and what it has to do with you."

In as few words as possible Fanny told the story of the Dalton tragedy as she had heard it from her mother, while Roy listened with absorbing interest.

"What do you think now of the great-great-granddaughter of 'Tina?" Fanny asked when the story was ended.

"I think her the sweetest, dearest little girl in all the world, and do not care a continental for the woman in white and blue ribbons, or the haunted house. You say there is only a cellar hole there now and that it belongs to you or your mother," Roy answered, throwing the cushion half way across the room and putting both arms around Fanny, who was crying, but who sat very still while he went on, "I'll tell you what we'll do when we are married. We will build a pretty cottage there,—a real up-to-date one, with bay windows and wide piazzas and give

'Tina a chance to perambulate under cover rainy nights. You say she takes such times to walk in preference to pleasant weather. I should think that white dress would be rather frayed and draggled and the blue ribbons slimpsy by this time."

He was making light of the matter and a load was lifted from Fanny's heart, for she had dreaded telling him the story which had weighed so heavily upon her since she heard it.

"It is so kind in you, Roy, not to care about that hanging," she said. "I have felt the rope around my neck so many times and have dreamed that I was 'Tina. I must look like her. She was blue-eyed and fair-haired and small, just like me, who am not a bit like mother. Her grave is in the Ridgefield cemetery, 'Tina's I mean, and mother sat there on the wall right by it when father told her the story. He didn't keep anything back, and held his head just as high when he said, 'My great-grandmother was hung.' His grandfather was the baby who cried for its mother. I've heard that, too, when I have been awake in the night and been so sorry for it. Mother says my father was very tall and fine-looking, and that I have some of his ways with my eyes and hands. I have dreamed of him so often since she told me, and sometimes it seems to me he is not dead. There is no proof except that notice in the paper and a letter mother had from the mines saying some of the bodies were so crushed they could not be recognized, and as my father was known to be in the mine and never seen again, it was highly probable he was dead. Oh, if I could find him! I think you'd better hunt for him than to be building a cottage to keep 'Tina from the rain!"

She spoke lightly now. Roy evidently didn't care and

the tragedy which had cast so dark a shadow on her life when she heard of it began to lessen in its proportions.

"I hear mother," she said at last. "I thought she was in the next room, but she is a little deaf. I don't believe she has heard all the foolish things you have said to me Mother, here is Roy," she continued, as the heavy portieres parted and her mother stood before her.

CHAPTER II.

MRS. PRESCOTT.

NATURALLY twenty-three years had changed her somewhat. The freshness and grace of youth were gone, with much of her brilliant complexion. Her dark hair was sprinkled with grey, and her eyes had lost some of the sparkle which had lured so many suitors to her side, but she was a very beautiful woman still, whom strangers looked at a second time, inquiring who she was. She had at first rebelled against wearing widow's weeds, but when she saw how becoming they were to her she became quite reconciled to her mourning and was beginning to feel reconciled to her widowhood, which gave her the freedom she had not enjoyed since her second marriage. She had paid a full penalty for her heartless act and had repented of her folly. There had been a year of so of perfect happiness with Mark Hilton and then the restraints of married life began to weary her It had been her boast that because her husband knew her so well he could never find fault with her, and there she was mistaken.

He was fond of her and proud of her and glad to see

her admired as long as the admiration was unsought, but when with the little arts she knew so well she tried to attract attention his jealousy was aroused, and gradually there came to be stormy scenes between them,—bitter quarrels when things were said on both sides which it was hard to forget. Finding that with all his apparent unconcern he was sore on the subject of his antecedents Helen used that as a lash and often reminded him of the difference in their social positions and the depth to which she stooped when she married him. Then they quarreled more fiercely than ever and the baby was made the instrument of goading Mark to madness. That it had a drop of blood in its veins which could be traced back to a scaffold was often a source of regret with Helen coupled with a wish that she had married Craig Mason instead of throwing herself away on a hotel clerk, with no family connections. Mark was not naturally bad-tempered; neither was Helen. They were simply wholly unsuited to each other. They had married in haste, trampling upon the rights and happiness of Craig Mason without remorse, and as a natural sequence reaped the consequence of their sin.

At last, after a sharp altercation in which Helen expressed a wish that she had never seen her husband, he left her, taking Jeff with him and leaving a note saying he should not return as he was tired of the life he was living. Urged on by her mother, who had never accepted Mark as a son-in-law, a divorce was easily obtained and Helen free from the tie which had become so distasteful to her. Chancing to know that Mark was in Denver she sent him a copy of the divorce and received in return the note of which Fanny had told Roy. After that she knew no more of him until she heard of a terrible explosion in some mine in Montana. Among the killed was Mark Hilton's name. Then in an agony of remorse she tried to verify the report. What she learned was that none of the bodies could be identified, they were so bruised and burned. Mark was known to have been in the mine and never seen after. Of Jeff nothing was known. He might, or might not, have been in the mine. In all human probability Mark was dead, and the divorce, of which she did not like to think, need not have been obtained. She was free without it and always spoke of herself to her friends as a widow, although she wore no black. If any of her old tenderness for Mark Hilton returned to her at times she gave no sign and was outwardly unchanged, except that she was very quiet and shunned society rather than courted it.

At her mother's request she returned to her home in New York and there at last met again the Walter Prescott whose name had been in her blue book as her possible husband before she met Craig Mason. In some respects he was like Craig, undemonstrative, caring little for society and much for books. He had never forgotten Helen and soon fell again under her spell. He knew of her divorce and would rather it had not been, but her beauty conquered him and she became his wife and mistress of one of the finest establishments in New York. With Judge Prescott, whom she respected and feared, she lived very comfortably. He was not a man to tolerate any nonsense. His wife, like Caesar's, must be above reproach, and from the first he was master of the situation.

Helen was very fond of Fanny, who was as unlike her as it was possible for a child to be unlike its mother. "She has not a feature like me, nor like her father, either, unless it is something in the expression of her eyes and the gesture of her hands," she often thought, as she studied

Fanny's face and wondered where she got her blue eyes and fair hair and the delicacy of her complexion and form. "I believe she gets it a hundred years back from 'Tina," she sometimes said, and then for a while rebelled against the heritage she had given her lovely daughter. "She shall never know of it," she thought, and kept it to herself until Judge Prescott's death, when it seemed necessary to tell Fanny of her real father.

Seizing upon something inadvertently spoken, Fanny, who was persistent and determined, never rested until she knew the whole story as her mother knew it. Over the father killed in the mines she wept bitterly, while the tragedy filled her with horror and for a time she refused to see anyone lest they should read in her face the secret which was making her life miserable. She had been so proud of being a Prescott and proud of her supposed father that it was hard to find herself suddenly stranded with no father, no name of which to boast, and she had dreamed many a night of the scaffold and of 'Tina, whom she was sure she resembled. "What will Roy say when he knows," had been in her thoughts all the long summer while she was with her mother in the quiet mountain resort. That Roy loved her she knew and that he would sometime tell her so she was sure. "And when he does I must tell him everything and he will not care for me any more," she thought. He had declared his love. She had told him everything, and he did not care; he could even jest about 'Tina and talk of a cottage to shield her from the weather. The revulsion of feeling was great, and Fanny's face was radiant with happiness, when Mrs. Prescott appeared suddenly in the door.

With a mother's intuition Mrs. Prescott had foreseen the probable result of Roy's intimacy with her daughter, and nothing could please her more than to see Fanny his wife and connected with the Mason family. Consequently when she entered the room and saw Fanny's confusion and Roy's exultation she guessed the truth and was prepared to hear all Roy had to say, as in a straight-forward, manly way he told her what his wishes were and asked her consent.

"Has she told you everything?" Mrs. Prescott said. "Your parents know it all, of course. They were a part of the drama played that summer which seems to me ages ago. Nor can I realize that I am the person who was guilty of that heartless escapade."

She was thinking of Craig Mason, while Fanny, who knew nothing of that page in her mother's life, thought only of her father, and said, "Oh, mother, you are not sorry you married my father? You can't be, if you love me. Where would I have been if you hadn't married him? He was nice, I know he was."

The brave little girl, who was fighting down all her pride of family and birth, would be loyal to the father she had never known and it touched her mother closely.

"I was thinking of the way I married him," she said, sitting down by Fanny and smoothing her hair, which was still a good deal disordered from contact with Roy's buttons and coatsleeves. "One always regrets the foolishness of youth which might have been avoided."

Turning now to Roy she continued, "When I married Judge Prescott it was his wish that Fanny should take his name, and mine to forget the past so far as possible. Your parents were abroad, but I wrote asking them to be reticent on the matter."

"And they have been," Roy answered quickly. "I never heard of Mr. Hilton until to-day; nor of his grandmother; nor do I care how many he had, nor how they died. I dare say half of mine ought to have been hung, if the truth were known. That has nothing to do with my love for Fanny. I want her, and right off, too,—the sooner the better. Father and mother knew my business here. I talked it all over with them and they would rather have Fanny for a daughter than anyone they know. When can I take her?"

He was very impetuous, and Mrs. Prescott could not repress a sigh as she looked at his flushed, eager face and remembered her own youth so far in the past.

"You can have my daughter," she said, "but not yet. She is not quite twenty and you are only twenty-two, both children in experience. You must wait a year at least; that will soon pass. I cannot spend another winter in this climate. I have tried Florida and do not like it, and have decided upon California, and Fanny will go with me. In June or July we shall visit the Yosemite, and when we return home it will be time to think of bridal festivities."

She was very firm, as she usually was when her mind was made up. All summer she had been planning this trip to California, intending, either on her way there, or on her return, to visit the mines in Montana where Mark had met his death. She would not like to admit to anyone the great desire she had to see some of the people who had known him and, if possible, to learn what had become of Jeff. For a brief space of time she had loved Mark passionately, and she always thought of him now with regret for the bitter things she had said to him. He had once told her there was in him, about equally balanced, the making of an angel or a devil, and a woman's hand would turn the scale. She had turned it and sent him to destruction, and the widow's weeds she wore were almost as much for Mark Hilton as for the courtly Judge Prescott. Sometimes in her sleep she heard Mark's voice calling to her from beyond the Rockies and bidding her come to him with their child. Again she sat with him in the ghost-haunted room in Ridgefield and promised to prove false to the vows made to Craig only the night before. On such occasions she would wake suddenly, bathed with perspiration and thank God it was all a dream. She did not wish Mark back. Their paths diverged more widely now than when they separated. It was her treatment of him which she regretted, and her many sleepless nights and restless days had undermined her health, until a change was necessary. She must go to California and Roy must wait for his bride until another year.

"Why can't I go with you? You need some man to take care of you, especially in the Yosemite, where the brigands are so thick that the stages are stopped every few days," Roy said.

But Mrs. Prescott was not afraid of the brigands, and didn't need a man as an escort, and Roy was compelled to acquiesce in waiting a year, which seemed to him as endless. Mrs. Prescott promised to bring Fanny to Boston before leaving for California, and with this to comfort him he left New York the following day, anxious to carry the glad news of his engagement to his father and mother. He made very short work of it.

"I have asked Fanny to be my wife, and she has consented," he said. "She is not Fanny Prescott at all, but Fanny Hilton. I know all about it, 'Tina and all, and don't care."

Craig and Alice did not care, either. To them it was an old story nearly forgotten, and they congratulated their son and at once forwarded a letter to Helen inviting her and Fanny to spend Thanksgiving with them.

CHAPTER III.

ANCESTRY.

It was a large dinner party assembled on Thanksgiving day to do honor to the little bride-elect, who bore herself with great dignity when the engagement was announced and congratulations heaped upon her and Roy. She would have liked to have been known by her real name, Hilton, but her mother objected, and as neither Roy nor his parents saw the necessity for the explanation it would involve she yielded to their judgment and was Fanny Prescott, as she had always been. Her mother could only stay for a few days in Boston, and on the morning of her departure Fanny said to Roy, who was to accompany them, "Let's stop at Ridgefield over a train. I want to see where father used to live. Mother can go on without us. Will you?"

Roy was willing, and when the villlage 'bus in Ridgefield went up the hill from the 10 o'clock train it carried two young people who were looking about them as curiously as people were looking at them. Ridgefield had not grown much within twenty-three years, but there had been some changes. An electric car now connected it with Worcester and the intermediate towns and this gave it a thriftier appearance. A few houses had been added in the side streets and a new and large hotel built on the Common. In front of this the driver stopped, while a smart clerk came hurrying out.

"Not here. Take us to the Prospect House," Roy said.

The clerk looked surprised as he turned on his heel, while the driver whipped up his horses, wondering why such swells, as his passengers undoubtedly were, should prefer the Prospect House to the Tremont. But it was none of his business, and he was soon at the Prospect House, which looked rather shabby and uninviting, with an air of neglect everywhere visible. The Tremont had killed it, and in his old age Uncle Zacheus had little heart to compete with his rival. A few boarders still clung to him, but transients were very rare, and when Roy and Fanny alighted from the 'bus and came up the walk he was greatly excited and called loudly to Dot to hurry up as somebody was coming. His welcome was cheery, as of old, as he advanced to meet the young couple.

"Glad to see you; yes, I be. Want a room? For one, or two? just married, ain't you?" he said, not remembering Roy at all in his flurry.

"No, oh no!" Fanny exclaimed, blushing crimson. "We are not married, and have only stopped over a train to see where father used to live. I am Mark Hilton's daughter, and I want you to show me his room and his office and everything, and then we are going to the cellar hole and the grave, and everywhere."

Uncle Zacheus was at first too astonished to speak and stared open-mouthed at the girl whose blue eyes fascinated and confused him, they were so bright and large and clear, and seemed to take in everything at once within their vision. His wife, who had stopped to slip on a clean white apron and smooth her hair before going to receive her guests, now appeared on the scene, and, at sight of her, Uncle Zach recovered his speech so far as to give vent to his usual ejaculation. "Wall, I'll be dumbed! Yes, I will!" he said, advancing toward Fanny and offering his hand.

For an instant she drew back. She had not expected

what she found. Everything was so different from her life that it was hard to associate her father with this place and this queer little man making so free with her. A look from Roy reassured her and she gave her hand to Mr. Taylor, who nearly crushed it before he let go his hold. Roy was exlplaining now and talking to Mrs. Taylor, who remembered him having been there with his father and mother, and finally succeeded in conveying that fact to her husband's rather hazy mind.

"Don't I remember them young folks who was here a few years ago? Wall, I guess I do, and this is their boy and girl? I don't understand it," he said; then, as it began to dawn upon him more clearly, he continued, addressing himself to Fanny, "I know now; you are Mark's girl, but you don't look like him, unless it's some trick with your eyes,—nor like your mother, neither. Who are you like, I wonder?"

He was scanning her very closely, and without at all considering what she was saying, Fanny answered him: "Perhaps I am like father's great-grandmother, 'Tina. Did you ever see her?"

"Bless my soul, child; how old do you take me to be?" and Uncle Zach burst into a hearty laugh. "I'm only eighty-three, and Miss Dalton,—that's 'Tina,—has been dead a hundred and twenty years; but I believe you *are* like her. They say she was han'som' as a picter, with blue eyes and yaller hair and clingin' ways."

Fanny was not particularly pleased to have her resemblance to 'Tina discussed, and Roy, who wished to change the conversation, said abruptly, "Can we go into the office where Mr. Hilton used to spend his time?"

"Certainly, and all over the house, too," Mr. Taylor replied, leading the way to the office, where Fanny examined everything and sat in every chair and looked over the register of years ago which was brought out for her to see.

Turning back to the summer when her mother was there her tears fell fast on the yellow page, where traces of her father's handwriting seemed to bring him near to her. Uncle Zacheus was crying, too. He did a good deal of that in his old age, but he apologized for it to Fanny, saying, "You must excuse me. I always cry when I think of Mark,—the best clerk a man ever had in a hotel, and when I heard he was dead, I cried myself sick. Didn't I Dot? And Jeff wasn't mentioned in the notice. He ain't dead. No, sir! I'm always expectin' him home. He'll come before I die. Yes, marm! You want to see where your pa slep'? You shall; yes, marm! but 'tain't no great of a place. You see them was good days, with the house so full that Mark had to sleep where he could catch it, close to the office; here 'tis."

He threw open the door of a very small and plainly furnished room, at which Fanny looked askance, mentally comparing it with her own and her mother's luxurious sleeping apartments. But she wouldn't flinch, and stroked the pillow and smoothed the patchwork coverlet and tried hard to keep her tears from falling again. Everything was so different from what her father's surroundings ought to have been. Even the saloon her mother had occupied and the pictures of Dot's ancestors failed to impress her. Everything was scrupulously clean, but the furniture was old, the carpets were faded, the paper was dingy, and there was everywhere an air from which she shrank. Accustomed to every luxury money could buy, she was an aristocrat to her finger tips, and the Prospect House, as she saw it on that November day, was not at all to her taste.

"Now, let's go to the ruin and the grave," she said to

Roy, who shrugged his shoulders, thinking he was bound on a rather gruesome business.

"I shall have to ask the way to both places, as I believe they lie in different directions," he said, and turning to Mr. Taylor he began to make inquiries as to the best way of reaching the Dalton ruin and the cemetery and where to find 'Tina's grave.

"Want to see that suller?" Uncle Zacheus exclaimed. "Why, all the timbers has fell in and there's nothin' left but a hole. I wonder it hain't been sold afore now, though nobody wants it, there's so much stuff told to this day about the ghost. They say she carries a candle now. In my opinion she's enough to do repentin', without spookin' round where she used to live. I beg your pardon, Miss Hilton. I forgot I was speakin' of your grandmarm, who lived more than a hundred years before you," he said to Fanny, who was pale to her lips.

She knew he meant no harm and tried to smile, but it was a pitiful kind of smile, which made Roy's heart ache for her.

"Poor little Fan," he said, when they were out in the street. "This is a hard day for you. Hadn't you better give up the ruin?"

"No;" she said resolutely. "I want to see what my father called his ancestral hall. It was there he asked mother to marry him. I made her tell me all about it. They sat on an old settee, and there were rats in the room. Oh, this must be where we turn, and there is the curb to the well they threw him in," she added, as they reached the lane which led to the ruin.

When walking through the village Fanny had kept apart from Roy, but now she clung closely to him as they went down the road till they came to what was once the front entrance to the house. Window frames, door posts, heavy joists and portions of the roof lay piled together, with the dried remnants of the last summer's weeds showing among the debris. The day was not cold for November, but the sky was leaden and there was a feeling of rain in the air. The trees were bare and the dead leaves lay in the path, or were piled against the fence and wall. There was no place to sit down and Fanny would not have sat if there had been. She was in a kind of dream, going over in imagination the events of more than a century ago. At last Roy brought her back to reality by kicking at a part of what might have been a pier to the wall and which, giving way, went crashing down into the cellar.

"What a pile of rubbish and what a place for 'Tina to promenade! I don't wonder she brings a candle. She would certainly break her neck in the dark if it had not already been broken," he said, without a thought as to how the last of his remark sounded.

But Fanny thought, and with a plaintive cry said to him, "Oh, Roy, how can you joke about my grandmother? You'd feel differently if she were yours."

"She is mine," Roy replied, "or is going to be, and what I said about her neck was rather mean. Honestly, though, Fan, you are too morbid over an affair which everybody has forgotten and for which you are in no way responsible. Let's get away from here."

"Wait till I've looked in the well," Fanny replied.

She went to the well and leaning over the curb looked down, shuddering at the thought of a human body struggling there and calling for help.

"I am ready now for the grave," she said, when her investigation of the well was finished.

"Must we go there?" Roy asked, rather dubiously.

"Yes, we must. I owe it to father. They are his people and mine," Fanny answered, and the two retraced their steps through the village to the Prospect House, where Uncle Zach stood on the piazza and said to them, "Dotty's getting dinner ready for you when you come back from the cemetry. Turn to your right and foller close to the wall clear down to the corner. They're sunk in some, I guess."

They found the graves without any difficulty, but, as Mr. Taylor had said, they were sunken and neglected. No one had cared for them since Mark went away. The grass around them was never cut and now lay in dry clumps upon them. The rose bush Mark had planted was dead and a huge burdock stood in its place. The headstones were weather-beaten and discolored, and that of 'Tina had partially fallen over. Fanny went down upon the ground and read the name "Christine Dalton." There was nothing to tell where she was born or where she died, and in her nervous, morbid state Fanny found herself pitying the woman who had gone to her grave dishonored and despised.

"Nobody ever shed a tear for you, I dare say, but I will," she said, and sitting upon the stone where her mother had sat with Mark Hilton when he told her the story of 'Tina, she began to cry very low to herself, so that Roy might not hear and laugh at her. "Where is he?" she said, when she had paid sufficient respect to 'Tina, and looking up, missed him from her side.

She saw him at last in the distance standing near the monument of Gen. Allen, and his loud call came to her across the rows of graves which intervened.

"I say, Fan, ar'n't you some connection to Gen. George Allen, who served in the Revolutionary War, was wounded at Bunker Hill and Saratoga, and did a lot more things, and died regretted by friend and foe?"

She did not answer, and he continued, "Come away from that damp, lonesome place. I got chilly there myself. Come up here and visit another ancestor, who, perhaps, wasn't any more respectable than those you are mooning over, but he has a stunner for a monument and an obituary as long as my arm."

Fanny was getting tired and cold, and went up the slope to where Roy was waiting for her.

"Yes, that is mother's grandfather," she said, rather cheerfully, as she looked at the monument and read the inscription upon it.

There was some difference between this costly stone and well-kept enclosure where a number of Allens were lying and the sunken, neglected graves under the shadow of the wall, and Fanny felt the difference, and her spirits began to rise in the vicinity of the Allens, who represented the aristocracy of the cemetery. Both belonged to her, the grand monument and the sunken graves, the Allens and the Daltons,—but the Allens were the nearest of kin,—they were like what she was born to and had been accustomed to all her life and she felt a thrill of pride on reading the eulogy on her great-grandfather, who had rendered such service to his country and been so highly esteemed by his fellow-citizens.

"Good blood there, of the bluest kind," Roy said, teasingly. "It ought to make amends for forty 'Tinas." Then, as the shrill whistle from the shoe shop came echoing across the fields, he continued: "Twelve o'clock; time we were going, if you have seen enough of your ancestors. I'm getting hungry."

He was very practical and led Fanny so adroitly from what he called "an ancestral fit" that she was quite herself by the time they reached the Prospect House. Mrs. Taylor had prepared a most appetizing dinner for them, which she served upon a small round table placed near a window and the stove, where they could have both warmth and light. All her best things were on duty and Fanny, who found the dinner excellent, began to change her mind with regard to the hotel. In the summer it must be very pleasant, especially on the broad piazzas, and perhaps she should come again, she said to Mr. and Mrs. Taylor, as she bade them good bye.

"Bless you, child, I hope you will," Uncle Zacheus replied, holding her hand and trying to keep back his tears which his wife told him he needn't shed so often unless he had softening of the brain, of which they were signs. "It is good for my old eyes to see young people. There don't many come since they built the big stone tavern on the Common. I began to run down when Mark went away. A good feller, that, and I cry when I think of him dead. I can't help it if 'tis sign of soff'nin'. I remember the old days when Mark and your mother and this young man's father and mother was here and the house was full of young voices and courtin' and love-makin' from mornin' till night. Your young man, —I know he is yourn by the way he looks at you,—has a good face like his father and mother. You'll be happy with him, and he'll be happy with you. Your face ain't like nobody's, but makes me think of some flower that is ever so sweet and lovely and modest,—I can't remember the name. 'Tain't a rose, nor a pink, nor a piney."

Roy laughed, and suggested, "Lily of the Valley."

"I swan, that's it. Lily of the Valley," Uncle Zach returned, and continued, "I s'pose I must say good bye and God bless you and make you happy. Good bye."

He turned to leave them, when Fanny took his hand again,—the one her mother had kissed years ago,—and pressed her lips upon it just as Helen had done.

"I'll surely come again," she said, and then hurried away, for it was getting near train time and they were going to walk.

That kiss was too much for Uncle Zach. Softening of the brain or no softening of the brain he must cry, and he did, while his wife derided him for his weakness.

"I shall cry if I want to," he said, evincing considerable spirit for him. "I never told you of it, but her mother kissed my hand three and twenty years ago when she went away and I've never seen her since, and never shall, nor this little girl, neither. She will come, maybe, but I shan't be here. I'm wearin' out. There's more ails me than softnin' of the brain. I'm old,—most eighty-four. I'm slippin' away from you, Dotty, and from the places I love so well."

Here his feelings so overcame him that he cried like a child, while his wife, touched by the sight of his tears, tried to comfort him.

"No you ain't slippin' away," she said. "You'll see 'em again. You are good for ten years more, and so am I, and I am seventy-eight. Wipe up, there's somebody comin'."

He wiped up, and under the combined effects of a traveller who wanted dinner and Dotty's assurance of ten years longer lease of life he was quite cheerful until he heard the rumble of the train which was to take Roy and Fanny away. Then a sense of loneliness came over him again and he kept whispering to himself, "Good bye, good bye, Mark's gal and Craig's boy. I shall never see you again. Good bye."

CHAPTER IV.

INEZ.

Mrs. Prescott had spent the winter in Southern California, and some time in April was registered at the Palace Hotel in San Francisco, with her daughter and maid. As her meals were served in her private parlor and she seldom stopped in the public reception room, she saw none of the guests of the house, except a few New Yorkers who were stopping there. Fanny, on the contrary, saw everybody, and flitted through the hotel like a sunbeam, with a pleasant word for those she knew and a smile for those she did not know. Her mother sometimes tried to restrain her from being so free with people, telling her that since she had heard of the circumstances of her birth she had developed a most plebeian taste.

"If I have it *tastes* good," Fanny would answer, laughingly, "and I am a great deal happier in liking people and having them like me than I was when I felt that the world was made for me and only a select few had a right to share it with me."

She was very happy and enjoyed everything thoroughly. Time was passing and only a few months remained before her return to Roy, who wrote her nearly every day. In his last letter he told her he had been to Ridgefield.

"I was in Worcester," he wrote, "and I took the electric, for I wanted to see Uncle Zach again. He is a case, isn't he? He had the rheumatism and can scarcely walk. Poor old man! He cried when he spoke of the days when our parents were there making love to each other. He was quite poetic in his lamentations. 'No more matin' of birds, here,' he said. 'They've all flew off to the Tremont House, leavin' me nothin' but some *dum* English sparrers.' He talked a great deal of your father and a boy Jeff. Said he didn't believe he was dead, and he should be perfectly happy if he were with him again, turnin' summersaults! That would be funny, as Jeff, if living, must be over thirty. Of course I visited your property, which, if possible, looks more dilapidated than when we were there last November. It has quite a fascination for me, and I really mean, with your permission, and your mother's, to build a cottage there, where we can spend a few weeks every summer.

"When do you go to the Yosemite? Do you know I have a queer feeling about that trip and am half inclined to take it with you. I have just seen a chap who two years ago last summer was waylaid by robbers. He says it's not an uncommon thing for the stage to be stopped. His experience was a bad one. Two ladies fainted from sheer fright and one of them was robbed while unconscious. A strange feature of this robbery was that the watch taken from the fainting woman and which had her name engraved upon it was sent to her by mail to the hotel where she was stopping. Most of the money taken was also returned to the owners who could least afford to lose it. A queer thing for marauders to do, and shows that they are habitues of the neighborhood and have facilities for learning the names and position of those whom they plunder. I hope you will not meet with an adventure of this kind."

On the morning when Fanny received this letter she was sitting by the window of one of the parlors in the hotel, reading it a second time, and feeling a little nervous with regard to the stage robberies of which she had heard something in San Francisco. A Firemen's Parade was passing, with all the paraphernalia of bands and hose carts and boys and a crowd generally, but she paid no attention to it until a clear, musical voice, with a slight accent, said to her, "Pretty, isn't it, Miss Prescott; and isn't father grand in his new suit? That's he,—the tall man who bowed to me when I kissed my hand to him. He is foreman of one of the companies."

Surprised at being so familiarly addressed by a stranger, Fanny looked up and saw standing by the next window a young girl whom she had seen several times in the halls and corridors and wondered who she was. She was tall and well proportioned. Her features were regular, her eyes dark and lustrous and veiled under very long lashes and surmounted by heavy brows which made them seem darker than they were. Her complexion was a rich olive, telling of a southern sun which must have warmed the blood of one or both of her parents. There was nothing impertinent in her manner. It was simply friendly, and Fanny, who was longing for some young person to speak to, answered pleasantly, "How did you know my name?"

"Oh, everybody knows that," the girl replied, "and if they didn't they have only to look on the register. I saw you the day you came and have watched you ever since when I had a chance and I wanted to speak to you so badly. I don't know why, only I did. It seemed to me I should like you, and I know so few young girls. Perhaps I ought not to have spoken to you, but you don't mind, do you?"

She was so frank and unsophisticated and her face was so pretty and pleasant that Fanny had no thought of being offended. She had been told by her mother never to talk with strangers and especially to the class to which this girl belonged. But Fanny usually talked to whom she pleased and as she attracted this strange girl so the girl attracted and fascinated her.

"Sit down, please, and tell me your name, inasmuch as you know mine," she said.

The girl sat down and folded her hands just as Fanny had a trick of folding hers. There was this difference, however,—the girl's hands were large and brown,—helpful hands, used to toil,—while Fanny's were soft and white and dimpled like a baby's. The girl was not at all averse to talking of herself and said, "I am Inez Raybourne. My father is an American. My mother was half Mexican, half Spanish,—with a little Gypsy blood in her. She used to call me Gypsy because I love the mountains and rocks and woods so much. Father married her near Santa Barbara, and her name was *Anita*. Isn't that a pretty name?"

Fanny said it was, and Inez went on: "She was a little bit of a body whom father could take up and set on his shoulder. He is big and tall, and I am big, too. I wish I was small like mother and you. Mother is dead, and I have been so lonely since she died."

Her eyes filled with tears which hung on her lashes as she continued: "Our home is in the Yosemite, not far from Inspiration Point, and perched on the hillside above the stage road, with a lovely view of the valley and the mountains. We call it Prospect Cottage and in winter we shut it up and come to the city. Before mother died we went sometimes to Santa Barbara, sometimes to Los Angeles. Now we come here and I help the housekeeper in part payment for my board. Father helps round the hotel, and Tom, too, when he is here."

"Who is Tom?" Fanny asked, and Inez replied, "Oh, he is Tom and has lived with us since I can remember, and is like a son to father. In the summer, when the hotels in the valley are full of visitors, they sometimes go on trails as guides with the people. Again they are off on some business, seeing to exchange of property, which keeps them away for days. Then I am so lonesome and afraid, too, if there is a robbery on the road. I have a splendid dog, Nero, to take care of me. He is young, but very large. He is here with us. Maybe you have noticed him lying in the office or the hall."

Fanny had seen a big dog around the hotel and had patted his head, for she was fond of dogs, but she was more interested now in what Inez said of a robbery.

"Do you mean stage robberies, and are they of frequent occurrence?" she asked.

"Sometimes, and sometimes not," was Inez's answer. "There was a dreadful one just before mother died, and I think the fright killed her. She had heart trouble and was here to-day, gone to-morrow. We were alone, and when the stage passed in the afternoon a neighbor who was on it came and told us how dreadful it was, with two ladies fainting and children crying and the highwaymen taking the watch of the woman who lay like one dead. He sent it back to her at the hotel, and the money to the others. Wasn't that queer?"

Fanny was thinking of what Roy had written her and exclaimed, "I have heard of that."

"You have!" Inez rejoined. "Well, the papers were full of it, and people were determined to catch the men, if possible. Mother was very nervous over it, but I never thought of her dying. We always said our prayers together, and that night she prayed that the men might be caught and the wicked work stopped. She seemed the same when she kissed me good night, but when I went into her room in the morning she could not speak. Father had come home late and was caring for her, rubbing her hands and arms, which had in them no power to move. 'Was it the fright of the robbery?' I said to father, who nodded, while she tried to speak and her eyes followed him in such a beseeching way. 'Do you want to tell us something?' I said. She nodded and made a motion to write. I brought her pencil and paper, but her nerveless hands could not hold the pencil and she died looking up at father so pitifully. He was so tender and kind to her, and cried over her like a baby, and himself put her in the coffin. It was such a little coffin I didn't realize till I saw it how small she was. We buried her on the hill back of our house where the light from our windows can shine upon her grave when we are there in the summer. In the winter it must be awful with the snow piled so high and all of us gone. Father was almost crazy for a while and walked the floor and sat by her grave and wouldn't eat. He staid home the rest of the season and Tom staid, too, most of the time. There were no more stages robbed that summer, and not many last summer; three or four at the most, and it so happens that I am always alone with Nero. Of course no harm can come to me but I feel nervous just the same."

Inez was talking very earnestly and rapidly, and her language was so good that Fanny felt sure she must have had better advantages than were to be had among the mountains and asked her at last where she was educated.

"I am not educated as you are," Inez replied. "I was at school in Stockton two years and have been to school winters in Santa Barbara and here. The rest I learned from father and mother. She had been in a convent and taught me Spanish;—that was her language. She spoke English brokenly, but so prettily. Tom brings me books to read and I know all about the east where father is to take me some day when we are able to stop at first-class hotels as guests. I am afraid, though, it will be a long time before we go. Father's business is not always very good."

"What did you say it was?" Fanny asked, and Inez replied, "Exchange of property. I don't know what that means, exactly, and when I asked Tom he said I hadn't brain enough to understand it, if he explained. He likes to tease me."

There was beginning to dawn upon Fanny a suspicion of the relation in which Tom stood to Inez, but she made no comment, and Inez continued: "I wish you knew father, he is so handsome for a man nearly fifty, and so kind to everybody. They worship him in the Yosemite and depend upon him a great deal. When a stage has been robbed he always gives his services to find the robbers. They have caught one or two who are in prison now, but they can get no clew to the men who have been such a terror to the neighborhood."

"Oh," Fanny gasped, "you frighten me so. Mother and I are going to the Yosemite in June and I should die if the stage I was in was stopped."

"I shouldn't," Inez replied. "I have been on the road with father a good many times and nothing happened, but if there did I shouldn't be afraid. I'd fly at the robber and try to kill him. Father laughs when I talk that way and says there is murder in my Gypsy blood. Perhaps there is. Any way I would not hesitate to kill a man who was robbing a coach. I'd shoot him like a dog."

Her mood had changed as she talked. The softness had left her eyes which blazed and flashed defiantly, and she took a turn or two across the room as if she were in fancy battling with some desperado.

"Don't look so fierce. You scare me," Fanny said, when Inez came back and resumed her chair.

"Do I? I cannot tell you how I feel when I think of the bandits who make our beautiful valley a dread to tourists who visit it. But they may not be there at all this summer. Don't worry about them. Leave your valuables here, especially your diamonds, if you have any. Then, if you are held up you have not so much to lose. If I knew when you were coming I believe I'd meet you in Milton, where you take the stage, or have father do it. He isn't afraid. He goes home to-morrow or next day. Tom has already gone. I go in two or three weeks. You must come to our cottage. It is lovely."

Inez's face was a very changeable one, now grave and serious and sad, then sunny and sweet, with a smile which changed its whole expression. Like most communicative people she was very inquisitive, and having told all there was to tell about herself she asked Fanny about herself, her home in New York, and how old she was. "I am seventeen," she said.

"And I am twenty. I thought you older," Fanny replied, in some surprise.

"So does every one, because I am so tall and big, like my father. Where is *your* father?" Inez asked.

"He is dead," Fanny replied, thinking of both Mark Hilton and Judge Prescott.

"Oh, I am so sorry for you; but you have a mother, and mine is lying among the hills," Inez said, beginning to talk again of her home and her hope that Fanny would visit her when she came to the valley. "You *must*," she continued. "I want you to see our cottage and mother's grave, and father and Nero and everything.

If you will let me see your mother I will ask her for you. People nearly always do what I wish them to."

Fanny could not promise for her mother. To her Inez was a frank, simple-hearted girl, a little too forward, perhaps, but this came of her surrounding circumstances and not from any innate ill-breeding. Mrs. Prescott would probably think differently.

"Mother is something of an invalid and does not usually see strangers, but I will tell her of you," Fanny said, and as a maid just then came to say lunch was ready she bade her good morning and left the parlor.

The acquaintance thus begun ripened into intimacy as the days went by, and the two girls saw each other often. Mistress and maid, a casual observer might have thought them, they were so unlike; the one, slight and fair as a lily and clad in garments of the latest style, with every mark of culture and refinement; the other, tall and strongly built, with a freedom of manner which betokened a child of the mountains rather than of the city, and a face singular in its beauty, and eyes wonderful in their varying expression, from a softness under their veiled lids, amounting almost to sleepiness, to gleams of passion which told of a strong nature which, when aroused, was equal to acts of daring from which Fanny in her timidity would have shrunk appalled. Inez took Fanny on frequent walks through the city which she knew so well and where so many seemed to know her. At first Mrs. Prescott objected to her daughter's intimacy with one who, in her estimation, was little more than a peasant girl. But Fanny was not to be shaken from her allegiance, and after some inquiries of the housekeeper with regard to Inez Mrs. Prescott ceased to object to Fanny's being so much with her.

"But don't bring her in here. Why should I see her?" she said, when Fanny asked that Inez might be presented.

"Because I want you know her, and see if you can tell what makes me feel so when I am with her."

"Bring her, then," Mrs. Prescott said, one day, "but don't let her stay long. My head aches and I am tired."

That afternoon Fanny went out with her maid on an errand, saying to Inez as she left the hotel, "When I come back I am going to take you to mother."

For a while Inez waited patiently, watching for Fanny's return. To call upon Mrs. Prescott was a great event in her life and something of which to tell her father and Tom when she got home. In the housekeeper's room and from the servants and some of the guests whom she knew, she had heard a great deal of Mrs. Prescott, who was said to be fabulously wealthy, and had such costly diamonds and wore such pretty negligées in the morning and such beautiful dresses to dinner, although there was no one but her daughter at table with her. Occasionally she had caught a glimpse of the lady on the rare occasions when she went to drive, but she was always so closely veiled that it was impossible to tell how she looked. Now, however, Inez was to see her, and she grew very impatient at Fanny's protracted absence.

"Maybe she has come and I didn't know it. I mean to go up and see," she thought, as the clock struck four and there was no sign of Fanny.

Going up to Mrs. Prescott's rooms she stole softly to the door, which was partly open. Fanny was not there, but she heard a sound as of some one in pain. Mrs. Prescott had complained of a headache all day and after Fanny and her maid went out it grew so much worse that she dropped the shades and lay down upon the couch, hoping to sleep. But the pain which was of a neuralgic nature increased so fast that she at last uttered the moan which Inez heard. Her first impulse was to go in at once; then, knowing this was not the thing to do, she knocked twice and receiving no answer ventured in. Mrs. Prescott, who was lying with her eyes closed, did not know she was there until she said, "Are you sick, and can I do anything for you?"

The voice was singularly sweet, with a tone in it which brought to Mrs. Prescott's mind vague memories of woods and hills and sunshine on a river and pond where the white lilies grew and where in her giddiness and pain she seemed for a moment to be sailing away into the shadow of the willows which drooped over the water. Just where the woods and hills and river were was not clear to her, and the picture passed as soon as it came. Looking up she saw a young girl standing by her couch, plainly attired in a gingham dress and white apron, with a fancy silk handkerchief knotted around her neck.

"One of the chambermaids," she thought and answered "There's nothing you can do unless you rub my head. It aches very hard. Are you on this floor?"

Inez looked a little puzzled and replied, "On this floor? No; I room with the housekeeper. I am Inez,— Miss Prescott's friend."

"Oh!" and Mrs. Prescott's eyes opened wide and a slight frown contracted her brow at what she thought an undue familiarity.

But something in Inez's face disarmed her and brought back the picture of the woods and hills and river, with herself younger and happier than she was now. Before she could reply, Inez continued: "I used to rub mother's head when it ached and she said it helped her. Father says I have a great deal of magnetism in my hands. I take it from him. Let me try."

She knelt on the floor as she talked and began to manipulate Mrs. Prescott's temples, which thrilled at once to the touch of her fingers.

"You are doing me good," Mrs. Prescott said, lying very still while Inez smoothed her hair and rubbed her forehead and talked in her low, musical voice of her dead mother and what she used to do for her.

Mrs. Prescott listened until she had a pretty accurate knowledge of *Anita* and her grave among the hills and the cottage among the rocks and Inez's handsome father. Then, as the pain in her head grew less, there came over her a feeling of restfulness and quiet. Inez's voice was like the murmur of a brook she had heard somewhere. The leafy woods and hills and river were all blended together. Inez's face, like something she had seen before, looked at her through the mist which was stealing over her senses and when Fanny came in she found her mother sleeping quietly, with Inez sitting by her and fanning her. After that Mrs. Prescott made no objection to her daughter's intimacy with Inez.

"Yes, she is very nice, with something charming in her voice and manner. It is her Spanish blood, I think," she said to Fanny, "but, of course, she is wholly untrained and knows nothing of the world. You could not have her for an associate in New York, but here it does not matter. Mrs. Ward, the housekeeper, tells me she is perfectly correct in her morals, and her father is highly respectable,—rather superior to his class which accounts for some things in Inez. I do not know that I shall object to your spending a day or so with her when we are in the Yosemite. I shall try and secure the services of her father as guide, if I go on any of the trails. They say he is exceptionally good."

This was said a few days after Inez had left for her mountain home and Fanny was expressing a wish to visit her. The trip was planned for the middle of June, and Fanny, who had become greatly attached to Inez, was looking forward to meeting her again with nearly as much pleasure as to the Yosemite itself.

———◆———

CHAPTER V.

IN THE YOSEMITE.

The Yosemite stage which left the Milton station on the afternoon of June 15, 18—, was full of passengers, all eagerly discussing an attempt made the day before to rob the coach between China Camp and Priest's. A tall, powerfully built fellow had sprung out from behind a clump of trees as the stage was slowly ascending a long hill, and ordered the frightened inmates to hold up their hands. This they did at once, with no thought of resistance, and he was about to relieve them of whatever valuables they had on their persons, when a young man who was sitting on the box with the driver, sprang to the ground and confronting the ruffain with a revolver compelled him to retreat and sent after him a shot or two, which, however, went wide of the mark. Mr. Hardy, the hero of the exploit, was well known in Stockton and the country generally and was among the passengers that afternoon. Naturally he was plied with questions with regard to the incident and asked how he dared attack the desperado.

"I don't know myself how I dared," he replied. "It was so sudden that at first I whispered to the driver, 'Go on; lick the horses, go on!' He was shaking like a leaf,— teeth actually chattered. Then it came to me what muffs we were to sit there quietly and be robbed, and without another thought I sprang at the man, almost landing on his head. Of the rest I remember nothing until my hands were being shaken and women were crying and thanking me as their deliverer. I only wish my shot had brought him down. It was Long John, no doubt, and his companion is pretty sure to turn up soon. I'd like to meet him."

He did not seem at all averse to talking, and the passengers listened breathlessly, conscious of a feeling of security as long as he was with them. Among those who seemed the most interested and anxious was Fanny Prescott, who sat on the same seat with the hero, and had grown very pale as his story progressed.

"Oh, mother," she said at last, "what if that dreadful man should attack us! What should we do? I wish we had left our diamonds in San Francisco. I don't believe, though, he could find them. They are —"

A touch on the elbow from her mother kept her from finishing a remark which elicited a smile from her companions. For a moment Mr. Hardy looked at her and then said, "If your diamonds are very valuable it would have been wise to have left them in safe keeping, but I do not anticipate any danger on this trip. The attempt of yesterday is too recent to be repeated so soon. The whole neighborhood is looking for the robbers, who are probably hiding in the woods."

For the rest of the afternoon the conversation was of the men who were the terror of the road between Milton and the valley. The older of the two was said to be tall, the other short, and as they had been heard to address each other as John and Dick, they were usually spoken of as Long John and Little Dick, and so daring and sudden were their movements and so seldom did they fail to execute their purpose that the mention of their names was sufficient to fill the stoutest heart with fear. Of the two Dick was the one most dreaded. He was so rapid in his movements, sometimes seeming to spring from the ground, again to drop from the trees and leap in the air like an athlete and doing his work so swiftly that the people scarcely knew what was happening until it was over and he was leaving them. Two or three times efforts had been made to rob the express box, but either the robbers were in too great a hurry, or the box had baffled their efforts, for the attempt had been abandoned and the attention of the bandits given to the passengers. No bodily injury had ever been done to any one, and in a few instances when some woman or old man had complained that all they had was taken from them, their purses had been tossed back to them by Dick, who would lift his hat gracefully and with a bound leave as quickly and mysteriously as he came. Long John was more deliberate, but stronger, and that Mr. Hardy single handed had put him to flight seemed incredible, and he was lionized and made much of, and the wish expressed by the passengers that he should go on to the valley, as with him they felt secure. At Chinese Camp, where they were to pass the night, he left them, with the assurance that, judging from the past they had nothing to fear from the marauders.

"I wish you were going with us. I feel so safe with you," Fanny said to him when she stood for a moment alone with him in the narrow, dimly lighted hall.

She was standing directly under the hanging lamp, which showed her face pale with anxiety and fear.

"Don't be afraid," he said, in a tone such as he would use to soothe a frightened child. "I know the habits of the wretches, and would almost stake my life against their molesting you on the trip to the valley. There may be more danger when you leave it. Better take the other road to Clarke's. It is safer and pleasanter, and, one word of caution, don't talk about your diamonds and where you keep them. You came near telling in the coach."

"I know I did," Fanny replied, "but I will remember in the future and I thank you so much for your advice. Good bye."

She saw he was anxious to leave her and offered him her hand, which looked very small and white as it lay in his broad palm. For an instant his fingers closed over it with something like a slight pressure and his face was a study, as if two sets of feelings were contending in his mind with an equal chance for the mastery.

Dropping her hand he said, "Are your diamonds very valuable?"

"Yes," Fanny answered quickly. "They are worth thousands of dollars and are sewed up in the ribbon bows of my hat. I don't believe they would think of looking there. Do you?"

He laughed a hearty, ringing laugh, and when Fanny looked inquiringly at him he said, "I beg your pardon. I couldn't help it. I thought you were not to tell where your diamonds were, and you have told *me!* But, never mind, you are safe. Good bye. I think we may meet again."

He bowed and left the hotel, while Fanny joined her mother in the small room allotted them. There had been a long discussion between them as to the disposition of the diamonds during their absence from San Francisco. Remembering what Inez had said Fanny wished to put them in a safe deposit company's vault while her mother insisted upon taking them with her. She didn't know about San Francisco. If it were New York it would be different, and she wanted them with her. She was one of those nervous women who feel that nothing is safe unless they can see it. Her baggage was always taken to the hotel and to her room, if she was only to pass the night. She knew then where it was, and the diamonds must go with her to the Yosemite. She had left most of them in New York at Tiffany's, and only had with her a small cluster pin, her rings and Fanny's, and her large pear-shaped ear-rings,—the heirlooms which Mark Hilton had taken with him when he left Ridgefield and which were to be Fanny's on her wedding day. After devising various places of concealment, Fanny finally decided to sew the diamonds in the knots of heavy ribbon on her hat, where their safety could be ascertained at any moment. This done, Mrs. Prescott felt quite secure and listened composedly to all that was said of the robbers. She had only brought money enough for the trip, and unknown to any one a part of that was twisted up in her back hair. She had nothing to lose or fear, and she slept soundly in her small quarters at Chinese Camp. Fanny, on the contrary, could not sleep and sat by the open window looking out into the night starting at every sound and wishing Mr. Hardy had not left them. She was not superstitious, but felt oppressed with a feeling of impending danger and wished many times that she was safely back in San Francisco.

At a very early hour in the morning the stage started, for there was many a mile of rocks and hills between the Camp and the valley, and the sleepy passengers shivering in the cool morning air took their seats, wondering what would befall them before the day was over. Nor were they in any degree reassured when, as they were ascending a long hill the driver suddenly stopped and announced to them, "This is where they had the holdup and that the clump of trees the robber was behind."

Involuntarily Fanny's hand went up to her hat while the passengers shrank into their seats as if to escape a danger. Then, remembering there was none they looked curiously at the spot and two or three alighted and walked around the trees trying to conjecture just where the brigand stood before he made his appearance at the horses' heads.

"If it had been the little one instead of the big one he wouldn't have been drove off so easy. I tell you Dick is a terror. Why, they say he can jump straight up and land in the coach, or the box, either. Must have been a circus rider," the driver said, while every passenger breathed a prayer to be delivered from the terrible Dick.

As long as they were in the open country they felt safe, but the moment they came near to ledges and woods they fancied a robber behind every tree and rock and were glad when as night was closing in they began to descend into the valley under the shadow of old Capitan and into a region of fertility and civilization. As soon as Mrs. Prescott was settled in her small room, which had once been a bathroom, and in which she declared she could neither breathe nor sleep, she made inquiries for Mr. Rayborne, the guide, as she wished to secure his services for herself and daughter whenever they went on trails:

"That is, if he is really as good as I heard he was in San Francisco," she said to the landlord, who replied, "There's none better in the valley. No, nor so good either. You see he's a gentleman, and people like that, but I doubt if he is home. He has not been round the hotel for a week. His cottage is two or three miles from here. I'll send and inquire."

"And please," Fanny began, "will your messenger take a note for me to Miss Rayborne. Do you know her?"

"Know Inez! I rather think we do," the landlord replied. "Everybody knows Inez; the wild rose of the valley, we call her. I knew her mother, too,—a pretty little woman,—went off like a flash. Heart trouble they said. The whole neighborhood turned out to her funeral, visitors and all. The hill was black with 'em. John,—that is Mr. Rayborne,—has never been quite the same man since."

He was inclined to be very talkative, but Fanny was in a hurry to write to Inez and finally left him in the middle of a sentence. When the messenger returned he brought a note for her from Inez, who wrote: "I am delighted to know you are in the valley, and sorry father is not here to guide you on the trails. Perhaps he will come before you leave. I am so lonely with only Nero for company. I thought of you when that robbery occurred and was glad you were not on the road. I have something to tell you about it when I see you. Father came home that night, but Tom has not been here since. I expect him in a few days. Write me when to come for you. Inez."

Mrs. Prescott was a good deal disappointed that she could not have Mr. Rayborne for a guide, and because she could not she did not go on a single trail. As she cared little for scenery and there were but few people at the hotel of what she called her set she was ready to leave at any time.

"Not till I have made my visit to Inez," Fanny said,

and after they had been at the hotel a week it was arranged that she should spend a day with her friend and be taken up the next morning by the stage which was to pass the cottage and leave the valley by way of Inspiration Point.

CHAPTER VI.

AT PROSPECT COTTAGE.

It was one of the loveliest of all the summer days in the Yosemite when Inez drove up to the hotel in a buggy which had seen a good deal of service and was not like anything Fanny had ever ridden in. But she did not care. She was delighted to see Inez, who appeared at her best on her native heath and received the warm greetings of those who knew her with the grace and dignity of a young queen. Mrs. Prescott was invited to accompany Fanny, but declined, and the two girls set off alone for Prospect Cottage. Inez was very happy.

"I am so glad to have this little bit of you," she said, giving a squeeze to Fanny's hand and then dropping it again. "And we will have such a good time to-day all by ourselves. I haven't much to do. I was up at four o'clock to get my work done, baking and all, and have made a lot of things I think you will like. One is huckleberry pie."

Fanny had never seen one, but was sure she should like it, and anything else Inez chose to give her.

"It won't be like the hotel, nor your New York home," Inez said, "I do everything myself and oh, isn't it lovely here among the mountains with this pure air which makes me feel so strong as if I should live forever."

She was very enthusiastic and Fanny, who also felt the invigorating effects of the atmosphere, entered into her enthusiasm and enjoyed everything, from the wild flowers they stopped to gather, to the musical brook, which went singing along in its rocky bed beside the carriage road.

"This is our house," Inez said at last, pointing to a cottage in a niche of the hills behind some trees which partially hid it from the highway which was below it at a little distance.

An immense dog came out to meet them, frisking about the buggy and barking his welcome.

"That's Nero. You saw him at the hotel," Inez said. "I leave him at home to watch the house when I go away. Good Nero, down, down," she continued, as she alighted from the buggy and the dog sprang upon her, trying to lick her face.

"Please go right in; the door is open. I leave it so, with Nero. I must unharness my pony. I'm my own chore boy as well as maid," she said to Fanny, who went into the cottage, followed by Nero, who, stretching himself upon the floor, whacked his big tail approvingly, as Fanny looked curiously around the room.

It was a model of neatness and order and showed many touches of a woman's dainty hand and, what surprised her a little, had in it some articles of furniture more expensive than she expected to find among the mountains. The wide door opened upon a piazza which commanded a magnificent view of the monutains and the valley below. A honeysuckle was trained upon the rustic pillars and a bowl of roses and ferns was standing upon a round table near which were two or three chairs,

This was evidently the living place of the family and Fanny sat down in one of the chairs to wait for Inez who soon came in flushed and bright and eager to talk.

"Yes, we sit here a great deal," she said, in answer to a question from Fanny. "Father likes a piazza; it reminds him of his youth, he says, but he looks so sorry when I ask him about his youth that I don't often do it, and I know very little of his boyhood. I asked him once if I had any relatives. 'No' he said, so short that I have never referred to them again. You must have a great many."

"Very few," Fanny said, and Inez continued: "Has your father been dead long?"

There was a moment's hesitancy before Fanny replied: "Judge Prescott, who died last year, was my step-father, whose name I took when mother married him. She was a Miss Tracy, and my own father was Mr. Mark Hilton. He died in the mines of Montana when I was a baby. I do not remember him."

"I am so sorry for you," Inez said. "I wish you could remember him a little. You must resemble him, as you do not look like your mother."

Fanny drew a long breath, and, with a thought of 'Tina, answered, "I am like one of my grandmothers."

Slight as was her knowledge of the world Inez's womanly instinct told her that Fanny did not care to discuss her family and she changed the conversation.

"I am going to get dinner now," she said. "Would you like to see me? I don't suppose you ever did a stroke of work in your life?"

"I never have,—more's the pity," Fanny said, as she followed Inez to the kitchen and watched her with the greatest interest, offering to help her.

"Not now," Inez said. "You may wipe the dishes

when dinner is over, and then we can have more time to visit."

Fanny wiped the dishes after the dinner, in which the huckleberry pie had a conspicuous place, and left its marks on her mouth and teeth. When the work was done there was a ramble among the hills, a visit to Anita's grave, which was covered with flowers and then, as the afternoon began to wane, the two girls sat down upon the piazza and watched the shadows deepening in the valley and the colors changing on the mountains from rosy tints to violet hues, while the sound of the waterfalls in the distance became more distinct as night drew on.

"Isn't the world beautiful?" Inez said, "and isn't it a joy to live. And yet I have a presentiment that I shall die young, like mother. She had heart trouble, you know, and I inherit it from her. A great shock of joy or pain might kill me. Then what would father do,—and Tom."

This was the first time she had mentioned Tom, and after a moment Fanny said affirmatively: "You love Tom?" and into Inez's eyes there came a bright, happy look as she replied, "I don't mind telling you that I am going to marry him sometime when he gets a little more ahead and can leave his present business. It was settled last winter. He is a good deal older than I am, but looks younger than he is and I look older. Strangers take me for twenty at least. I have always known Tom and always loved him, I think. I have sometimes fancied that father was not quite pleased. He has never said anything except that Tom was too old for me and that I ought to see more of the world before marrying. Tom is my world. There is a pretty house in Stockton which he is going to buy, when he is able, where we can live in the winter, but we shall come back here in the summer."

"What is his other name? I've never heard. You have always called him Tom," Fanny said, and Inez replied, "Why, Tom Hardy. Funny you didn't know, and he is the one who kept Long John from robbing the coach the other day. That is what I was going to tell you. I am so proud of him. The papers are full of his praises. Father says there is not another man in the valley who would dare attack that giant of a fellow. Tom hasn't been home since, and I'm dying to see him. I have felt nervous every time I have thought of the risk he ran. What if he had been shot!"

Inez's cheek grew pale as she thought of the danger her lover had escaped, and before she could say any more Fanny exclaimed, "Is that Mr. Hardy *your* Tom? I know him. He was on the coach with us from Milton to Chinese camp and told us all about it. I'm glad he is your Tom."

Inez's confidence with regard to Tom reminded Fanny of Roy, and in a few minutes Inez had heard all about him and the wedding which was to take place during the holidays.

"I am so glad for you. It is nice to be engaged," Inez said; "Mr. Mason is of course very different from Tom, but I am satisfied with him, and I do hope he will come to-night and father, too. I think they will. I am keeping supper back a little in case they do, as they are always hungry. What is it, Nero?" she added, as the dog sprang up in a listening attitude, and then darted off through the brush towards the highway. "I believe he heard them. Yes, he did," Inez cried, as a peculiar whistle, loud and clear, sounded in the direction Nero had taken. "That is Tom! He always whistles to let me know he is coming. I hope father is with him. There they are! Hallo, father!

Hallo, Tom!" and she was off like the wind to meet the two men coming up the steep path from the road.

One was tall and walked as if he were tired, with his head a little bent. The other was short and slight and walked with a quick, springing step, as if he never knew what fatigue was. He was dressed differently from what he had been in the stage and there was a jaunty air about him generally, but Fanny would have had no trouble in recognizing him as the hero of the hold-up. Inez threw her arms around her father's neck, kissing him many times; then, with a glance backward to see if Fanny were looking on she put up her lips for Tom to kiss, and holding a hand of each of the men came toward the house, swinging her arms and theirs back and forth like some happy child, while Nero bounded in front and barked his approval.

"Father, this is Miss Prescott, my friend I have told you so much about. She is spending the day with me," she said, as Fanny came forward to meet them.

"My daughter's friend is very welcome," Mr. Rayborne replied, his voice so pleasant and the expression of his face so kind that Fanny was both surprised and fascinated.

She had not expected a guide to appear just as he did, and she let her hand rest in his a moment, while she looked into his eyes, which held her with their peculiar expression. When she first met Inez she had experienced a feeling as of looking at herself in a different guise, and the sensation returned to her in the presence of Inez's father. Over him, too, there came a strange feeling of interest as he looked at her. She was not at all like Inez. She belonged to an entirely different world, of which he was once a part, years and years ago, it seemed, but which came back to him very vividly with Fanny Prescott standing beside him. He was always gentlemanly, but he seemed to gain a new access of dignity, which both Tom and Inez noticed, as with a few more words of greeting and a bow he left her and walked into the house. It was Tom's turn now, and Fanny did not wait to be introduced to him.

"I know you already," she said, "and I am so glad to see you again here, with——"

She glanced at Inez, who blushed and said, "She means here with me. I've told her about us. You don't care!"

"Of course not; why should I?" Tom said, throwing his arm around her.

Disengaging herself from him, Inez said she must see about their supper and left him alone with Fanny. He was very friendly and talkative; asked when she came to the cottage and how she liked the valley and when she expected to leave. Then with a few commonplace remarks he, too, left her and she saw no more of him or Mr. Rayborne until supper was announced. When that was over they all repaired to the piazza, which a full moon was flooding with light. Nothing had as yet been said of Tom's exploit in Fanny's presence, but when alone with him in the kitchen Inez had caught his hand and said to him, "You don't know how proud I was when I heard of your bravery. How did you dare do it? They say it was Long John,—almost twice your size. Wer'n't you frightened?"

"A little, at first," Tom replied, releasing himself from her and going out to a bench near the kitchen door where Mr. Rayborne was sitting and where he, too, sat down and began to talk in a low tone.

"He is so modest he does not wish to hear about the hold-up," Inez thought, and was rather surprised when, after they were seated upon the piazza, Tom said to

Fanny, "What of your diamonds? Are they still in the bows of ribbon in your hat?"

"Yes," Fanny answered, "and I have sewed them in more securely, so I know they cannot drop out, and I don't believe anyone would think to look for them there. Do you?"

"Hardly," Tom said. "It's a unique hiding place; and you leave us to-morrow?"

"Yes," Fanny answered, "but not in the Milton coach. We are going to Clark's to stop a few days and visit the big trees. You don't suppose those dreadful robbers will waylay us on the route, do you? Long John, and little Dick! I shudder when I hear them mentioned. I wish you were going with us."

"Can't you go?" Inez asked, as the conversation progressed and Fanny became more and more nervous.

"I would willingly," Tom replied, "if I had not an engagement, and besides I might not be of any use a second time. My hands would probably go up with the rest and stay up."

"Nonsense, Tom! You know better. You would tear at them like mad. I wish you'd go. Your engagement will keep."

"I'm afraid not, and thousands of dollars are involved in it," Tom replied.

"Oh-h! So much money?" Inez gasped, thinking of the pretty house in Stockton, which Tom would soon be able to buy, if he were getting rich so fast.

"I do not think Miss Prescott need to feel any alarm," Tom continued. "The road to Clark's is perfectly safe. There are not as many rocks and trees to hide behind, and then the country is being thoroughly scoured to find the maurauders. There is a larger sum offered for their arrest than ever before."

"I hope they will be caught and hung," Inez said energetically. "Some people think they live right around us, and know every foot of ground. I never told you, did I, that Mrs. Smithson said one of them was seen in the woods back of our cottage last summer. You and father were gone, and I was awfully scared. Do you believe they live here in the valley? Just think of talking with them and not knowing it!"

"I shouldn't wonder if you had seen them hundreds of times," Tom said laughingly, while Mr. Rayborne arose and went into the house saying it was getting chilly and he was tired.

He had taken but little part in the conversation beyond assuring Fanny that she had nothing to fear. The most of the time he had sat apart from the young people, with a look on his face which troubled Inez, who wondered why he was so silent.

"Are you ill, father dear?" she said, following him to the kitchen and putting her hand on his head.

"No, daughter," he answered: "there's nothing the matter:—a little tired, that's all. Go back to your friend,"

"Isn't she lovely?" Inez asked, still smoothing his hair. "I wish you could see her mother, she is so grand and handsome and proud looking. She wanted you for a guide, and because she could not have you she didn't go on a single trail. She had heard you were a gentleman and preferred you to some of the rough guides in the valley. I wish you had been here."

Mr. Rayborne was not particularly interested in Mrs. Prescott. He was more anxious for Inez to leave him and was glad when, with a goodnight kiss, she went back to the piazza and he was alone with his thoughts. He could not account for the feeling which had come upon him, bringing memories of people and events which had but little in common with what he was now. Through the open door came a breath of wind laden with the perfume of flowers from Anita's grave, and as he inhaled it he thought of the dead leaves of a rose he had gathered long ago and been foolish enough to keep through all the years of change which had come and gone since he hid them away in the first stage of his youthful passion. Leaving the house he went to Anita's grave and standing there alone with the dark woods in the background and the moonlight falling around him he talked, sometimes to himself and sometimes to the dead at his feet.

"Little Anita," he whispered, "I wish I were lying beside you with all the past blotted out. And there is more of that past than you ever suspected. I loved you, Anita, and when your dying eyes looked at me I knew what they said and swore I would do your bidding. But a stronger will than mine has controlled me until now when I am trying to break the bands of steel. What is there in that girl's face and voice and gestures which makes me struggle to be free. Is there a God, and would he help me if I were to ask him? I used to pray in the old church, miles and miles and miles away across a continent, but I fear it was only a form. God wouldn't have let me fall so far if he ever had my hand in his. If I were to stretch it out now would he take it and help me?"

He put it out as if appealing to someone for aid; then dropped it hopelessly and said, "No, I've sinned too deeply for that. If I am helped at all I must do it myself, and I swear it here by Anita's grave that not a hair of that girl's head shall be harmed if I can prevent it, and I think I can. It says somewhere, 'Resist the devil and he will flee from you,' but I guess the one who said it didn't know Tom Hardy!"

It was late when he re-entered the house. Inez and

Fanny had gone to their room and were asleep, but Tom still sat on the piazza, with his feet on the railing and his hands clasped behind his head.

"I knew he'd wait for me," Mr. Rayborne said, "but I've sworn, and I'll keep my vow, so help me God."

He did not know that he had prayed and that God was helping him as he went to that midnight interview with Tom Hardy. There was an earnest discussion carried on in low tones lest the sleeping girls should be wakened. Then the discussion became more spirited, and angry words passed on Mr. Rayborne's side. Tom always kept his temper, but was in deadly earnest and nothing could move him. He had no sentimental feelings, he said, with regard to a white faced, blue eyed girl, whom neither of them had either seen or heard of before, and did not propose to let a fortune slip through his fingers on her account. He had made inquiries and there had seldom been a richer party leaving the valley than was to leave on the morrow. If Mr. Rayborne did not choose to join him he would go alone.

"And if you do," Mr. Rayborne replied, "by the old Harry I'll circumvent you if I can, and if I can't and you succeed I'll give both of us up to justice and end this accursed life into which I allowed you to lead me."

Tom laughed and replied, "I have no fear of that. You like your good name and your liberty too well to be willing to spend the rest of your days behind prison walls, an object of greater contempt because you have stood so high in the community, trusted and respected by everyone; and then there is Inez. Would you voluntarily ruin her life with a knowledge of her father's shame?"

Tom knew what cords to touch to make the man like clay in his hands. For once, however, he had gone too far. The white faced, blue eyed girl, as Tom designated

Fanny, was completing the work which Mr. Rayborne had for some time been agitating. She was Inez's friend. She had been his guest. She trusted him, and she should not be harmed. But how to hinder it was a question which he revolved over and over again in his mind as, after leaving Tom, he sat by his window, suffering all the horrors of remorse, and once burying his face in his hands he cried, "God help me. He heard the thief on the cross; maybe he will hear me who am worse than that thief."

*　　*　　*　　*　　*　　*

The early morning was breaking in the east and on the mountains there was a glow of sunrise. Tom was up and Inez, too, busy with breakfast as the stage for Clark's passed at a comparatively early hour. Mr. Rayborne had not been in bed at all and looked white and tired as he went out to the bench where he made his ablutions. Tom was there, trying to force down a feeling which was warning him of danger. Still he had no idea of giving up his enterprise. It had been planned for days in every particular, and he would not abandon it now. He would rather have Mr. Rayborne with him, if he could, although he was getting a little clumsy and sometimes handicapped his more agile companion with his deliberation. If he would not go, then Tom would go alone,—he was resolved on that,—and said so to Mr. Rayborne when they met by the rude washstand.

He had no fear of being circumvented by his colleague, and bidding him good-bye, kissed Inez, who came to the door just as his conversation with her father ended, and went down the hill whistling "The girl I left behind me," while Mr. Rayborne looked after him with a feeling of pain and apprehension.

"I have sown the wind and am reaping the whirlwind, and I wish I were dead," he thought. Then he repeated a name which only the winds heard. "What would *he* say, and he trusted me so fully. I am glad he don't know. It would kill him. Nobody knows, but God and Tom. I am glad God knows; it seems as if he would show me some way to stop it."

Just then Inez came to tell him that breakfast was ready, and bathing his hot face and eyes again in the cold water which trickled in a little stream down from the hills, he put on as cheerful a face as possible and went in to meet Fanny just coming downstairs with something in her smile which made him think again of the withered rose leaves and a summer he would have given much to recall.

"Where is Mr. Hardy?" Fanny asked, as she missed him from the breakfast table.

"He was obliged to go away very early on account of that appointment he told us about. He left a good-bye for you and bade me tell you he might perhaps meet you on the road," Inez said.

"Oh, I hope he will. I grow more and more nervous about the journey," Fanny replied, glancing at Mr. Rayborne, who was silent and preoccupied.

His head ached, he said, and finishing his coffee he left the table and the girls were alone.

"He is not himself this morning. He never is when he has one of his hard headaches, and this I guess is worse than usual," Inez said apologetically. "Tom wanted him to go with him, and I think they had some words about it, for just before he left I heard Tom say 'I believe you are a coward.' Queer for father and Tom to quarrel."

Fanny did not reply except to lament that Tom's engagement must keep him from going with her.

"Perhaps father will go," Inez suggested, and going out to the bench where he sat with his head down she said, "Can't you go with Miss Prescott as far as Clark's? The ride will do you good."

Inez could not see how white he grew as he answered, "*I* go! *I*,—and meet Tom on the road?"

She did not know what he meant, and looked at him in wonder. Suddenly starting and brightening up he exclaimed, "It has come to me at last. *You* shall go to Clark's and return on the late stage. If there is not room for you inside you can go on the box with the driver. That's the best place for you. Keep your eyes out everywhere, and if a bandit attacks you, don't throw up your hands, but scream in your natural voice."

Inez could not understand why he was giving her so many directions. She only knew she was delighted to go.

"I cannot be of use like Tom, if anything happened," she said to Fanny, "but father has told me what to do, and I'm not afraid."

She hurried through her morning's work, her father's dinner was planned, and she was ready some time before the stage was seen in the distance a quarter of a mile away. Mr. Rayborne went with the girls to the road and waited until it drew up. Every inside seat was taken except the one reserved for Fanny. Mrs. Prescott who always looked out for herself, had appropriated a corner seat in the rear of the stage, where she could lean back against the cushion. She had a headache, as usual, and with her veil over her face she looked up enough to greet her daughter, who said, "Inez is going to Clark's with us. There is not room for her inside, and I am going outside with her."

Immediately a young man arose and offered his seat

to Inez, whose father said in a low tone, "Stick to the box."

"And I shall stick, too," Fanny said. "The view is much finer outside, and Inez can tell me the places."

The two girls were soon seated and the driver was about to start when with a roar Nero came down the hill, jumping at the horses' heads and then at Inez.

"Here, Nero, here," Mr. Rayborne called while Inez pleaded for him to go.

"I can bring him back to-night, and he never has a chance to go anywhere," she said, but her father was firm and the dog followed him rather reluctantly to the house and disappeared in the direction of his kennel, which Tom had built for him.

"Nero is the last one to be there if anything happens. He is so affectionate and demonstrative and sure to mix in the melee that recognition would be inevitable, and I would spare Inez that, if possible," Mr. Rayborne thought, as he sat down in his silent room, which had never seemed so lonely before. Nor had the past ever crowded upon him so thickly as it did now, filling him with remorse as real as it was bitter. Every leaf in his life was turned with its dark record from which he recoiled with horror. Away back in another world it seemed to him there were bright spots and he saw himself, looked up to and respected and happy, leading what looked to him an ideal life compared to what he was leading now.

"Oh, for those days. Oh, to be young again and innocent," he said aloud, and his voice sounded so strange that he half started from his chair and looked around to see where it came from. "I don't like being alone," he said. "Nero is better than no company. I'll call him."

He went to the rear door, and called two or three times, "Nero! Nero!" then whistled, with the same result. Nero neither answered, nor came. He had gone to his kennel and lain down at first, then, as no one was about, he struck off into the woods, looking back occasionally to see if he were watched. Once in the woods and out of sight of the house he started rapidly in the direction of the road, keeping out of it until he saw the stage in the distance. Then he took the road, and in a few minutes was barking his delight at the horses and at Inez on the box. He had often tried to follow his master and Tom, of whom he was very fond, but had always been ordered back. Now, he had succeeded in eluding them, and was out for a holiday, which he enjoyed hugely, sometimes keeping near the stage and again making a detour into the woods and disappearing altogether for a time. When he did not return to the cottage Mr. Rayborne knew where he had gone. There might no harm come of it, and perhaps the dog's presence would do good, he thought, and as the hours crept on he waited in feverish impatience for the news which he knew would travel fast if there were any news to travel.

CHAPTER VII.

ON THE ROAD TO CLARK'S.

It was a good road and a pleasant road and Fanny and Inez enjoyed themselves immensely. There was a halt at Inspiration Point for the grand view and a last look at the beautiful valley. Then the stage lumbered on slowly for it was full and the horses not the fleetest in the world. It had been cloudy for an hour or so, and after a time rain began to fall in a soft, misty shower. This roused

Mrs. Prescott, who said Fanny must come inside, while the young man who had at first offered his seat to Inez insisted again that she should take it, while he went outside. The exchange was made and the young girls were riding side by side with their backs to the horses and Inez next to the wheels. The shower lasted but a few minutes before the sun came out so brightly that Inez, whose eyes were not strong, tied over her hat a thick, blue veil which concealed her face entirely. There was no thought of fear among the passengers. The road to Clark's was considered safe and more than half the distance had been gone over. Mrs. Prescott was asleep in her corner; Fanny and Inez were chatting together as girls will chatter; Nero, tired of jumping at the horses and Inez, was off in the woods chasing a rabbit, and the driver had ceased to be on the watch for any trouble.

"We are gettin' through all safe," he said to his companion beside him. "It's about time for them rascals to show up again, and I didn't know what might happen." They were nearing a sharp turn with a ledge of rocks beside it and he was gathering up the reins the better to manage his horses round the curve, when suddenly the word "Halt!" rang out on the air, and a man wearing a mask came from some quarter no one could tell where, he moved so rapidly and with so much assurance. Stepping to the horses' heads he stopped them and pointing a revolver at the driver, bade him make no effort to go on

"Little Dick!" was whispered among the terrified passengers, who never thought of disobeying his command, "Hands up, every one of you!"

They all went up, except those of Inez, close to whom the bandit was standing. At the sound of his voice she started violently, and clutched at the veil upon her hat trying to tear it off.

"I am very sorry, my good people, to disturb you, and I assure you none of you will be harmed, nor shall I detain you long if you at once give up whatever valuables you may have on you persons,—money, watches and jewelry. Perhaps I'd better search you myself, as it is not convenient for you to use your hands while you are holding them up. Step out quietly and it will soon be over. These two young ladies first, please. Shall I help you?"

He bowed toward Inez and Fanny, extending one hand to them and with the other covering them with his revolver. Fanny was paralyzed with fear, and half sliding from her seat, tried to hide behind Inez, to whom she said, "Oh, what shall we do?"

Inez made no reply. She had succeeded in tearing the veil from her face, which was white as a corpse, while in her eyes was a look of horror, but not of fear. Turning toward the man inviting her so politely to descend she gave a shriek more appalling than the word "Halt!" had been, and bounding from the stage in front of him, struck his arm so heavy a blow with her fist that his revolver was thrown at a little distance from him and lay upon the ground. Both started for it, but Inez reached it first. Snatching it up she looked steadily into his eyes, which the mask did not conceal.

"Go," she said, "or I will shoot you like a dog. I always said I would kill any one I found doing this dirty work, and I have found *you!*" Then, to the passengers, who, in their fright, were still holding up their hands, she continued: "Drop your hands! Cowards! to fear this one man! You see I am not afraid of him."

The man stood as if turned into stone, until she said to him again, "Go, I tell you, before I fire, or Nero sees you. He is here."

This last was spoken so low that only the brigand heard it, looking round quickly and then back at Inez. Her cheeks were flushed; her eyes were blazing, and her white teeth showed between her parted lips as she advanced toward him like some enraged animal, with the revolver aimed at his head. It seemed as if he wanted to speak, but she gave him no chance, and at her second imperative "Go," and mention of the dog, he went, not very rapidly at first, but walking like one whose strength had left him.

At this point Nero, who had given up his rabbit, came panting back, surprised, if dogs can be surprised, at what he saw. The passengers had all alighted and were surrounding Inez with warm encomiums for her bravery. Nero seemed to know she was the central figure in the group and gave her a loud, approving bark, which was heard by the bandit, who half turned his head and then quickened his steps to a run. But Nero, who had caught sight of him, was after him with yelps and cries and barks, which the passengers thought meant mischief. Inez knew better, and fierce as was her anger she would, if possible, prevent a recognition which would involve so much.

"Nero," she tried to call, but her tongue refused to move, and she could only give a low cry of alarm as the dog bounded upon the back of the man, with such force that he was thrown down and his mask fell off.

In a moment he was on his feet, keeping his back to the passengers and beating Nero off, while Inez, who had found her voice, called to him peremptorily to come back, saying to those around her, "We do not wish to see him torn to pieces before our eyes."

Very unwillingly Nero obeyed and came back just as the bandit disappeared among the trees. Up to this time

Inez had stood rigid like one in catalepsy,—the revolver in her hand and her eyes strained to their utmost as she watched the receding figure. Her heart was beating wildly in her throat. There was the roaring sound of "Halt!" in her ears, shutting out every other sound so that she scarcely heard the words of commendation from those around her.

"Inez," Fanny said, "don't look so terribly! It is over now. He has gone. Sit down, before you faint."

"Yes, that is best," Inez gasped, while many hands were stretched out to keep her from falling, as her eyes closed and her body began to sway.

They put her down upon the grass and Fanny took her head in her lap, while every bag in the coach, which had a restorative in it, was opened, and its contents brought out. Brandy, whisky, camphor, cologne, bay rum, lavender water, witch hazel and hartshorn were tried by turns with no effect. She still lay in a death like faint and they could see the rapid beating of her heart as it rose and fell irregularly.

"Loosen her dress," some one suggested. They loosened it and she breathed easier, but did not recover and her face was growing purple when the sound of horses' hoofs was heard and Tom Hardy came leisurely galloping round the curve in the road on the bay mare Inez had driven the previous day.

"What is this? Another hold up?" he said, dismounting quickly and joining the excited group, each one of which began to narrate the particulars in his and her own way.

To those nearest to her Fanny said in a low tone, "He is her lover, and the man who saved the other coach as she has saved us."

It scarcely took an instant for this to become known

to all, and Tom was at once nearly as much an object of interest as Inez, and a way was made for him to go to her.

"Why, it is Inez! How came she here?" he asked in a perfectly steady voice, but his face was white and his hands shook as he knelt by the still unconscious girl, calling her name and rubbing her cold face.

At the sound of his voice she opened her eyes and looked at him with an expression of loathing and despair.

"Oh, Tom, Tom," she cried, and the anguish in her voice haunted Tom to his dying day.

"I am here, Inez," he said, very tenderly. "What can I do for you?"

She made no reply, but looked up at Fanny as if asking what she knew or suspected. Fanny suspected nothing, and her tears fell fast and hot upon Inez's face, which she kissed again and again until a faint color came back to it; the heart beats were less rapid, and she tried to get up. Every one was ready to help her, Tom with the rest, but she motioned them all aside, and standing erect said with an effort to smile, "I have made quite a scene. My strength gave out at last. I am all right now. What became of my hat?"

Three or four hurried to bring it to her, while Tom said to Fanny, "Where is yours?"

It had fallen off in her excitement and lay at some distance from her where it had been stepped on two or three times and badly crushed. Tom picked it up, brushed it very carefully, straightened it as well as he could and then put it on Fanny's head, saying, as he did so, "I think it is all right."

He seemed much more cheerful than at first, and patted Nero on the head, saying. "You here, too? I wonder you did not go after the ruffian.

"He did," Fanny explained, "and knocked him down and would have torn him to pieces if Inez had not called him off."

"Why did she do that? She might have let him hold the villain till he was captured. There are surely enough men here to have secured him," Tom said, speaking so low that Inez did not hear him.

She was leaning against a tree, with Nero at her side. He had seemed suspicious of Tom and declining his advances had gone to Inez, looking at her inquiringly as if asking the cause of the commotion.

"I wish he had held him," Fanny said, vehemently. "but I wish still more that you had met us earlier and this would not have happened. You ought to have seen Inez when she sprang over the wheel and confronted the robber. She was grand and her eyes were terrible as she marched straight up to him as if she were not a bit afraid. I think she would have fired if he had not turned and ran."

Tom made no reply except to say, "I wish I had come earlier," then, addressing Inez he asked if she would go on to Clark's, or go home.

"I must go home," she answered quickly. "It is the best place."

Fanny at once offered to go with her, but Inez declined.

"No, no," she said. "I want to be alone."

"How will you go? You cannot walk so far," someone asked, and Tom replied, "She will take my horse and I shall walk."

By this time the driver was getting anxious to be off. and the passengers gathered around Inez, bidding her good bye, telling her they should never forget her bravery, and calling her the heroine of the valley, as Tom was the hero.

"Don't, don't," Inez said, putting up both her hands. "Don't thank me. I didn't think of saving anybody. I was wild. I was desperate. I—I am not a heroine. Don't talk about me. Don't let them put me in the papers. I can't bear it."

There was a hard look on her face which softened when Fanny came up to say good bye. Drawing her closely to her Inez sobbed like a child.

"It was so bright yesterday, and this morning I was so happy. It is so dark now, and will be always. Good bye, and God bless you. I don't believe I shall ever see you again."

"Yes, you will," Fanny answered. "We are to spend a few days at Clark's, and if you do not come there I shall drive over and call on you, and then there is New York in the future."

Inez shook her head. She knew there was no glad future for her and her tears fell like rain as she watched Fanny getting into the stage, helped by Tom, who lifted his hat very politely as the stage drove off, the passengers looking back and waving hands and handkerchiefs to Inez until the turn in the road hid her from view. Nothing was talked of the rest of the way but the attempt at robbery and Inez's wonderful courage and presence of mind.

"We ought to do something to show our appreciation; make up a purse, perhaps, if she is poor," some one suggested, and Fanny quickly interposed, "They are not poor in that way. Money would be out of place. Make her a present which she can always keep."

This met with general approval, and it was decided

that as soon as Fanny returned to San Francisco she should purchase a handsome watch, with Inez's name and the date of the attempted robbery on the case. The money was to be contributed at Clark's, where the stage arrived nearly an hour behind its usual time. All the passengers were to continue their journey that day except Fanny and her mother. The latter was in a state of utter prostration and went at once to her room and to bed. During the scene on the road she had sat half fainting in the coach, alighting once when all the rest did and then, seeing she could be of no use, creeping back to her corner and feeling that she was doing her duty when she passed out her golden stoppered salts as her contribution to the many restoratives offered to Inez. Her trip to the Yosemite had not been very pleasant, and she was glad she was so far on her way back to the city which suited her better.

"I shall always feel grateful to that girl," she said to Fanny, as she was getting into bed. "She saved us from a great unpleasantness. Think of being ordered out of the stage and searched by a masked blackguard with a revolver in your face. He would have found nothing of value about me except a few dollars. The diamonds were safe in your hat. I watched it all the time until it rolled off into the mud. Mr. Hardy picked it up. I did not see him very closely, but thought he seemed a very gentlemanly fellow, who had seen more of the world than that girl he is to marry. I think he could do better."

Fanny did not hear the last of her mother's remarks. In her fright and excitement over the robber and Inez she had not given the diamonds a thought until her mother brought them to her mind. Her hat was still on her head and snatching it off she passed her hand over the bows of ribbon in quest of the little linen bag. IT WAS GONE! The strong thread with which it had been sewed to the hat had been wrenched apart from the ribbon and it had slipped out, when or where no one could tell. The diamonds were lost, and the hotel was soon in a state of nearly as great excitement as there had been on the road. Many suggestions were offered, one of which was that when the hat was stepped on by the heavy boots of some of the party, as it evidently had been, the stitches had given way and the bag fallen out. This seemed feasible, and with a gentleman and a guide from the hotel Fanny went back to the scene of the adventure, looking all along the road and going over every inch of ground near the spot where the stage had been stopped. There were footprints of the people and Tom Hardy's horse and a spot in the spongy soil where Nero had stretched himself at full length, but the diamonds were not there. Very unwillingly Fanny broke the news to her mother, who at once went into hysterics so violent that a physician was called, and all that night Fanny and Celine were kept busy attending to her. It was not the value of the diamonds she deplored so much, she said, although that was great, as the fact that the ear-rings had been in the family so long and were to have been Fanny's on her wedding day. Fanny, too, was very sorry for her loss, but thought less of it than of Inez, whose face haunted her as she last saw it, so white and drawn, with an expression which puzzled her. She would like to have driven over in the early morning to inquire for her, but her mother was too weak and nervous to be left and she was obliged to wait for the daily stage which she hoped would bring her some news.

CHAPTER VIII.

MARK HILTON.

When the stage disappeared from her sight Inez was standing as motionless as a statue, with a look in her eyes which made Tom half afraid to go near her.

"Inez," he said, at last, as she did not move. "Inez, shall we go now?"

"Bring up the mare," was her answer.

He brought her, and pointing to the stump of a tree near by Inez continued, "Take her there."

He took her there, and held out his hand to help Inez mount. She motioned him aside and seated herself in the saddle, which did not inconvenience her at all, as she was accustomed to it. She was shaking like a leaf, but did not know it or feel any fatigue as she started on the road, followed by Tom and Nero. The latter alone seemed to have any life in him. He was glad to go home and showed his gladness by barking and jumping alternately at Inez and the mare. At last, as no attention was paid to him, it seemed to occur to his canine sagacity that something was wrong and had been all the time, and he, too, subsided into silence and trotted demurely by Inez's side. Once when a feeling of dizziness came over her, making her sway in the saddle, Tom, whose eyes were constantly upon her, put his arm upon her waist to steady her. Recoiling from him as from a viper she said, "Don't touch me, Tom Hardy, nor speak to me until this mood is past. Your revolver is in my pocket. Father says there is murder in my blood, and I might kill you."

Tom fell back behind her, while she straightened herself and sat erect as an Indian, but made no effort to guide the horse, who took her own gait, a rather slow one, with which Tom could easily keep pace. What his thoughts were during that long walk it were difficult to guess. His hands were in his pockets and his head was down, hiding his face from Inez, who glanced at him once as the mare stopped a moment under the shade of a tree and he passed on in advance. If, as her father had said, there was murder in her blood, it was boiling now and had been since she bounded from the coach.

"I could rid the world of him so easily," she thought, and her hand went into her pocket, but with a sob which seemed to rend her heart in two, she drew it back, and whispered, "I have loved him so much. I cannot harm him now."

They had reachd a point from which the cottage could be seen, with her father on the piazza looking in their direction. At sight of him Tom turned to Inez and said, "You are not to despise your father as you do me. I led him into it. I am to blame."

Inez made no answer, but her face softened a little; then hardened again when, as she drew near the cottage, she saw her father coming to meet her. He had felt all the morning that the crisis he had so long expected was close at hand. The net of sin he had woven was closing round him and, but for his daughter, who believed in him so fully, he did not care how soon it enfolded him and he stood unmasked before the world which now respected him so highly.

The reader has, of course, long suspected that Mr. Rayborne and Long John and Mark Hilton were one. How he came to be what he was he could scarcely tell. He had loved Helen Tracy devotedly. He sometimes thought he loved her still in spite of the bitterness which had sprung up between them, he hardly knew how or why, as he looked back upon it. She had thought herself safe with him because he knew the worst there was of her. But because he knew it he was, after the first few months of feverish adoration were over, more on the alert, perhaps, than he should have been. He did not trust her and she knew it and grew restive under his watchful surveillance. He had no right to distrust her,— no right to be jealous,— no right to criticise her actions, and because he did, she, in a spirit of retaliation, taunted him with his birth and position and poverty, until he could endure it no longer and left her, half resolving, before a week was passed, to go back, for his little baby daughter had, if possible, a stronger hold upon him than her mother. Then his pride came up and he said, "I'll stay away till she sends for me. She knows where I am." But she did not send, and from some source he heard she was getting a divorce. This hurt him more than all the hard words she had ever said to him, as it cut him off from her forever. But there was still the baby. "For her sake I'll be a man and some day I'll go to her and tell her I am her father," he thought.

Alas for the mistakes which change the current of one's whole life. Chancing upon a Chicago paper in which were comments upon the recent divorce of "the beautiful Mrs. Hilton, so well known in fashionable circles," there was mention made of her recent bereavement in the death of her little girl. Mark could not remember when he had cried before, but he did so now. Everything was swept from him,—his wife, his home, and his infant daughter.

"God has turned against me, if there is a God," he said, "and I care nothing what becomes of me now."

For days he was in a most despondent mood, scarcely

eating or sleeping, and paying but little attention to anything passing around him. Jeff, who had come with him from Chicago, roused him at last by suggesting that they go to the mines of Montana. Although so young, Jeff was beginning to have a great influence over Mark, who felt so discouraged and hopeless that it was pleasant to lean upon some one even if it were a boy. They went to Montana and into the mines, but on the day of the accident both were away at some distance from the scene of the disaster, prospecting for themselves. When the news reached them and Mark heard that he was supposed to be dead and that Jeff was missing, it was the latter who said, "Let's *stay* dead and missing, and take another name, and go on further west or south, and begin new with the world. I think it will be fun."

The boy's advice was followed, and John Rayborne and Tom Hardy went to California, where Anita Raffael came in Mark's way. She was an orphan,—alone in the world,—with no home but the convent in which her father had placed her at school before he died. With Mark it was at first only pastime to talk to the little half Spanish, half Mexican, when he chanced to meet her. Then something in her lovely face and soft, dark eyes began to appeal to him, and he accidentally discovered how much he was to her, and how forlorn she was in her convent home, where she was like an imprisoned bird beating its wings against the bars of its cage in its efforts to escape. No one was unkind to her; no one could be, she was so gentle and sweet. She was unhappy because she wanted freedom, and when Mark asked her to be his wife, she took him gladly, and was so loving, and happy and gay, that he never repented the act. She was not like Helen, nor was he like the Mark Hilton who had won the famous beauty. He was John

Rayborne, and Anita was his wife, and their home was in the Yosemite, where she persuaded him to go, for she loved the wild, mountain scenery and made their cottage a bower of beauty, with her skillful hands and perfect taste. When she heard of a stage robbery she would get furious and stamp her little feet and denounce the robbers in her broken English, while Mark laughed at her excitement and asked, "What would you do if I were to take to the road some day?"

"Kill you first, and then die myself," she answered, with no more thought that such a thing could be than Mark himself had then.

For a time he drove the stage in the summer between Milton and the valley, and was once or twice stopped on the road when Jeff was with him on the box. Thus, both "knew the ropes," as Jeff said, criticising the manner of the attack and pointing out a better way, while Mark laughed at him, and without meaning what he said, suggested that he try it.

. Giving up stage-coaching, he became a guide, and then——. There was a deep, dark gulf after the then, and he always shuddered when he recalled the day when he joined Jeff in what he called a mere lark. Jeff had tried it alone, and, unknown to Mr. Hilton, to see if he could do it. He had profited by what he had seen on the road and laid his plans carefully as to what he would do in certain circumstances. As a boy he had picked pockets for fun, and he stopped the coach on the same principle, finding that the gymnastic perfomances of his youth were a help to him in the rapidity with which he could do his work and disappear. The stage which was the object of his first attempt was chosen because there was only one passenger in it, a clergyman, who had prayed aloud while he was being searched.

"The old cove's watch was silver, and he had only twenty-five dollars in his purse, and I gave them back to him. I never meant to take a blessed thing, and my revolver wasn't loaded," he said to Mark to whom he related his adventure.

The boy, who had horrified Uncle Zacheus by saying he'd like to be a robber and had astonished Alice by offering to pick her pocket, had developed into a man with a will so strong and a manner so enticing that Mark was like clay in his hands. It was, however, some time before he was persuaded to try what he could do at a hold-up. He found he could do a great deal. The excitement and danger were exhilarating, especially when Jeff was with him and by his wonderful activity bewildered the passengers until they could have sworn there were half a dozen men instead of one demanding their money. It was exhilarating, too, to help search for the brigands and hear all that was said of them and make suggestions as to the best means of capturing them. The downward grade once entered upon, it was comparatively easy to continue it until he was steeped in crime so deep that to go back seemed impossible. Sometimes when Anita's arms were around his neck he would put her from him quickly with a feeling that he was not worthy to touch one so pure and innocent and who trusted him so implicitly. It would kill her if she knew the truth, but she never should know it, he thought, and for her sake and his daughter's he was deciding to quit his mode of life when her sudden death paralyzed for a time every faculty of his mind and left him without the ballast he needed.

Returning home late one night after an absence of two or three days he had been talking with Jeff of a recent robbery and the necessity there was to keep quiet for some time to come, the country was so thoroughly aroused and so large a price was offered for the capture of the men. A slight sound, more like the cry of a wounded animal than of a human being, attracted his attention, and hurrying into the next room he found Anita senseless upon the floor. She had been sitting up after Inez was in bed hoping he might come home and had fallen asleep so that she did not hear him when he came in; neither did he see her, or suspect that she was in the next room. His voice must have awakened her, but what she heard he never knew. That it was enough to kill her he was sure. Everything which he could do for her he did, but although she recovered her consciousness she never spoke again except with her eyes which followed him constantly and were full of the horror she could not express. After she died he remained at home the entire summer, but when the next season came round Tom persuaded him to take up the old life, which would give him excitement if not peace of mind. Many were the ruses resorted to to throw people off the track should they ever chance upon it. The attack of Mark upon a stage and Tom's defence was one of them, planned by Tom, who was ringleader in everything. No one suspected them and their popularity hurt Mark nearly as much as suspicion would have done. But nothing touched him like Inez's faith in him. She was his idol, on whom he lavished all the love he had ever given to Helen and Anita. Of her engagement he secretly disapproved. That Tom would leave nothing undone to make her happy he knew, but that his beautiful young daughter should marry a man for whose capture thousands of dollars were offered was terrible. But he was powerless. To betray Tom was to condemn himself, and either would kill Inez as her mother was killed.

And so matters were drifting when chance threw Fanny Prescott in his way and something about her reminded him of the days when he had walked with Helen Tracy through the woods and pastures of Ridgefield, and when Uncle Zacheus had believed in him implicitly, disclaiming all taint of heredity which might have come to him from 'Tina. He had no thought that Fanny was his daughter, but she was like the people he used to know,—like Helen and Alice and Craig, and she sent his thoughts back to them with a vividness which almost made him feel that he was like them again. He would not harm her, nor have her harmed.

"It's no use talking," he said, when Tom unfolded his plan of stopping the coach in which she was to leave the valley. "I'm tired of it all, and would give half the remainder of my life if the scroll could be unrolled and all the black writing erased."

To this resolution he stood firm, wondering what he could do to prevent the catastrophe. It came to him like an inspiration to send Inez with the driver, knowing that with her tall figure she would be readily seen from the point where Tom would probably stand concealed and make his observations. That something might happen he feared when he found that Nero had gone after the coach. He would recognize Tom and springing upon him in his delight, as he had a habit of doing, he might unmask him and the secret be revealed. To threaten to do this himself was one thing, and to have it done was another, and he was waiting impatiently for the result when he at last saw Inez coming up the path on the bay mare. Her face was pallid as a corpse and her eyes so unnaturally large and black that he could see their blackness in the distance and felt himself shrinking from meeting them. Tom was near her, with his head bent down and his feet dragging heavily as if walking were difficult for him.

"I must face it," Mark said to himself, and hurrying to meet them he asked what had happened.

"Don't ask *me,* and don't touch me," Inez answered, motioning him away. "Tom, your colleague, will tell you."

She sprang from the horse and went into the house without looking at her father, who turned to Tom for an explanation.

CHAPTER IX.

MARK AND TOM.

THE explanation was given concisely and fully, with nothing added or withheld. As he listened Mark felt that he had neither strength, nor muscle, nor nerve left. His sin had found him out, and the iron grip of the law could not have hurt him as he was hurt with the knowledge that Inez despised him.

"You think she knows everything?" he asked in a strange voice, for his tongue felt thick and heavy.

"Everything. The game is up, and I wish I had died before I began it; died in the old hogshead where I slept when you found me," Tom replied.

He was shaking with cold, notwithstanding that drops of sweat were on his face and hands, and his hair was wet as if drenched with water.

"It is an accursed business," he went on rapidly, "and I am sorry I dragged you into it. I was never so bad as some might think and I did it less for gain than for the excitement of seeing half a dozen men cower before a little fellow like me and a pistol which half the time was not loaded. That was the case to-day with the revolver Inez picked up and held at my head before she pocketed it. You should have seen her when she bade me go before she shot me like a dog. I never loved her as I did at that moment when I knew I had lost her. Once on the road when she seemed about to fall from the saddle and I tried to help her she threatened to shoot me again, reminding me that my revolver was in her pocket. Do you remember how I used to stand on my head when anything sudden pleased me? Well, I felt like trying it again when I imagined Inez's surprise to find the chambers empty if she tried to kill me. She said you had told her there was murder in her blood. Do you think that Dalton woman's fingers were tingling to shoot me?"

Tom was talking at random, scarcely knowing what he was saying. But it did not matter. Mark was not listening to him. He had heard all he cared to know and was wondering how he could meet Inez and what she would say to him. He knew she had gone to her room, but could hear no sound of her moving. Once the thought came to him, "Is she dead? Has the shock killed her as it did her mother?" and he started to go to her. Then as he heard the opening of a window he resumed his seat. Outside, the bay mare had been patiently standing waiting to be cared for, and at last, as the care did not come, neighing loudly and pawing on the ground. Mark heard her and rising mechanically went out to her, glad of something to do, which would for a few moments divert his mind from himself. Over the mare's stall a halter was hanging, and Mark looked at it attentively and tested its strength and wondered if it would hold him and how he would look dangling there, and if his feet would not touch the floor and so defeat his purpose. Satan was tempting him terribly and might have won the victory if there had not come to him a second time that day thoughts of Ridgefield and the old man who had loved and trusted him, and who, he had no doubt, had prayed for him when he supposed him still alive. The north piazza of the Prospect House, with Craig and Alice and Helen and the pleasant hours spent there came up before him and brought the tears to his hot eyes, cooling and healing and driving the tempter away.

"'Tina's great-grandson must not hang himself. That would be heredity with a vengeance," he said, laughing an unnatural laugh. "Only Inez knows it, and my whole life shall be devoted to convincing her of my repentance," he thought, as he left the stable.

There was a grain of comfort in this, and the future did not look quite so dark as he went back to the house and sat down with Tom, who neither moved nor looked up at him as he came in. He, too, was thinking of the future and the past; of Ridgefield and his happy boyhood there; of Mrs. Taylor's teachings, which, although occasionally emphasized with a box, had lodged in his memory, and were repeating themselves over and over in his brain. But beyond all this was a thought of Alice, who had been so kind to him,—who had defended him against Mrs. Tracy, saying there was no harm in him and she would trust him anywhere.

"What would she think of me now, all smirched and stained as I am? Would she speak to me as she did that morning when we gathered the pond lilies and she smoothed my hair?" he thought, and his hand went up to his head to the spot where Alice's hand had rested so long ago. "I can feel it yet," he said to himself. "It kept me then from mischief; it shall help me now."

Then he thought of Inez. She was lost to him so far as the life he had hoped for was concerned. He might in time learn to live without her, but he could not live and see her cold and hard towards him as she had been that morning.

"I would rather die," he thought, "than know she would never again look upon me except with hatred and distrust."

Had he been in the stable and seen the halter which had suggested suicidal thoughts to Mark there might have been a tragedy added to that day's doings. But the halter was out of sight and Tom wrestled with his remorse, which, to do him justice, did not arise alone from the fact that Inez knew and despised him. He was genuinely sorry and could not understand how he had become what he was. In his nature there was enough of hopefulness for a rebound from the depths of despair if he saw a ray of light, and after sitting for more than an hour in perfect silence he arose and going up to Mr. Hilton said, "If we were in a boat that was sinking, we'd get out of it, if we could. Let's do so now. We have been on the down track and touched the bottom. Let's try the upward slope. Let us *be* what the world thinks we are,—honorable, upright men. I have helped to pull you down. I will try to help you up, and maybe——— I don't think I ought to take His name on my lips, but you know whom I mean, and He, perhaps, will help us. I used to learn a lot about Him in the Sunday School in Ridgefield, and it is coming back to me now. What do you say? Shall we strike hands on a new deal? No one knows but ourselves and Inez. She will not tell. We shall carry the burden of our secret always, but maybe it will grow lighter in time."

He offered his hand to Mr. Hilton, who took and held it a moment, but said nothing. He was still shifting the blame to some extent upon Tom's shoulders and cursing himself for having been so weak as to be led by him. Releasing Mark's hand, Tom began walking across the piazza with his hands in his pockets, when he touched something hard and started as if a serpent had stung him.

"By George, I had forgotten this in my excitement," he said, taking out a small linen bag and laying it upon the table which stood upon the piazza. "See," he continued, taking out the diamonds Fanny had guarded so carefully.

In an instant Mr. Hilton was on his feet and facing Tom threateningly.

"Tom, you villian!" he exclaimed, "you robbed her after all, and have been prating to me of a new life and Sunday School lessons learned in Ridgefield. You hypocrite, I could strike you dead, if it were not for adding murder to my other crimes! Why did you do it, and how?"

Tom could not resent Mark's anger, and could scarcely speak aloud as he replied. "I don't know why I did it. When I picked up her hat and straightened it and felt the stones something I could not resist made me take them. My fingers tingled as they used to do in Ridgefield when I picked pockets for fun. A legion of devils were urging me on and all the while I was saying to myself 'I shall get them back to her somehow,' and I will. They must be very valuable."

He held up the ear-rings which glowed and sparkled in the sunlight, emitting sparks of color which played upon Mark's face, which was ghastly now with a cold sweat standing upon it and a look of terror in his eyes. Surely he had seen those jewels before,—so large, so white, so clear, and pear shaped, with the old fashioned setting which Helen would never have changed. He could not be mistaken. He had seen them too often and clasped them in Helen's ears too many times not to know them now.

"Tom," he said in a whisper, for his throat seemed closing up. "Tom, these are the Tracy diamonds,— my wife's diamonds. Don't you remember them?"

Tom had been too young when he left Mrs. Hilton to know much about her jewelry. It came back to him now, however, that her ear-rings were very large and of a peculiar shape. These might be the same, and if so how came Fanny Prescott by them? He put the question to Mark, who did not answer. The conviction that he had Helen Tracy's diamonds was strengthening every moment, and if so *who* was Fanny Prescott? Something like half the truth began to dawn upon him, making him so faint that the ear-rings dropped from his hands and he sat down gasping for breath. That Helen had married again and that Fanny was her daughter he suspected, but not that she was his. That little child was dead. He saw it in the paper. This girl was Helen's. Helen had been near him,—in the valley,— past his house,—and he had not known it. He did not care for her, he thought, but he did care for her daughter, if the girl were her daughter.

"Inez may know something. I must see her," he said, starting for her room.

Once on the stairs he stopped, afraid to meet her. Then, knowing it must be he went on and knocked at her door.

CHAPTER X.

INEZ AND HER FATHER.

When Inez heard Tom's voice and saw him standing near her she knew him at once and felt for a moment as if her heart stopped beating; then there was a sensation as if it were turning over rapidly, as she had seen a wheel turn in machinery, and swelling as it turned, until her throat was full and she could not breathe. Of what happened next she had only a confused recollection. Somebody shrieked, but whether it was herself, or Fanny she did not know. Somebody leaped from the stage and confronted Tom with a revolver. That was herself. She was clear on that point. She had threatened to shoot him and knew there was a feeling in her heart which would have let her do it, if he had not gone as she bade him go. Then Nero came, and with him a reaction of feeling and her thought was to save Tom from recognition, for he was still the man whom she loved, and she called the dog back and watched Tom till he disappeared from sight, straining her eyes while he was visible among the trees as if she would hold him as long as possible, for never again could he be to her what he had been. Then a great darkness came over her and she felt Fanny's tears upon her face and heard the sound of many voices talking of her, and among them at last Tom's; Tom, himself, in the clothes he had worn away that morning, when he kissed her good-bye, as he would never kiss her again. The impulse to kill him was gone. She must save him now from suspicion, for more than he was involved in the terrible thing which had happened.

Rallying all her strength she saw the stage depart

leaving her alone with a despair which made her cover her mouth with her hands lest she should cry out and bring her friends back to her. With a feeling of disgust she drew away from Tom's touch when he would have helped her and felt again a disposition to kill him if he came near her. All her Spanish and Mexican blood was at fever heat, nor did it abate at the sight of her father who was equally guilty with Tom. Ignoring his offer of help she went at once to her room and threw herself upon the bed in an agony of despair. Everything had been swept away, leaving a darkness so profound that she could see no light in the past or future. She loved Tom. She worshipped her father, and had been so proud of both, and both were brigands. She said the word to herself, pressing her hands first upon her temples, which throbbed with pain and then clasping them over her heart which burned like fire and beat so loudly that she could hear every beat and thought it sounded like a muffled drum.

"Brigands!" she repeated, while from every corner of the room the word came back to her till the air was filled with it.

She understood everything, for her mind had gone rapidly over the past, gathering up proof here and there until all was plain to her,—the double lives of the two men, who were all she had to love, and the knowledge gave her nearly as much shame as pain that she should have been so deceived. She knew now why her mother died so suddenly, with that awful look on her face as her palsied tongue tried in vain to speak. She had discovered the truth and it had killed her.

"Happy mother, to die!" she moaned. "I wish I could die too. Oh, father, I thought you a king among men, and Tom, too. I was so happy yesterday and this morning, with no thought that I was a brigand's daughter,—that the men I wished could be caught and hung were father and Tom! Oh, I cannot bear it. I feel like a debased creature, whom no one would speak to, if he knew, and I loved Fanny so much, and she liked me some. But that is all over now. Tom meant to rob *her,* the only girl friend I ever had—Oh-h! I cannot bear it."

Her agony was intense as the horror grew upon her and she was burning with excitement and fever. There was a feeling in her as if she could not breathe, and every heart beat was like a heavy blow. She had opened a window and she tried to rise again and go to it for air, but could not, and she fell back upon her pillow with her eyes staring at the pointed ceiling of her room. It was a pretty room, furnished with many articles her father had bought for her and which she knew were expensive. Fanny had liked it and her presence there had lent a halo to everything. But Inez loathed it all now, knowing where the money came from which had bought these luxuries which a poor mountaineer's daughter ought never to have.

"I can't stay here. I must go away and earn my living somewhere," she was thinking, when she heard her father's knock upon the door.

He was coming to explain, she thought, and she did not want an explanation. Nothing could change the shameful facts, and she did not look at him as he came in and sat down beside her. Her hand was lying near him and she drew it away quickly as if afraid he might take it. He saw the motion and interpreted it aright.

"Inez," he began, "have no fear that I will touch you. I am not worthy to sit in the same room with you, and I am not here to make excuses; I want to ask what you know about Fanny Prescott. Who is she? I mean, who was her mother?"

Inez was too stupified and bewildered to wonder at her father's question and replied, "Her mother was a Miss Helen Tracy, of New York. Judge Prescott was her step-father, whose name she took when her mother married him. Her own father was a Mr. Hilton, who was killed in the mines of Montana when Fanny was a baby—Father, father, what is it? What is the matter?" she exclaimed, as her father fell forward upon the bed. Everything was for the time forgotten in her anxiety for him as he lay like one dead.

"Tom, come quickly," she cried, "Father is dying."

But life was strong within him, and he soon recovered, but tore his cravat from his neck and unbuttoned his vest to help his breathing, which was nearly as labored as Inez's had been.

"Tell me again who she is! Tell all you know!" he said, while Tom looked inquiringly at him and at Inez, who repeated what she had said of Fanny Prescott.

Tom, who was standing up, dropped into a chair as if he had been shot, while Mr. Hilton exclaimed, "Oh, Inez, Fanny is my daughter and your sister! For I am Mark Hilton—married first to Helen Tracy and divorced when our baby was a few months old. I thought she was dead. I heard so. Oh, my daughter, my daughter!" he cried in alarm at the look on Inez's face as she listened to him. He had told everything with no thought of the effect it might have upon her. She had borne all she could bear, and with this fresh blow she lay for hours, not fainting, but dying it seemed to those who cared for her so tenderly,—the wretched father, the remorseful Tom, the kind neighbors who had been called in, and the doctor summoned from a hotel. The news of her bravery in confronting the robber had spread rapidly and the shock it must have given her was the cause assigned by the physician for the state in which he found her. There was also heart difficulty inherited from her mother, aggravated by the strain upon her nerves, he said. She was young. She might pull through, but the utmost care must be taken not to excite her in any way. All night a light shone from the window of the room where she lay with no sign of life except a feeble fluttering of the pulse and a low moan when her father spoke to her. Once when an allusion was made by some one to the adventure on the road and the belief expressed that the robbers would be captured if the whole state rose up to do it, she opened her eyes and looked at Tom, who was sitting at the foot of her bed. Her lips moved with a sound her watchers construed into "Do," but which Tom, with his senses quickened and on the alert, knew was "Go," and meant that he should fly before he was captured. But he was not that kind and would not have gone with Inez dying if he had known that all the police in San Francisco were on their way to take him.

Just as day was breaking there was a change for the better, and the women, who had cared for Inez during the night, left with a promise of returning as soon as possible. When no one was in the room but her father Inez whispered, "I want Fanny."

"Yes, daughter," Mark answered, feeling himself a strong desire to see her.

Then he remembered that if he would secure the daughter he must meet her mother,—once his wife. Could he do it, stained with sin as he was, and to find whom every foot in the valley had been gone over. There were placards out now he was sure in San Francisco and Stockton, offering thousands of dollars for his capture and that of his confederate. He had seen them before, and with Tom had stopped and read them, but never with a feeling that it was really himself that was meant. It had always been somebody else. Now it *was* himself,—Mark Hilton,—who was wanted, and he could not meet Helen face to face. It was true she would not know the depths to which he had fallen. She would only be surprised to find him alive and very low down in the scale from what he was when she called him her husband. He could bear her look of proud disdain after her first fright was over, but, knowing himself as he did, he feared he could not meet her without betraying himself in some way. Tom could do it, and Tom must go. But Tom refused outright, and Mark was nearly beside himself.

As the morning wore on Inez grew more and more restless, asking for Fanny and if she had come and if they had sent for her. About noon the doctor came and found her fever so high that he said to Mr. Hilton. "If that young lady can come she may save your daughter's life."

Mark could hesitate no longer. "I am going for Fanny," he said to Inez, and will certainly bring her back."

He found the hotel full of excited people, all talking of the hold up of the previous day and all inquiring for Inez, of whose serious illness they had heard when the morning stage from the valley came in. He was told that Mrs. Prescott was in her room, but Fanny had gone with a party to visit the big trees.

"I am not a card man now," he thought, as he said to a servant, "Tell Mrs. Prescott that Mr. Rayborne wishes to see her," and then sat down to try to quiet his nerves which tingled as if red hot lead was pouring through them.

It was years since he parted from Helen in bitter anger, but he was not thinking of that time now. His thoughts were back in Ridgefield and the summer morning when he saw her on the north piazza and fell under the spell of her wonderful eyes. He could see the mischief in them now as they had looked when she said to Uncle Zach "Which is Mark and which is Craig? You did not tell me." He could see Craig dropping his straw into his tumbler of lemonade as he sprang up to meet her and himself knocking his head against Craig's as each seized the same chair for her. He remembered, too, the rose in her ribbons and knew that somewhere among his belongings the faded leaves and dried calyx were hidden away. It was strange how every detail of that morning came back to him as he sat waiting the return of the servant, who, when he came, said to him, "The lady will see you. Second floor, No. —, to the right."

CHAPTER XI.

MARK AND HELEN.

Mrs. Prescott had nearly recovered from the fright of the previous day, but had not felt equal to joining the party to the Big Trees. She seldom joined any party. Her room was comfortable and she preferred to stay in it, and when Mark's message was brought to her she was sitting by her window watching some people who had just arrived.

"Mr. Rayborne?" she repeated. "Who is he? I know no such man."

"He is the father of the young lady who saved the coach yesterday," the servant replied.

"Oh, yes, I remember now. Show him up." Mrs. Prescott said, with a feeling of annoyance that she was to be bothered with so commonplace a man as Mr. Rayborne must be.

As she had been in her room all the morning she had not heard of Inez's illness and really had not thought much about her, as the loss of her diamonds was uppermost in her mind. Of course she was grateful to her for what she had done and by and by when she felt equal to it she meant to write her a note and tell her so. She had contributed generously towards the watch to be bought for her and should make her some present on her own account. This she thought quite sufficient without a call from the father. Then it occurred to her that he might have come with some news of the diamonds, or at least he could be of use in finding them, and she was more willing to see him.

"I wonder what kind of man he is," she thought. "Rough, of course, though they said he was well educated and very gentlemanly for a guide," and immediately her old nature began to assert itself.

There was enough of coquetry left in her to wish to look her best before any man. Going to the glass she pulled down her frizzes a little more in order to cover some rather deep lines in her forehead,—straightened her collar, pinched her cheeks to bring more color to them,—threw a fleecy white shawl over her shoulders and sat down with her back to the door. The carriage was now driving away and she was still watching it, when a voice she had never forgotten and which made her start from her chair, said to her "Helen."

For a few moments Mark had been standing in the open door looking at her to see if she had greatly changed.

"A little faded, but very handsome still and proud as ever," he thought, as he saw her profile and the pose of her head and shoulders.

He had loved her with all the strength of his youth, and though there was a gulf between them which could never be crossed, something of the old feeling prompted by memories of the summer days in Ridgefield stirred within him as he watched her. She had expected Mr. Rayborne to knock, and at the sound of her name she sprang up and turning looked for a moment steadily at the intruder, while her face grew white as her shawl.

"Who are you?" she asked, taking a step towards him.

"Have I changed past recognition? I should have known you anywhere," he replied, with a smile she could not mistake.

"Mark," she whispered, for she could not speak out loud, "How came you here, when you have been dead so many years?"

"To you, yes," he said, coming nearer to her. "To you, yes; but very much alive to myself and others. That notice of my death was a mistake. I was not in or near the mine, but I let it pass. I preferred to be dead to you and my old life. With Jeff I came to Southern California, taking another name and marrying a little Spanish girl, Anita——"

"Marrying, when you knew I was alive! Oh, Mark!" Helen interrupted him, while the hot blood stained her cheeks and the fire which leaped into her eyes made her like the Helen Tracy of his Chicago home when she was roused.

Mark smiled at this flash of jealousy and replied, "You forget the divorce which made me free to marry. It was kind in you to see that I had that privilege. You sent me a copy of the decree you know. And then you married again. Why shouldn't I? Anita was very lovely and sweet. She is dead."

"I thought you dead, too," Helen replied, angry with him, angry with poor little Anita, and angry at herself for showing her anger. "Where did you come from, and why are you here?" she asked, glancing at the door in fear lest Fanny should come in.

"Didn't the servant tell you Mr. Rayborne wished to see you?" Mark said.

"Mr. Rayborne, yes; but not Mr. Hilton. Are you Mr. Rayborne? Is that the name you took?" she asked, and he replied, "Yes, I am Mr. Rayborne, and I am here at Inez's request. She is very ill,—dying, we fear,—the shock was so great. She wishes to see her sister."

For an instant Mark's eyes, which usually moved rapidly from one object to another, were still and held the woman as if a spell were thrown over her. With a sensation of numbness in every limb Helen gasped, "Inez, your daughter! and sister to my Fanny! How do you know that?"

She was almost prepared to deny Fanny's paternity, but Mark's reply prevented it.

"Fanny told Inez that her own father, Mark Hilton, whom she could not remember, was killed in the mines of Montana and that she took Judge Prescott's name when her mother married him. Do I want more proof than that? I suppose you changed her name from

Frances to Fanny, which was natural enough. Sit down. You don't look able to stand."

He brought her a chair and put her in it with his old time courtesy of manner, while Helen began to cry. To find Mark alive was not so bad. Indeed, she was glad, for his supposed death in the mines had always weighed upon her as something for which she was in part responsible. But to find him a guide, a mountaineer, was galling to her pride. Her Apollo had fallen from his pedestal, not only in position, but in looks. He was still fine looking, but there were signs of age about him which her quick eye detected. His hair was tinged with grey, and he was not as erect as when he carried her through the rain. He had grown old and Helen found herself feeling sorry for it and sorry that he had lost the jaunty, city air he had when she last saw him. All this, however, was nothing to the fact that he had another daughter, who was Fanny's sister and whom Fanny would claim at once if she knew of the relationship. She must not know, and Helen was about to speak, when Mark said to her, "You remember that the divorce was mentioned at some length in the gossipping papers, and in one of them sympathy was extended to you for the loss of your little daughter."

"Yes," Helen answered. "She was very ill and said to be dead by one of the nurses. The reporters were very busy and seized upon every item, whether true or false. The story was contradicted in the next day's issue."

"Just so. I saw the first, and not the last, and thought her dead. With her gone and you lost to me, as you were, and with no home or friends, it is not strange that I wanted to get away and be forgotten," Mark said. "In California it is comparatively easy to do this. For a long time I would not look in a New York or Chicago paper if one came in my way, and so I missed seeing the announcement of your marriage with Judge Prescott and supposed you were still Mrs. Tracy, if living. I believe you dropped my name when you dropped me."

Helen assented, and he went on: "There is no look in Fanny's face like you, or like me, but she interested me strangely when I saw her, and sent my thoughts back to Ridgefield and to you, and the long ago, which I could wish blotted out, if it were not for Fanny and the love she and Inez bear each other. I have never heard a word of you since I came to California and did not know whether you were dead or alive. I have avoided eastern people lest I should stumble upon some one who knew me. I have acted as guide unwillingly, for fear of meeting an old acquaintance. Fortunately I never have. I had no suspicion that Fanny was my daughter until yesterday, when Inez came home, more dead than alive and I asked particularly about her friend. Inez's mother died with heart trouble, which she inherits. I have always known this and tried to guard her from strong excitement. The fright yesterday was too much for her and she does not rally from it."

"Does she know of—of—the relationship?" Helen asked falteringly, as if the word hurt her pride.

"I told her when I learned who Fanny was; she is very anxious to see her sister. Can she go?" Mark said.

"No, oh no," Helen cried, wringing her hands. "She must not go. It would all be known,—the relationship, I mean. She thinks you dead. Let her think so. She knows all about you—way back."

"To 'Tina?" Mark asked, and Helen answered him. "Yes, to 'Tina. I told her everything when Judge Prescott died. I had to, she was so persistent after she knew a little. She is to marry Roy Mason, son of Alice and Craig. You remember them?"

It was a strange question to ask, and Mark laughed as he answered it.

"I have reason to remember Craig, as he has me. I suppose you have met him often. I should like to have seen the first meeting."

"It was nothing to see," Helen answered. "He was Alice's husband and any love he ever had for me was dead, as it should be."

"And you didn't try to see if you still had power to move him?" Mark said ironically, while Helen's eyes flashed with anger.

"What do you take me for? I had been divorced and widowed as I supposed. I was Judge Prescott's wife, and we met almost as strangers. I would as soon think of moving the Sphinx, as I used to call him, as of moving Craig Mason. Are you satisfied?"

Mark bowed and asked, "What has Fanny's engagement with Craig's son to do with her going to Inez?"

"Much," Helen replied. "The Masons are very proud, and I don't know what the result would be if they knew of your change of name and of a daughter who would claim relationship with Roy. Leave Fanny alone, I beg, and go your way."

She was standing before him with tears in her eyes which looked just as beautiful as they had looked twenty years ago, and he might have yielded had there been no one but himself to consider. When he remembered Inez he was firm as a rock.

"We will let Fanny decide. I will wait for her," he said, and turned to leave the room.

Helen called him back. She knew the result if the

matter were left to Fanny. Nothing could keep her from Inez.

"Mark," she said again, going close to him and putting her hand on his arm.

He felt it through his coat sleeve and wanted to take it and wanted to shake it off. He did neither and said to her, "Well, what is it?"

"You are a man of honor," she replied.

He knew he wasn't, but rejoined, "Well?"

"And you are a gentleman," she continued.

Mark thought of the many times she had told him he was not a gentleman, but he merely repeated the word "Well?" while she went on: "If I let Fanny go, promise not to tell her who you are. There's no knowing what she would do, and I could not bear to have everything come out as it would with Fanny calling you father and all that. I did many wrong things when we lived together, but I never meant half as bad as I talked, and when I thought you were killed in that dreadful way I was very, very sorry. I was going to stop in Montana on my way home to see if I could find any one who knew you. I am telling you this to show you that I am not as bad as you think. Let the past be dead and buried, and don't let Fanny know. Will you, Mark?"

She had both hands on his arm now and was looking at him with an expression he could not resist.

"I promise that neither Inez nor I will tell her," he said, "but do you know how hard it will be for me to see her and not tell her I am her father?"

"Yes, I know; but it is better so. You must see that it is."

He did see it when he remembered what he was,—a man from whom Fanny would shrink, if the veil were lifted as it had been from Inez.

"Fanny shall not know from me," he said, and with this fear gone Helen began to speak of what all the time had been in her mind,—her diamonds.

Had Mark heard that they were lost from Fanny's hat and could not be found? "My ear-rings were with them. You remember them? I was going to give them to Fanny on her wedding day."

Every word she said cut like a knife, but Mark managed to answer naturally that he had heard that the diamonds were lost and to assure her that he would do whatever he could to find them and so would Mr. Hardy.

"Oh, yes,—Mr. Hardy,—your daughter's *fiancee*," Helen rejoined,—the young man who saved a coach from being robbed as your daughter saved ours. Fanny thinks highly of him."

Mark responded with a bow, and something in his face made Helen ask quickly, "Mark, is Tom Hardy Jeff?"

"Yes, but let him stay Tom Hardy until he chooses to declare his identity himself. He will try to trace your diamonds," Mark said, in a constrained voice.

Helen bowed her acquiescence, but looked puzzled. Everything was puzzling,—everything annoying,—and her brain was in a whirl, making her wish to be alone.

"Good bye," she said to Mark, bowing him from the room. "It is too late for Fanny to go to the cottage to-night, but you will see her to-morrow. Remember your promise."

She was trembling so she could scarcely stand, and when he was gone she threw herself upon the couch and sobbed hysterically for the trouble which had come upon her so unexpectedly. In the heyday of her youth and beauty, when her path was strewn with bruised hearts she had asked ironically if there were not a passage in the Bible which said "'Vengeance is mine, I will repay,' saith the Lord." When Mark deserted her and she went through the notoriety of a divorce, she had felt that she was being paid, but that was nothing to this last instalment of the payment, and the proud woman writhed under the chastisement, indignant at Mark,—she scarcely knew for what, unless it was for having married Anita, and indignant at Inez for being Fanny's half sister. It was some time before Fanny came, and when she did she found her mother in bed in a chill, with cramped hands, blue lips and cold feet, and Celine attending to her with hot drinks and hot water bags and shawls. It was some time before Mrs. Prescott was sufficiently quiet to tell her of Mr. Rayborne's visit and Inez's serious illness.

"I dare say he exaggerated the case and probably the girl is better by this time," she said. "I promised you should go and see her to-morrow, but if I feel as I do now, I cannot allow it."

Fanny, who had heard of Inez's illness before she came up to her mother, made no reply, but in her little wilful heart she said "I shall go," and she did. She knew her mother's nervous condition, which she could not understand, would not last long, and that Celine would do all that was necessary. Probably she should not stay more than the day. It would depend upon how she found Inez, she said to her mother, at whose bedside she stood just as it was growing light. It was a long drive to the cottage, and as she wished for as much time as possible with Inez she had stipulated with the landlord to have a conveyance ready for her at a very early hour.

"Good bye, mother," she said. "I am going now. You look a great deal better than you did last night. Celine will take good care of you till I come back. Good bye."

She stooped and kissed her and then hurried away, while Helen began to cry, not so much because Fanny had gone, as from a growing conviction that the truth would come out, and then, what might not Fanny do? Acknowledge her father, of course, and probably insist upon taking Inez to New York and introducing her as her sister. The thought brought on a nervous headache which kept her in bed all day, bemoaning her fate and wishing she had never come to California. Mark would keep his word, she was sure, but she distrusted Jeff, whom she had never liked. And he was Tom Hardy, and Mark was Mr. Rayborne. The change of names affected her unpleasantly and when at last she fell asleep they kept repeating themselves over and over in her troubled brain,—Mr. Rayborne and Tom Hardy.

CHAPTER XII.

FANNY AND INEZ.

INEZ, who had passed a restless night, had been told the conditions on which Fanny was permitted to come to her, and this detracted somewhat from her anticipated pleasure in having her there. But her father had given his word, and it was sacred to her. All night Mark had staid by her, while Tom sat outside, trying to devise some means of returning the diamonds without exciting suspicion. He could hear Inez every time she moved or spoke, and that was some comfort. Once, during an interval when the pain in her heart was not so great, she said to her father, "Tell me how it happened, and when? The other marriage, I mean, and tell me about Tom,—when he was somebody else."

Mark, who shrank from this ordeal which he had feared might come, said to her, "You are not strong enough, daughter. Wait awhile."

"No," she answered. "There is no waiting for me. I want to know now how you came to marry that proud lady. Were you like her? Like her people, I mean? and was Tom with you?"

Very briefly Mark told as much of his story as he thought necessary, omitting Tina and the finding of Tom in Boston where he rescued him from the street. Everything was softened and the life at Ridgefield dwelt upon at length, while Inez listened as to an interesting romance. It did not seem quite real to her that her father was once in a position so different from that which he now occupied. The change of names troubled her and twice she repeated "Mark Hilton,—Jefferson Wilkes," as if accustoming herself to the sound. Once when her father made an allusion to the present as if to explain, she said, "No, no. I cant' bear that, now or ever. There is no excuse. You are my father, and I must love you always,—and Tom, who is not Tom at all!"

Tom was on his feet and in the room in a moment, standing where she could not see him, as she went on very slowly, for her breathing was difficult.

"It seems odd, but I am glad you were once a gentleman like those at the hotel, and lived in a grand house like Fanny's, but I like better to hear of the woods and river and meadows and ponds in—what was the place?—Where Tom gathered the lilies."

"Ridgefield," Mark replied, trying to stop her as he saw how exhausted she seemed.

"Let me talk while I can," she said. "I can't speak of the past when Fanny comes if she is not to know you are her father. No one need to know it or the change of names. You are Mr. Rayborne, and Tom is Tom. I cannot hink of him as Jeff, or you as Mr. Hilton. You are father and he is Tom till I die."

"She does care for me a little. Thank God for that," Tom thought, as he crept back to his post on the stairs.

It was beginning to get light, and not long after sunrise a buggy driven by an employee from Clark's stopped at the foot of the hill leading to the cottage. Mark saw Fanny as she ran up the path, and went to meet her. In her flushed, eager face there was a look which he had seen often in his own face when he was a boy, and this it was which made him call her "My child" as he led her into the house and told her how low Inez was and how necessary that she should be kept quiet and not excited in any way.

"Her mother died of heart trouble. Inez may go the same way if we are not careful," he said.

"I will be very careful," Fanny answered, as she followed him to Inez's room.

The curtains were drawn over the windows, but it was light enough for Fanny to see the great change in Inez. Her eyes were sunken, but unnaturally bright. There was a drawn look about her mouth and her cheeks had lost much of their roundness, but were red with fever spots, which contrasted sharply with the pallor of her lips.

"Fanny, oh Fanny! I am so glad you have come," she said, trying to rise and opening and shutting her fingers rapidly. Then exerting all her strength she threw her arms around Fanny's neck and burst into tears while her father tried to quiet her. "Don't stop me," she said. "I must cry or my heart will burst, and my head, too,—it aches so hard. Fanny, Fanny! You don't know all your coming to me means. Now put me back on my pillow and sit where I can see you without turning my eyes. I am tired all over."

Her arms fell helpless on the bed and she scarcely seemed to breathe.

"I don't understand it," Fanny said in a low tone to Mr. Hilton.

Inez heard her and before her father could reply she whispered, "Don't try to understand, or speak of it. Just sit by me."

All day Fanny sat by her, knowing that whenever Inez's eyes were open, they were fixed on her with a look which began to make her uncomfortable.

"What is it, Inez? Is there something you want to tell me?" she asked at last.

Inez did not answer at once, but her hand moved slowly towards Fanny's, which chanced to be lying on the bed near her. For a time she regarded it intently, evidently contrasting its whiteness and softness with her own larger brown hands.

"We are not much alike, but you love me and are not ashamed of me," she said.

"Ashamed of you!" Fanny repeated. "Why should I be?"

"And you will stay with me? It can't be long," Inez continued.

"Yes, I will stay," Fanny answered involuntarily.

Then she remembered her mother, who was expecting her back that night, or the next day, at the farthest. What would she say?

"I'll stay a week any way. Inez must be better by that time," she thought, and wrote to her mother to that effect, suggesting that if she were not comfortable at Clark's she go on to San Francisco, where she would join her later.

Mrs. Prescott was greatly agitated when she received this note, and insisted that Celine should go to the cottage and bring Fanny away. She would have gone herself, but for the dread of meeting Mark again and being compelled to see Inez and possibly Tom. She could not go, but Celine must. Celine, who had been in the family since Helen was a young lady, understood her perfectly, and understood Fanny too. If the latter had made up her mind to stay with Inez, she would stay, and after a little she succeeded in making her mistress see that it was better to let her daughter alone.

"But I shall not go to San Francisco and leave her behind. I am very comfortable here and shall stay till she joins me," Mrs. Prescott said, adding after a moment's thought, "I don't know what the surroundings are at that cottage. Plain, of course, and not what Fanny is accustomed to. She will be worn out with the watching and the change. I think you'd better go and see to her."

This was a great concession and Fanny felt it as such when she received her mother's letter offering Celine.

"It is kind in you, mamma," she wrote in reply, "but Celine is not necessary. There is a woman in the kitchen and I don't know what I should do with a maid. I am waited on now by everybody as if I were a princess, and Inez couldn't see strangers. Keep Celine for yourself, and don't worry about me."

After the receipt of this note Mrs. Prescott settled down to wait Fanny's pleasure and fret at the prolonged delay. Inez did not improve, except that her voice was a little stronger and Fanny could talk with her longer at a time and not tire her. One day after the stage had passed Tom brought a small package sent from San Francisco to Inez in care of her father. It was the watch which a lady had been commissioned to buy as a testimonial of the gratitude of the passengers who had been in the stage on the day of the hold up. Fanny had hoped to select it herself, but when she saw it she felt that she could not have chosen better. It was a little diamond jeweled stem winder, with Inez's name on the inside lid and the date of the hold up.

"Something for you from San Francisco," Fanny said as she put the box on the bed before Inez, whose eyes grew very bright and questioning when she saw what it contained.

"A watch! the thing I have always wanted. How did it come to me? I don't understand," she said.

Fanny explained why it was sent and how glad the passengers were to send it. It was the first time any allusion had been made to the attempted robbery. Mr. Hilton had warned Fanny not to speak of it and she had been careful not to do so. Now she said as little as possible and was glad that Inez did not seem greatly excited.

"I'll keep it under my pillow," she said, and several times that day Fanny saw her looking at it, particularly at her name and the date. "I wish 'July —' wasn't there. It brings the dreadful day back to me, and I see him and hear him and hear my scream, which must have filled the valley," she said.

"You will get over that when you are stronger," Fanny suggested.

"Maybe," Inez replied, and Fanny noticed that after that the watch lay a little away from her instead of under her pillow.

The next morning Inez handed it to her, saying, "Will you think me foolish if I ask you to take it away. Doesn't it tick very loudly?"

Fanny did not think so, and Inez continued: "I had father put it on the bureau and the table and at last in the drawer last night, but I could hear it saying '*halt, halt,*' just as *he* said it. I am sorry, but I can't bear it. Take it away."

With a feeling of disappointment Fanny took it from her and said, "Shall I give it to Mr. Hardy to keep for you until you are better?"

"No, no; oh no, not to Tom; anything but that," Inez exclaimed, and greatly puzzled Fanny put the watch in her travelling bag down stairs where she was sure the fancied *halt* could not be heard.

Inez's attitude towards Tom had troubled Fanny from the first. She never asked for him, and if he came into her room and spoke to her, his visit was sure to be followed by a chill, or headache. At last Fanny spoke of it to Mr. Rayborne, who replied, "Inez is rather fanciful. It is part of the disease to turn against your best friend. Perhaps Tom had better stay away." After that he staid away, but Fanny frequently found him near the door when she went out and in.

"I am here to see if there is anything I can do," he said in explanation, offering to go for whatever she wanted and saving her many steps up and down the stairs.

Towards her father Inez's manner was different. She seldom spoke to him, but she allowed him to sit by her and once she took his hand with a look in her eyes which he could not misunderstand, and he said to her, "Yes, daughter, I promise before Heaven *that work* is finished for me and Tom, too. I can answer for him."

Fanny's step was heard outside and he stopped abruptly, but Inez seemed brighter and better for what he had said. He was constantly in the sick room, frequently sitting in the shadow where he could see not only the fever stained face with the sunken eyes in which the shadow of a great horror was still visible, but the fair, blue eyed girl who filled him with pride and an intense desire to take her in his arms and call her his daughter.

CHAPTER XIII.

THE SISTERS.

TEN days passed and there was no real improvement in Inez. Occasionally she would rally and inquire about the household matters, showing that she had some interest in them, but these moments were always followed by sinking spells when life seemed nearly extinct. The doctor was greatly perplexed.

"A strong girl like her ought not to be so affected by a scare," he said. "I don't understand it. She seems to have lost her grip and makes no effort to get hold of it, and then the weather is against her."

It was very hot those July days, hotter and dryer than it had been in the valley for years, and Fanny began at last to droop in the heat and confinement. They sent to Stockton for a nurse and this relieved Fanny from her constant watch in the sick room, where Inez lay a part of the time half unconscious of what was passing around her and talking very low to herself. Once Fanny thought she caught the word *Ridgefield* and wondered how Inez knew anything of that place.

"I mean to ask Mr. Rayborne," she thought, and went to find him.

The sun was setting and a cool breeze was blowing down from the mountains and she stepped out upon the piazza for a moment to enjoy it. While there she heard Mr. Rayborne and Tom enter the sitting room from the kitchen. They were talking of her, and Tom's voice was rather loud as he said, "I think it a shame that for the whim of a proud woman you cannot tell her that you are her father and Inez her half sister! Do you think she would be ashamed of you? She is not that kind."

For a moment Fanny felt as if she, too, had heart disease. She could not move and there was a prickly sensation in her hands and feet. Then she recovered herself, and in a moment was confronting Mr. Rayborne with the question, "Are you Mark Hilton, and is Inez my half sister?"

Mark could not reply, but Tom did it for him. "I am bound by no promise," he said, "and will tell you the truth. He *is* Mark Hilton, your father if Helen Tracy is your mother. He was not killed in the mines, and Inez is your half sister. She knows it and your mother knows it, but would only permit you to come here on the condition that you were kept in ignorance of the relationship. I am hampered by no conditions. I have told you and it may save Inez's life."

Tom had freed his mind and walked from the room, leaving father and daughter alone. Mark waited for Fanny to speak first, but she could not. The prickly sensation had returned. Her tongue felt thick and her hands cold and stiff. She had thought so much of her own father since she heard of him, and had pictured him often in her mind as the Apollo her mother had described. She had regretted that she could not rememher him, and now he was here before her, and was not at all like her idea of him, nor at all like Judge Prescott, nor Roy, nor any man she had ever known socially. He was still fine looking, with the manners of a gentleman, but he was a miner,—a stage driver,—a guide,—with another name than his own. All this passed through her mind, and with it a thought of 'Tina. There was some proud blood of the Tracys in her veins, and for a second it asserted itself strongly. Then, with a long breath, like one shaking off a nightmare, she went forward and said, "If you are my father,—kiss me!"

Mark felt as if all his life which he would forget were slipping from him and leaving him the man he used to be, while he held his daughter to him and cried over her as if his heart were breaking. When he grew calm he told her all he wished her to know of himself since he parted from her mother, whom he screened as far as possible from blame. After her father left her Fanny returned to the piazza and sat down alone to think and try to realize what she had heard and the new position in which it had placed her. One fact stood out vividly before her. *Inez* was her sister, and she was glad, and began to build castles of the future when Inez would be able to go to New York. No thought of separation occurred to her. Inez was hers to care for. With the advantages of a city she would make a brilliant and beautiful woman. She was much younger than she looked. A year or two at school would be desirable and then she would live with Fanny and Roy, "and marry Tom?" Fanny whispered interrogatively.

There was no one to hear,—no one to answer,—except Fanny herself, who began to rebel against a marriage which before had seemed suitable enough, if the parties were satisfied. She had admired Tom for his apparent bravery, his pleasant face and genial manner, but as a brother-in-law he was not so desirable. She could mould and cultivate Inez, but not Tom. He was too old. She must take him as he was, if she took him at all; not as Tom Hardy either, but as Jeff Wilkes, who, her mother had told her, was a strange boy with strange ways, whom she had never liked. That her father had changed his name displeased her, but she did not resent it in him as much as she did in Tom, who she felt nearly sure had suggested it. But he was Inez's *fiancée*. She must accept him and make Roy accept him, too. She did not anticipate much trouble there. Roy would think what she wished him to think, and Tom was really better looking than half the men of her acquaintance if they were shorn of their city dress. This comforted her, and when at last Tom came out and talked to her as he could talk when he chose, she began to feel quite reconciled to him as a prospective brother-in-law.

It was too late for her to see Inez that night, but very early in the morning she was at her bedside, calling her sister and telling her how glad she was and that now she must get well fast so as to go to New York in September, when she and her mother went home.

"No, Fanny," Inez said. "I shall never go to New York. It is lovely in you to suggest it and to be glad I am your sister. You don't know what joy it is to have you call me so, and to believe you love me. In some circumstances I might have gone with you for a while, for I should like to see the eastern world where father and Tom were born. He must be Tom to me always, and it will not be long. I am going as mother did, only not so sudden. I am younger and stronger, but I know I am dying. I feel as if part of me were dead already and there is nothing to rally from. The tree struck with lightning twice does not recover. I have been struck twice, once in the stage when——oh, Fanny, I can't talk of that without my heart standing still. The second shock was different and came when I heard that father and Tom were somebody else, and you my sister. I was so weak that it was like another blow. For your sake I'd like to live, although our paths would be apart. Yours in the great, busy world, and mine here with father. I wish I could see your Roy, but it is too much to think he would come across a continent."

Inez had thought all this out the previous night after her father told her that Fanny knew of the relationship, and now that she had said it she sank into a state of great exhaustion, during which Fanny staid by her and every time she put her hand on Inez's head, or spoke her name, the sick girl's eyes opened with an expression of unutterable joy, and the pale lips whispered "My sister!"

That night Fanny wrote to her mother: "I know everything from 'Tina to the present time. Tom has told me that Mr. Rayborne was Mark Hilton, my father, and Inez my sister. *My father* told me the rest, and I do not believe there is anything more for me to learn about myself. At first I prickled all over and could scarcely speak. Now I am very calm and glad and should be happy if Inez were not so low. I think she is going to die, and I cannot leave her. I shall write to Roy to-morrow and tell him everything. I hope he will come. I want him to see Inez."

After this Fanny devoted herself entirely to Inez, taking quite as much care of her as the hired nurse. But it was of no avail. Inez grew weaker every day and baffled both the physician from Stockton and the specialist from San Francisco, who had been called to see her.

That there was serious heart trouble, complicated with slight paralysis, both agreed, but neither could understand why the stage fright alone should have affected her so strangely. If love and care and tenderness could have given her back her life she would have had it, but nothing could save her. Every night she seemed weaker, and every morning her face looked thinner and her hands more transparent as they lay just where they were put, for she had but little power to move them now.

"They are almost as white as yours, but not so small," she said one afternoon to Fanny, who was rubbing and bathing them. "They have been strong hands and done a heap of work, but will never do any more, and it is better so. I've thought it all over and do not want to live. I'd rather go to mother, who is waiting for me. She'll be glad to see me. I know what you want to say," she went on as Fanny tried to interrupt her. "You would take me to New York and try to make a lady of me like yourself. But I am not like your people. I could never be like them and they would wonder how you came to have a sister like me, and tongues would be busy and you would feel hurt, and Roy, too. I should like to see him before I die. Do you think he will come?"

Fanny had not heard from him since she wrote and told him of Inez and her father and it was time she received a letter. She was quite sure, however, that he would come, "and take me by surprise, most likely," she said to Inez, who was exhausted and disposed to sleep. Fanny, too, felt the need of rest and air and went out upon the piazza to enjoy the sunset. She was very tired and a little homesick, with a great longing for Roy. "If he would only come," she was thinking, when in answer to her thought Roy came rapidly up the walk and stood at her side.

CHAPTER XIV.

ROY.

Fanny's letter had reached him in Ridgefield, where, with his father and mother, he was spending a few days at the Prospect House. Its contents electrified them all and no one more than Uncle Zach.

"Mark and Jeff both alive!" he said. "I never b'lieved Jeff was dead. He ain't the kind, but for Mark, that I sot such store by not to be killed is queer and I've mourned for him as I would for Johnny. And he took another name, and married another woman and had another girl! I didn't think that of Mark! No, marm, I didn't. And he is Fanny's father? I'll be dumbed! I'd like to see him, though, and Jeff, too. Like fust rate to see him turn a summerset on the grass again. Give 'em my respects and tell 'em to come home and bring that girl if they want to. Ridgefield air and Dot will soon bring her round. She must be a clipper to spring at a robber like that. No wonder she's got heart disease. It makes mine wobble round to think of it."

Uncle Zach had his remarks mostly to himself, as Roy was talking excitedly to his father and mother of the journey he was going to take at once.

"Fanny needs me, and I am going," he said, and he started that night, and several days later reached Clark's very hot, very tired, very dusty, and very impatient to see Fanny. "You say she is still in the mountains. How long does it take to get there?" he asked Mrs. Prescott, whom he had surprised as she was taking her lunch in her room.

She was very glad to see him, for she was getting tired

of waiting for Fanny and anxious as to what the result of the waiting might be. She was not hard enough to hope Inez would die, but could not help thinking that if she did one possible annoyance would be removed, and this thought was in her mind when Roy came suddenly upon her, overwhelming her with so many questions that for a few minutes she could only listen without replying. When at last she had a chance she repeated all that had happened since she came into the valley, dwelling most upon the loss of her diamonds for which Roy did not particularly care. He was more interested in Fanny. Once or twice during his rapid journey it had occurred to him that his newly found relatives might prove awkward appendages if Fanny insisted upon having them near her. But he put the feeling aside as unworthy of him.

"If she can stand it, I can," he thought, and began to wonder what manner of people his father-in-law elect and sister-in-law might be.

Craig and Alice had both said that Mark was a gentleman and Roy accepted that so far as it went. He might have been a gentleman when they knew him, but he had passed through many phases since and there was no guessing what he was now, except that he was Fanny's father, and as such must be respected. Mrs. Prescott did not help to reassure him and in all she said he detected a keen regret for what had happened, and that it was Inez who troubled her most. Mark would never intrude himself upon her, but Fanny would insist upon taking Inez to New York, if she lived, as she probably would.

"And if she does, oppose it with all your strength. We cannot have it. And bring Fanny away at once," she said to Roy, when he left her for his drive to the cottage.

The sun was down when he reached it, but there was still light enough for him to see the gleam of a white dress upon the piazza. Something told him it was Fanny, and quickening his step he soon had her in his arms, smothering her with kisses, while she cried for joy. He did not at first notice how worn and pale she was, he was so glad to see her and so struck with her surroundings.

"By Jove, isn't it queer to find you here? and how white you are," he said at last. "This will never do. I must get you away at once."

"Not while Inez lives," Fanny answered, in a tone Roy knew it was useless to combat.

"Is she so very low?" he asked. "Tell me all about it. You have written a good deal, and your mother told me a lot, but I want to hear it from you. It's the strangest thing I ever heard."

Fanny told him everything from the day she first saw Inez up to the present time. When she described the hold-up she was very earnest and dramatic, and Roy's blood tingled with admiration for the heroic girl who had braved a masked robber and was perhaps paying for it with her life. Two or three times he asked questions which Fanny thought irrelevant to the subject, but for the most part he listened quietly till she was through.

"You are glad you have found your father?" he said, during a pause in the conversation.

"Glad? Of course. Why shouldn't I be?" Fanny replied. "I once told you I believed I should find him. He is not like you, nor Judge Prescott, nor anybody I ever knew, but he is *mine,* and you must like him."

"I intend to," Roy said, "and now fire away at Tom. What is he like?"

If there was sarcasm intended Fanny did not know it, and answered readily, "He is nice, too,—though not like father. I don't quite know what I mean, only he is different. I am sorry for him. He was to marry Inez, you know, and now that can never be, and what I don't understand is that he seldom comes into her room, and when he does she is sure to have a chill. She used to ask me often where he was and when I said, 'Do you want to see him?' she'd say, 'No, I only want to know if he has gone out.' I told him of it and he said, a little irritably, 'Tell her I'm always in the house.' That seemed to quiet her. Strange, isn't it?"

Before Roy could answer, Fanny exclaimed, "There's father," and Mark Hilton appeared, looking surprised at the sight of a young man, with his arm around his daughter.

"Father, this is Roy,—come all the way from Boston," Fanny said, and the two men were soon shaking hands and looking keenly at each other in the moonlight which fell upon them.

Roy saw a tall man, with a slight stoop, who must have been handsome once and was good looking still, with something in his language and manners indicative of education and a knowledge of good society. Mark saw a boyish young fellow, with innocence and purity written on his face, and thanked God that Fanny's choice had fallen upon him. At first he was a little reserved, for he never grasped the hand of an honest man that he did not experience a twinge of shame, and this was very strong in the presence of Roy, who, as Craig Mason's son, was allied with the past, and whose frank, honest eyes were studying him so closely,

If Mark felt any trepidation in meeting Roy, Tom felt it in a greater degree. He guessed who the young man was on the piazza with Mark, for he knew Fanny had written him to come, and for a minute he shook like a leaf. Then steadying himself with the thought that he had nothing to fear from Roy, he went forward to meet him as he came in, greeting him cordially and seeming wholly at his ease. When supper was over the three men began chatting together as familiarly as if they had known each other all their lives. Roy casually mentioned Ridgefield to Fanny, saying he had left his father and mother there, and both Mark and Tom began to ply him with questions concerning the town and Uncle Zacheus and Dotty.

"You know we lived there years ago and are interested in the place," Mark said, and Roy told them all he knew, and then at the first opportunity plunged into the subject uppermost in his mind—the robbers and the hold up on the road.

This was something of which neither Mark nor Tom cared to talk. But they could not help themselves. No matter how adroitly they tried to turn it aside Roy brough it up again, with all the eagerness of youth, to whom such things are interesting.

"I wonder the robbers have never been caught," he said. "We do things better in Boston. Why don't you get a detective from the east? There's Converse,—nearly equal to Sherlock Holmes. He only needs the slightest clew,—sometimes a word, a look,—to follow to the end. He'd unearth them quick. I believe I could run them down myself, give me time."

"Why don't you try and get the reward? It is a big one," Fanny asked. "People think they live here."

"Here!" Roy repeated, glancing around the room, as if in quest of a robber in some of the shadowy corners.

"Not in this house, you stupid," Fanny said, laughingly, "but in the neighborhood,—among the mountains,—and that we possibly meet them every day. The very idea gives me the shivers, and I never see a strange man that I do not think, perhaps you are one of them. It would be dreadful if I had ever been near them, or spoken to them."

"Is there nothing in their appearnce to mark them?" Roy asked, and Fanny replied, "Nothing but their size. One is very tall; that is Long John. The other is short; they call him Little Dick. He attacked us. You know I told you that before."

There was a lamp in the room and Tom and Mark were sitting where its light fell upon them. Roy had not noticed them particularly until Fanny spoke of the size of the robbers. Happening then to glance that way he was struck with the expression of Mark's face and saw the look which passed between him and Tom.

"By Jove!" he exclaimed, under his breath.

Then, as Fanny looked inquiringly at him he covered his blunder by fanning himself with his hands and asking if the room were not very hot and close.

"Let's go outside, where it is cooler," he said.

Fanny was glad to go and Mark and Tom were glad to have her and be rid for a while of their inquisitive guest.

"How much longer could you have stood that," Tom asked Mark, whose face was bathed in perspiration, and who only replied, "I think it is getting rather hot;" then he went out at the rear door and strolled off into the woods with Nero for company, while Tom stood his ground, deciding to make himself so agreeable to Roy that he would forget the detective Converse and the robbers and his intention to "run them down."

Meantime Roy and Fanny were walking along the road in the moonlight, Fanny supremely happy and trying to answer the many questions Roy was putting to her about the hold-up in which she had a part. She thought she had told him all about it, but here he was asking her such funny questions; "How did Inez look when she confronted the robber? How did the robber look? that is, how tall was he?"

"Tall as I am?" he asked, and Fanny replied, "Oh, no; he was about as tall as Tom, and slimmer. He wore a sweater which made him look small."

"How did Tom look when he came up?" was Roy's next question.

Fanny couldn't enlighten him much there. She didn't think of Tom, she was so absorbed with Inez. She knew he picked up her hat, which was frightfully jammed, and straightened it, and put it on her head. Then she spoke of her diamonds, wondering how they could have gotten loose and if she would ever find them.

"Tom is still hopeful that after a heavy rain they may come to light and has promised to look for them."

"I hope he'll find them," Roy said, and continued: "By the way, what am I to call him and your father? Do the people know he isn't Tom, and that your father is not Mr. Rayborne?"

"No," Fanny said. "Inez wanted them to stay as they were, Mr. Rayborne and Mr. Hardy. They know father was divorced and that I am the daughter of his first marriage and took my stepfather's name at his request; that is all they know, and they wouldn't care, if they knew the whole. I think divorces are wrong, but they are common, and a lot of people left their real names east when they came here."

"Queer set Fanny has fallen among. I wonder what father would say," Roy thought, as they walked back to the house, where only Tom was waiting to say good night.

Alone in his room Roy thought over all he had heard and seen and drew his own conclusions.

"I may be wrong," he said. "I hope I am. Mr. Rayborne does not look like a highwayman. Fanny's father, too. It can't be, but I don't quite like Tom's face, it is too cunning and that look he gave Mr. Rayborne meant something. I wish Converse was here. No, I don't. There's Fanny! It would kill her, as it is killing Inez, if I am correct in my surmise. I'll get her away from here as soon as I can, but while she stays *I* stay and watch! There will be a kind of excitement about it."

For one so young Roy was a shrewd observer and was seldom wrong in his estimation of people. He was fond of detective stories, and often thought how he would act in such and such circumstances. A suspicion, of which he did not like to think, had fastened itself upon his mind, and in trying to combat it he at last fell asleep.

The next morning, when he met Mark and Tom by daylight, they both looked better to him and were so genial and gentlemanly and kind that he mentally asked pardon for having harbored an evil thought against them. Tom was particularly friendly and proposed a drive through the valley, as the day was fine. To this Roy acceded readily, saying he would be ready as soon as he had seen Inez. At the mention of her name Tom's face grew so sad that Roy said to him, "Fanny has told me of your engagement to her and I sincerely hope Inez will live to keep it."

"Never," Tom answered, and turned away, while Roy followed Fanny up to Inez's room.

Inez had passed a fairly good night, and was very anxious to see Roy. Fanny had brushed her hair and put on her one of her own pink and white dressing jackets, which brought out the beauty of her face, notwithstanding her hollow eyes and sunken cheeks.

"She looks like a picture," Fanny thought, as she led Roy to the side of the bed.

No introduction was needed and none was given. Inez's hand was lifted slowly to Roy, who took and held it in both his own. He knew the great black eyes, which looked blacker from contrast with the pallor of her face, were studying him closely, but he had nothing to conceal and met her scrutiny unflinchingly.

"Roy," she said. "I am so glad for Fanny that you are her Roy, and glad you are here."

He could not say he was altogether glad to be there except to be with Fanny, but he told her how sorry he was to find her so ill and that he hoped she would soon be better. He knew they were idle words, for death was written on every lineament of her face, but he must say something. Inez shook her head, but did not reply, and Roy, thinking to please and interest her, said, "I am going to drive with Mr. Hardy, who has kindly offered to show me the beauties of the valley."

At the mention of Tom Inez closed her eyes as if to shut out a painful sight.

"Tired? Ar'n't you?" Fanny said, motioning Roy to leave, which he did, willingly.

Sick rooms were not to his taste; he was happier with Tom, who proved a most agreeable companion, and talked so well and so intelligently on every subject and seemed imbued with so good principles that Roy mentally asked pardon again for having distrusted him. Of the hold-ups Tom did not like to talk, and said so.

"The last was fraught with so much disaster to Inez that I never think of it without a shudder," he said, while of the first, in which he had been the hero, he made light, saying people had magnified what he did, and praised him too much. "I don't believe it was courage. I was mad," he said, "and flew at the man without thinking what the consequence might be to me. I hope we are done with the rascals and tourists can hereafter visit the valley in peace."

Then he began to talk of the east and of Ridgefield and to relate anecdotes of his boyhood and his experience with Uncle Zach and Dotty. Mark, too, came in for a share in the conversation. And here Tom was very eloquent.

"Seeing him now, broken with hard work and crushed with anxiety for Inez, you can have no idea of the grand man he was when he lived in Ridgefield. Everybody respected him, and under right influences he would have staid what he was. No man will stand being nagged continually and twitted with his birth and poverty. I beg your pardon," he added, as he saw Roy scowl, and remembered that he had been making insinuations against his mother-in-law elect; "I mean no disrespect to Mrs. Prescott. She was proud and beautiful, and greatly admired, and not always on the square. Her daughter is not at all like her."

"I should think not," Roy answered, dryly, and then Tom spoke of Roy's mother and the good she had done him as a boy.

"If I had followed her advice I should have been a better man, but what is done is done and cannot be changed. Do you believe a bad man can become a thoroughly good one?"

The question startled Roy, who felt unequal to meet it, but who answered with a gravity beyond his years, "It depends upon what he has done. If reparation can be made he should make it, and—. Yes, it seems to me a bad man may become a good one. Of course the memory of the bad would always cling to him, making him sorry for the past and most sorry when the world was praising him."

Roy had no idea how his words were stinging Tom, who answered quickly, "That's just it. Memory! If we could kill that; but we can't. Hell must be made up of memories."

Again the suspicion of the previous night began to creep into Roy's mind, but he cast it aside, while Tom roused himself from his melancholy mood and began to point out the lights and shadows on the mountains and asked if Roy would like to try a trail on the morrow. Nothing could suit Roy better, and for the next two or three days Tom went with him from mountain to mountain and was as gay as if no harrowing memory were intruding itself upon his mind. At last Roy suggested that they go to the scene of the last hold-up and look again for the missing diamonds. At first Tom hesitated. That spot was like a haunted spot to him, but there was no good reason for refusing, and they set off together for the scene of the attempted robbery. Once there Tom grew very communicative, rehearsing the proceedings even more dramatically than Fanny had done when describing them to Roy. Here was the stage. Here the robber stood waiting for it, and commanding the driver to halt and the passengers to hold up their hands. Here

Inez sat and sprang over the wheel with a shriek which must have frightened the brigand quite as much as the revolver which proved not to be loaded, and here she lay fainting with her head in Fanny's lap when all was over."

"Were you here through it all? I thought you came later," Roy said, and Tom, who saw he had made a mistake, colored and stammered. "Sounds as if I was here, don't it? You know, I happened along after the rascal had left, and a more frightened lot of people you never saw. I have heard Inez describe the scene so graphically that I feel as if I were a part of it."

"I do believe you were," Roy thought.

"Where was Fanny's hat when you picked it up? We will look for the diamonds there, first," he said.

Tom's face was flushed, but his manner was composed and natural as he pointed out the spot where he had rescued the crushed hat from the mud. The grass was growing there now, and there was not a spot within a radius of many yards where the diamonds could have dropped and lain hidden.

"Some one of the crowd must have taken them," Roy said, with conviction, when they ended their search and sat down upon a fallen tree to rest. "Yes, somebody took them here, and I will not leave California till I know who the thief is. I believe I'll send for Converse. I suppose he could visit the valley like any ordinary person, and keep his eyes open. The diamonds were to have been Fanny's on her wedding day."

"And when is that to be?" Tom asked.

Roy was not sure, but some time between Christmas and New Years.

"I hope she will have them by that time," Tom said, throwing down the stick with which he had been poking in the grass and bushes, and going back to the buggy preparatory to returning home.

It was rather a silent drive, for they were both tired and a shadow had come over both, distrust on Roy's side, and on Tom's a dread of what the hot-headed young man might do. It was the second time he had mentioned Converse, the Boston detective, and Tom felt that his sin might be finding him out, and saw no escape from it except by suicide, of which he had thought more than once, but had always put the tempter behind him, with a vehemence which kept him at bay. His Ridgefield training had not wholly lost its effect, nor the advice Alice Tracy had given him when she gathered lilies with him on the river or tramped through the woods to visit the hornet's nest and the turtle bed in the pond. Those days were very vivid to him now with Alice's son beside him and a look like her in his face and blue eyes. He liked the boy, as he designated him, and was still a little afraid of him or what he might do. Roy, on his part, was thinking, "A first-rate fellow whom I can't help liking, any more than I can help putting things together, but if he is bad so is Mr. Hilton, and on Fanny's account I'd better keep quiet."

In this state of mind they reached the cottage where they found Fanny waiting for them on the piazza, greatly excited and alarmed.

"Inez is much worse," she said, "and wants to see Roy alone."

CHAPTER XV.

AT THE LAST.

Inez had been better that morning and had asked to sit in her chair near the window where she could look out upon the mountains and the valley. Fanny was brushing her hair and talking to her, when she asked, as she often did, "Where is Tom?"

"Gone to drive with Roy," Fanny said. "I believe they were going as far as the scene of the hold-up. Roy is anxious to see the place, and look for my diamonds. But it is of no use. If Tom can't find them, he can't."

"The diamonds? What diamonds?" Inez asked quickly.

Fanny had been warned not to talk to Inez of the hold up. Consequently, with the exception of the day when the watch came, she had never mentioned it until now when she spoke of it in connection with her diamonds. It was of no use for her to try and waive the subject. Inez could not be put off, and she finally explained that when she reached Clark's the diamonds were missing. The stitches in the ribbon bow of her hat had been broken and the linen bag had slipped out somewhere on the road.

"I have given them up," she said, "and now only care to have the robbers caught. Roy talks of sending for a famous detective from Boston, but I hardly think he will. He is a rash boy any way and would like nothing better than such an adventure as we had."

As she talked Fanny was admiring the gloss and texture of Inez's hair, and wondering how it would look twisted on the top of her head after the fashion then beginning to prevail.

"I am going to do your hair in the latest style, if it will not tire you too much," she said, going for some hair pins.

There was no answer and when she came back with the pins she saw that Inez's head was turned to one side and lay motionless against the chair. She had not heard of the loss of the diamonds until now, when in an instant she saw the whole scene again, and knew where the diamonds were. The thought of the detective Roy was to send for added to her excitement. Tom was worse than she had supposed him to be, but she could not have him arrested. His downfall would implicate her father and Fanny would be involved in the disgrace. All this went rapidly through her mind until unconsciousness came and she knew no more until she was in bed, with her father and Fanny and the nurse bending over her with restoratives.

"Was she excited in any way?" Mr. Hilton asked, and Fanny replied, "I think not. I was brushing her hair and telling her that Roy had gone with Mr. Hardy to look for the diamonds. I had forgotten that she didn't know they were lost. It might have been that, but I think it was the fatigue of sitting up too long."

Mr. Hilton made no reply, but he knew what caused the faint which lasted so long and left Inez with no power to move except her head and one hand which from the wrist beat the air constantly. It was still moving feebly up and down, when Roy went to her and asked what he could do for her. Fanny had come up with him and with a motion of her head Inez dismissed her; then said in a whisper, with long, painful breaths between each word, "Don't try to find the robbers, nor send for a detective. I shall be gone, but Fanny will be here. Don't do it for her sake. *My* father is *her* father. She will have the diamonds back."

Roy looked surprised. His talk of a detective had been mostly talk, and he told Inez so, assuring her that nothing should ever be done which could hurt Fanny, or compromise her father or Tom. She knew he understood her and that she was giving away those whom she loved better than her life, but she was giving them to Roy, who loved Fanny.

"Thanks," she said faintly. "You will keep what I have said to yourself, and never let Fanny, nor any one, know. I can trust you?"

"To the death," he answered, taking her shaking hand, which was as cold as if the shadow stealing into the room had touched that first and turned it into ice.

"I knew Tom was a rascal all the time, and Mr. Hilton, too, but my word is pledged and I shall keep it. Think of Fanny here in a den of robbers. It can't be long, though. The poor girl is about done for," Roy thought, as he tried to soothe and quiet Inez.

"Go now, and send Tom," she said at last, and, glad to escape, Roy went quickly down the stairs and delivered the message to Tom.

It was the first time she had asked for him, and he felt much as a criminal feels when going to execution. He had no idea what she wanted and was rather relieved when she said to him, "Do you love me still?"

"More than I can tell you. Oh, Inez, I am so sorry for it all, and have nothing to offer in excuse," he replied, bending over her until his face touched the hand which was still moving very slowly, and whose fingers stirred his hair as they moved.

"Don't try to excuse, or explain" she said. "Bury the

the past in my grave, and begin a new life. Make restitution as far as possible. Give Fanny her diamonds!"

Tom started violently. "How did you know she lost them?" he asked, and Inez replied, "I do know, and it has put out the little flickering flame there was left of my life. Get them to her somehow."

"I have intended to do this all the time, and I assure you she shall have them," Tom said.

"And the others," she continued; "If you know who they are and where they are, send them what belongs to them, or its equivalent. You and father, both; I cannot talk to him. I leave it with you."

She was asking impossibilities and Tom knew it, but he promised that so far as he could he would do all she wished.

"Tom," she whispered, after a moment's silence, "Come closer; it is hard for me to talk; the lump in my throat chokes me so."

Tom bent closer to her, while she went on: "I have loved you so much and thought you so good and never suspected the truth. Tom, oh, Tom, kiss me for the sake of what we have been to each other, and when I am gone, be the good man I used to think you were. Stay with father and take care of him. He needs you. Good bye. Go now. I am so tired."

In an agony of remorse Tom kissed the face where the moisture of death was gathering fast. Then he left her, and when he saw her again she was like a beautiful piece of marble, with a smile on her lips which told of perfect peace. Mark and Fanny watched by her until the great change came, and the hand which had beaten the air constantly was stilled forever, its last stroke falling on the head of her father who knelt beside her. In his heart was anguish such as few men have ever known.

Not once had she reproached him. If she had he could have borne better than he could the look in her eyes and the way she shrank from him at times. Once when Fanny was absent from the room for a moment she said to him, "Poor father, I know you are sorry, and I have loved you through it all, but I can't bear it. I must die. It is better so, for things could never be again as they have been. I couldn't be happy here, nor anywhere. I want to go to mother and to God. Stay with Tom; he will be kind to you. Don't go with Fanny, if she urges it, —with her and Roy, I mean. You could not go to her mother."

She had done what she could for all of them, and felt that her work was finished. For an hour or more she lay with her eyes closed and with no perceptible motion in her body except the slow beating of her fingers, and when they stopped she was dead. When sure she was gone Mark broke down entirely, while Fanny and Tom tried in vain to quiet him.

"Let me alone," he said. "I must have it out by myself. Nothing can help me but time."

Leaving the house he spent hours among the hills, walking up and down while the rain, which had begun to fall, beat upon him unnoticed. He did not think of the storm, or the darkness, and stumbled over rocks and bushes until benumbed with cold and wet with the rain he returned to the house, an old man, so broken that he would never be himself again. He let Tom and Roy and Fanny make the arrangements for the funeral, while he sat in the room with Inez, sometimes talking to her, sometimes to himself, and sometimes to Anita, by whom Inez was buried on one of the loveliest mornings of the late summer. There were few visitors in the valley, but all the people in the sparsely settled neighborhood turned out to the funeral, as they had done to her mother's. The house was filled with the flowers they brought, some from the woods and some from the gardens which were stripped to honor the dead. Early in the morning on the day of the funeral there came from Stockton a box of exquisite roses and a pillow of flowers, with Inez's name in the centre. The moment she heard of Inez's death Mrs. Prescott had telegraphed for the flowers, urging haste and fearing lest her gift should not be in time. As the funeral did not take place until the third day after Inez's death, they were in time, and neither Fanny nor Mark would have had any doubt as to the sender, if her card, "Mrs. Helen Tracy Prescott," had not accompanied them.

"Look, father," Fanny said. "See what mother has sent."

She put the roses upon the table and left the room for vases in which to arrange them. When she returned one was gone, but there were so many she did not miss it, or suspect that it was between the lids of the family Bible which Mark had not opened before since he recorded Anita's death. Helen's thoughtfulness had touched him closely and the rose he took was for her sake and the old time when he had nearly ruined himself with the roses bought for her in Ridgefield. When the short service was over Roy, who longed to get away, suggested to Fanny that they should leave that afternoon, as her mother was anxious for her return. There was no good reason for her staying longer, except to be with her father, who, putting his own grief aside, said to her, "Much as I want you to stay I think you should go to your mother. It was kind in her to let me have you so long. Tell her so, and thank her for the flowers she sent to Inez."

Fanny would like to have asked him to come to New York, but she knew this could not be. Her father and mother had separated themselves from each other, and the gulf between them could never be recrossed. But she could have him in her own home, when she had one, and she urged his coming to Boston and felt piqued that Roy did not second her invitation. He was busy strapping his satchel and pretended not to hear. Mark understood perfectly, and while thanking Fanny for her kindness, knew he should never trouble Roy, and knew, too, when he said good bye to Fanny that in all human probability he should never see her again. For hours after Tom, who took Roy and Fanny to Clark's, was gone, he lay on Inez's bed, wishing he, too, were dead and lying by the new-made grave from which a faint odor of roses occasionally reached him. It was like a breath of Helen, —a perfume from the years of long ago, and he could have shrieked as he recalled those days, remembering what he was then and what he was now. It was dark when Tom returned, and not finding Mark in the house he went to the grave where he was standing with folded arms and his frame convulsed with sobs.

"Mark," Tom said, stretching his hand across Inez's grave, "Mark, it is we two alone forever."

"Yes, we two alone forever," Mark answered, grasping Tom's hand, and holding fast to it as a drowning man holds to a spar. "Alone forever, with our secret to keep, and here by Anita's grave and Inez's, both of whom I killed, let us swear that henceforth we will be honest men and try in some small measure to redeem the past."

"I swear it! I promised Inez that whatever restitution could be made we would make," Tom said, and for a few moments the clasped hands were held above the grave, while the heads of the two men were bowed low as if each were ratifying the solemn vow.

CHAPTER XVI.

MARK AND TOM.

It was the morning of Fanny's wedding day and the house in Madison Avenue was a scene of great excitement. Flowers and ferns and palms, and florists arranging them, were everywhere. Presents were constantly arriving until the room set apart for them could scarcely hold any more. Cards had been sent to Fanny's father and Tom, who were in San Francisco, Mark at the Palace Hotel and Tom in a wholesale grocery. A pretty remembrance had come from each, with a letter from Mark wishing his daughter every possible happiness. So far as practicable Tom's promise to Inez had been kept. Only a few of the people robbed were known to him or Mark by name. To these at intervals money had been sent, which produced nearly as great a sensation as the hold-ups had done. That the brigands had reformed or left the country was evident and Mark and Tom often heard the subject discussed, but Mark never joined in the discussion, or in any other. He was a silent, broken man, doing his work faithfully, but keeping apart by himself, with a sad, far-away look on his face, as if his thoughts were always with the two graves on the mountain side of the Yosemite.

Tom, whose temperament was different, was more social. It was seldom, however, that anything called a smile to his face, for he, too, was nearly always thinking —not so much of Inez's grave as of the scene on the road and her face as it looked at him when bidding him go before she shot him, as she would shoot a dog. Just before Christmas he asked leave of his employer to go for a day to Salt Lake City. On his return he said to Mark, "It is all right. They are on the way."

A few days later, and on the morning of the wedding day, Fanny and Roy were sitting together behind a forest of palms and azaleas, when the door bell rang for the twentieth time within an hour.

"Another present, I'll bet you," Roy said. "We shall have enough to set up a bazaar."

"I hope it isn't a clock. I have four already," Fanny rejoined, going forward to take the carefully sealed package sent by express from Salt Lake City.

"Salt Lake City!" Fanny repeated, examining the package curiously. "Do we know anybody there? What do you suppose it is?"

Roy could not explain the presentiment he had as to what it was. He had expected something of the kind long before this, for he remembered that Inez had said, "Fanny will have her diamonds."

"Open the package and see what it is," he said.

The seals of wax were broken, the box opened, and Fanny gave a start of surprise as she saw the linen bag she had sewed with so much care into the ribbons on her hat.

"Mother! Look here! The diamonds!" she cried, laying them one by one on her mother's lap.

They were all there and unharmed except as they were a little dim for want of cleaning.

"Who could have found them and sent them?" Fanny kept saying.

Roy felt sure he knew, but said nothing, while Mrs. Prescott suggested that the person who found them intended at first to keep them,—then, failing to dispose of them, decided to send them to New York.

"Yes, but how did he know where I lived, or that I was to be married to-day?" Fanny asked.

Roy tided over that difficulty by saying, "Easy enough, your mother advertised for them to be sent here if they were found, and the man or woman, whoever it is, happened to forward them in the nick of time. Providential dispensation, don't you see?"

He was decking Fanny with the jewels as he talked, and she accepted his theory as she accepted everything from him.

"I shall write to father this very day that I have them. He will be so glad, and Tom, too. I dare say the poor fellow has hunted over every foot of ground between that place and Clark's several times."

Roy's shoulders always gave a little shrug when Fanny talked in this strain, and he now left her while she wrote a few hurried lines to her father telling him her diamonds had come and asking if he had any idea who sent them.

"I am so happy," she wrote, "for in a few hours I shall be Roy's wife. I wish you could be here, and Inez. Oh, if she were only alive she would be my maid of honor and eclipse me with her beauty. Dear Inez. It makes me cry every time I think of her up among the mountains with the snow piled over her grave, and I so happy here with Roy. Think of me to-night and bless me, dear father. Mother is to give me away, but I shall fancy it is you. Good bye. Your loving daughter, Fanny Hilton, soon to be Fanny Mason."

Mark read this letter to Tom, who said after a moment, "She is a splendid girl. I don't think she takes after her mother."

"Or her father, either," Mark rejoined.

"Where does she get her lovely traits of character?" was Tom's next remark, and for the first time since Inez died a smile broke over Mark's face, as he replied, "It must be from 'Tina. From all descriptions I have had of that unfortunate lady Fanny looks like her."

"I guess she does," Tom said, then added, "I am glad the diamonds reached her safely. That chapter is closed and a great weight off my mind. I wonder if Inez knows?"

"Of course she does, and is glad as we are," was Mark's reply, and the diamonds were never mentioned again between them.

Mark was failing, and after he knew the diamonds were safe with Fanny, he began to go down rapidly.

"I feel as if I had been broken on the rack until every joint was loosened and every nerve crushed," he said to Tom. "There is nothing to live for. Inez is dead; I shall never see Fanny again, and it is better so. But I do long for the hills and ponds of Ridgefield and Uncle Zach and Dotty. Do you think they'd be glad to see me? They don't know what I am. Nobody knows but you and me."

Tom wasn't so sure about Roy. He believed that young man had his suspicions, and was equally sure he would keep them to himself.

"I know Uncle Zach and Dotty would be glad to see you, and in the spring we will go there," he said to Mark, who, buoyed up with this hope, counted the weeks as they passed away, knowing the while that his strength was slipping from him and leaving him so weak that he staid all day in his room where Tom came every night to see him, and Mark, who had forgotten all the blame he had ever attributed to him, clung to him, as if he had been his son.

"I shan't go to Ridgefield. I've given that up," he said to Tom one day in March. "It's the cottage now in the valley I want to see. How soon do you think we can go there?"

Tom didn't know, and his face was very grave as he looked at his old comrade, who was so surely dying. Spring came early that year and as soon as it was at all practicable Tom took Mark by easy stages to the cottage. He had been there himself to see that it was made ready for the sick man and had passed a most uncomfortable time. He was neither a coward, nor superstitious, but during the three days and nights he spent alone in the cottage he suffered what he called the tortures of the damned. He heard or saw Inez everywhere. Saw her flitting in and out from room to room; heard her singing as she used to sing in her glad girlhood, and felt her kisses on his cheeks just as he felt them on the night of their betrothal. They were real kisses then which made his pulse beat with ecstasy; they were shadowy kisses now, which burned where they touched him, while his lips were purple with cold. Once he called to her, "Inez, Inez, do you know I am here?"

Then in his disordered imagination he fancied he heard again the shriek which had curdled his blood when she sprang over the wheel and confronted him.

"I am not afraid," he said to himself, "but I wish Mark was here, or even Nero. I ought to have brought the dog, although he does not take to me as he used to do. I believe he knows something. Lucky he can't talk."

A week later Mark was there in the old familiar place,

where everything spoke to him of Inez. He had no such fancies as Tom, and took Inez's room for his own, sleeping in her bed, sitting in her chair by the window watching the light of the first summer days as it crept over the mountains, and knowing it was for the last time. Once he went to the closet where Inez's dresses were hung, and taking them down looked at them with eyes, which could not shed a tear. On the one she wore on the day of the hold-up he gazed the longest. It was the last in which he had ever seen her and he recalled just how she looked in it when he helped her to a seat by the driver and remembered with a pang her soiled, crumpled condition when she came back with a look on her face he would never forget. There was a bit of dry mud still clinging to the skirt and he brushed it off carefully and shook from the dress every particle of soil and dirt and hung it away with the other gowns, leaving the closet door open so that from his bed where he lay a good part of the time he could see them and feel through them a nearness to Inez.

Everything he could do for him Tom did, and the two men lived alone through the months of May and June, when the tourist season commenced and the valley was again full of life and stir, and pilgrimages were made to Inez's grave as to the grave of a saint. It was covered with flowers and some of these Mark pressed and sent to Fanny, who wrote to him every week and whose letters helped to prolong his life. But like Inez, he had lost his grip, and early in July he died quietly, like going to sleep, and there were three graves on the hill behind the cottage.

Tom was alone, with only Nero for company. Since the hold-up he had fancied that the dog avoided him. He had been much in Inez's room during her illness and constantly with Mark until he died. He had stood by Inez's grave when she was lowered into it and had lain by it for days after as if watching for her reappearance. And now he and Tom stood by Mark's grave, the only mourners there, and Tom's hand rested on Nero's head as if asking for sympathy, which the sagacious animal gave. He seemed to know they were alone, and when the burial, which took place at sunset, was over and the people gone and Tom sat in the gathering twilight with his head upon a table and his hand hanging at his side, Nero crept to his feet, licking his hand and rubbing against him as he had not done in a year. Then Tom cried, as he said, "Bless you, Nero: if you have forgiven me I am not quite alone in the world. We will stick together, old fellow, but not here. You may like to sit by their graves, wondering why they don't come back, but I can't endure it. I am going away and you are going with me,—miles and miles away, old chap, where it will not be as lonesome as it is here, and where one at least will be glad to see me."

A letter received by Mark from Fanny a few days before he died had decided Tom upon his future, and three weeks later, when a carriage full of tourists came from a hotel to see the grave of the girl who was always spoken of as "the heroine of the valley," the cottage was closed and Tom was gone.

CHAPTER XVII.

IN RIDGEFIELD.

Fanny and Roy had been married amid flowers and music and crowds of people and the grand event chronicled in the Boston and New York papers. That the bride's own father was living was not mentioned. The reporters had not gotten upon that item of gossip and Helen did not enlighten them. Fanny was the only daughter of Judge and Mrs. Prescott, and when she read one of the lengthy articles describing the wedding and her dress and her mother's dress and dwelling at length upon the position and wealth of the Tracys and Prescotts and Masons she rebelled against it almost as hotly as years before Uncle Zach had rebelled against the advertisement her father had written of the Prospect House.

"I wish I had kept my own name, or taken it when I knew who I was. I am not Fanny Prescott," she said, hotly, while Roy rejoined, "Of course not. You are Fanny Mason, my wife."

They went to Florida where they spent the winter and Roy grew brown as a berry with being so much on the lakes and rivers and Fanny grew bilious eating too many oranges, and both were perfectly happy. Early in the spring they returned to Boston, where they staid with Roy's father until June, when Fanny suggested that, instead of goinig to some fashionable watering place, they spend the summer in Ridgefield. Her father had sent her a deed of his Dalton property, and now that she owned it she began to have an effection for the old ruin and wanted to see it, she said to Roy, who answered, "All right. I'd rather go where I can have you to myself than to a hundred watering places where everybody will be admiring the beautiful and accomplished Mrs. Roy Mason; that's what the reporters would call you."

"Horrid!" Fanny said. "I'm not beautiful, and I haven't a single accomplishment. I am just Fanny,— your wife," and she nestled close to him, with a look in her blue eyes which told Roy how much he was to her.

They stopped at the Prospect House more for the sake of its association with their parents than for the real comfort there was there now. The ruling spirit, Dotty, had been stricken with paralysis, and was more helpless than Uncle Zach, who, a martyr to rheumatism, sat in his wheel chair all day, unable to walk more than a few steps at a time, with the help of two canes. He had received cards to their wedding, and had sent his regrets in a long letter in which he deplored the fact that he could not get some good out of his "swaller-tail, which he wore to Craig's weddin' when he didn't or'to wear it, and which was as good as new." Mention, too, was made of Dot's plum-colored satin, which was now too small for her, especially the sleeves. He was glad they remembered him. An *invite* was good to stay home on, and he was their respectful and venerable friend to command. Zacheus Taylor, Esquire, and poor Dotty's X mark, "for she can't use her hands to write more than that."

Uncle Zach had grown childishly weak with his trouble and his years, and received Roy and Fanny with floods of tears, lamenting Dotty's inability to serve them.

"I never expected to see you both agin, and when you was here together I told Dot so," he said; "but here you be, and I'm mighty glad. I'm havin' hard sleddin'. Old age ain't a pleasant thing, with rheumatiz' and paralysis, and maybe soffnin' of the brain, and the tarvern all run down,—and Dotty played out."

The best the house afforded was theirs, he said, and he insisted upon their taking the saloon, as he still called the parlor Mrs. Tracy had occupied.

"You'll be better off there by yourselves," he said. "The boarders ain't what they used to be. The Tremont has got the big bugs."

Poor Dotty couldn't talk much or move, and Fanny spent hours with her, anticipating her wishes by her looks and greatly smoothing her path to the grave. Roy staid a good deal with Uncle Zach, who asked numberless questions about Mark and Jeff.

"I wish they was here. I want to see 'em, and so does Dot, though she can't say so. Strange how I miss her talk and blowin' me when I deserved it. I'm like a ship without a captain, but my laigs trouble me the most. Feel like sticks when I try to walk, and Sam Baily don't push me even, at all,—jolts awfully over the stones. Yes, I wish they was here. Mabby they'd come, if they knew how used up Dotty and I be. Jeff could lift her and wheel me. Write and tell 'em I want 'em."

Roy was not very enthusiastic on the subject, but he made no objection when Fanny wrote what Uncle Zach had said and added her own entreaties for her father to come.

"I don't suppose you will care to see mother often," she said, "but you can see *me*. I shall have a home of my own in Boston and we are going to build a cottage near the old ruin,—Roy and I,—and shall spend a part of each summer here."

It was two weeks before an answer came, not in Mark's handwriting, but in Tom's.

"Oh, Roy. Father is dead. Read what Tom has

written. I can't," Fanny said, as she glanced at the letter and then passed it to Roy, who read: "Stockton, June — 18— Mrs. Mason, Dear Madam:

"It is my painful duty to inform you that your father is dead. He has been failing ever since Inez died, but did not wish you to know it, as it might mar the pleasure of your wedding trip. He was always thinking of you and Inez. He was very ill when your last letter came, but it pleased him to know that you wanted him, and Mr. Taylor, too. If he had lived and been able, I think he would have gone to Ridgefield and taken care of the poor old couple. His death occurred three days after the receipt of your letter, which he kept under his pillow with Inez's watch, which you are to have.

"I know he died a good man. I wish I were half as good. He talked a great deal of you, and once or twice spoke of your mother. He said, 'Tell Helen I am sorry for any pain I caused her, and that I always think of her as she was that summer at the Prospect House.'

"We buried him by the side of Inez and Anita, and crowds attended his funeral. Now, I am alone, with only Nero left of all which once made my life so happy."

Uncle Zach shed floods of tears when Fanny read this letter to him.

"Mark dead and lyin' away off there among the mountains and the robbers," he said. "They or'to have brought him here and buried him with his kin. I'd of given him a big monument. Yes, marm, I would. I liked Mark, if he did alter his name, and I feel as if I had lost a son, don't you?"

He was looking at Roy, who did not feel as if bereft of a son, and not much as if he had lost a father, but he was very sorry for Fanny. Her grief was genuine. She had built many castles in the future when her father would come to her and these were all swept away.

"Do you think I should wear black?" she asked, "and that father ought to be brought east and buried here? Inez and Anita must come if he does."

Roy shivered, as he thought of the three coffins landed at the station and himself superintending their interment in the angle of the wall near 'Tina.

"No, darling," he said, kissing Fanny's tear stained face. "I do not want you to wear black, nor is it necessary, and it is much better for your father and Inez to be among the hills of the Yosemite where they lived than to be brought here. Sometime we will go and see the graves and I will have a suitable monument erected to their memory.

"By their loving daughter and sister," Fanny rejoined, drying the tears which were like April showers, she was so sunny and sweet.

Tom's letter was sent to Helen, who was about starting for Narragansett Pier with a party of friends. Just how it affected her it was hard to tell. She gave up the trip to Narragansett, saying she was not feeling well and preferred to remain at home. If she cried, no one saw her. If she were sorry, no one knew it. She was too proud to show her real feelings, or talk of a past which was buried, but her eyes were very heavy and her face very pale as she sat behind the closed blinds of her house, at home to no one, and supposed by most of her friends to be out of town, as she usually was at that season. Fanny urged her coming to Ridgefield, and she replied, "Not yet. It would bring back a past I wish to forget. Your father is dead, and I have no hard feeling towards him. We were both in fault. I was self willed, and thought because I had money I must not be crossed.

He was a man who could not yield quietly to be governed in every particular by a woman. But let that pass. I am glad you knew him and glad you revere his memory."

This was quite a concession for Helen, and showed that much of her proud spirit was broken. When she heard how fast Mrs. Taylor was failing as the summer wore on she sent her little notes of remembrance, with boxes of flowers and delicacies of various kinds. These pleased Uncle Zach, but it was difficult to know whether his wife realized the attention. She always seemed glad when Fanny was with her, but nothing brought so happy a look to her face as the appearance of Uncle Zach in his wheel chair, and her eyes rested constantly upon him when he was with her, but she couldn't speak to him or return the pressure of his hand when he laid it on hers.

"She can't do nothin' she wants to," Uncle Zach said pathetically. "I'd like to kiss her, but I can't stand alone and should tumble on to her, if I tried."

"I'll help you," Fanny said, and passing her arms around him she held him, while he bent down and kissed the old wife whose quivering lips returned the kiss and tried so hard to speak.

That night she died, and no young husband ever made a bitterer moan for his bride of a few months than did Zacheus over his Dotty. "The greatest woman in the world for runnin' a tarvern and keepin' a feller straight." he said amidst his tears, which fell continually, sleeping or waking. He did not think of her as old and wrinkled and grey haired, but as she had been in their early married life, when she was slight and fair, with long curls in her neck and around her face. "The prettiest girl in town as she is now the most remarkable woman. I shall get along somehow, I s'pose," he said to Fanny, "but it is very dark with Dotty gone, and Mark, too, and Jeff, and Johnny in the cemetry goin' on sixty year. If he had lived he might have had boys to stay with me. As 'tis, I am all alone. It isn't pleasant to be old and helpless and all alone and cold as I am most of the time with this pesky rheumatis'."

To this Fanny could offer no consolation. She couldn't stay with him always, nor could she take him with her when she left Ridgefield. He was indeed alone in his old age, dependent upon hired help, who might not always be kind to him. And this he seemed to feel nearly as much as Dotty's death.

CHAPTER XVIII.

DOTTY'S FUNERAL.

"ALONE and cold, with no one to care for me," was Uncle Zach's constant lament, as he sat shivering by Dotty's coffin during the days which preceeded her funeral.

Craig and Alice were both with him and this was some comfort, while the flowers sent in great profusion made him feel, he said, as if he was somebody, and he wished Dotty knew. Greatly to Fanny's surprise and delight her mother came in the morning train, and the honor of having her there with Craig and Alice partly compensated Mr. Taylor for his loss. It was the first time Helen had been in Ridgefield since she left it twenty-four years ago, and naturally her presence aroused much interest and curiosity in those who remembered her. When she heard of Mrs. Taylor's death a sudden impulse seized her to go to the funeral. Almost anything was better than staying at home alone as she was doing. If Roy built that cottage she must of course go there some time, and she might as well make this her opportunity. So she went and in her crape, still worn for Judge Prescott, she looked grand and handsome and dignified, and cried a little over Dotty and more over Uncle Zach in his wheel chair. He persisted in calling her Miss Hilton and talking to her of Mark, until Alice suggested to him that it might be better to give her her real name and to say nothing of Mark, as it could only bring up unpleasant memories.

"Jess so,—jess so. Yes, marm. You are right, and it shows how I am missin' Dotty to tell me what is what," Uncle Zach replied.

After that he laid great stress on Miss Prescott when he spoke to her, as she was brushing his hair and arranging his necktie for the funeral. She had asked to do this for him and as he felt her fingers on his forehead and about his neck, he burst out suddenly, "It brings it all back, when you was a young gal makin' the house so bright. You ain't a widder, nor Miss Prescott to me, and I won't call you so."

"Call me Helen, please. I feel more like her here than I have in years," she replied.

She was very kind to him and arranged that he should go to the grave in the carriage with Roy and Fanny and herself. "The very best and easiest there is in town," she said to the undertaker.

"But, but," Uncle Zach interposed, "I could no more git into a kerridge than I could fly. I must be wheeled. Dot won't mind. She knows how stiff I am."

It was in vain that they urged upon him that he could be lifted into a carriage. He insisted that he couldn't.

"If I go at all, it must be in my chair, with Sam to

push me," he said, and that settled it, and his chair was wheeled into its place in the long procession which followed Dotty to the grave.

It took some time to get all the carriages into line and ready, and while they were waiting a stranger came rapidly across the street and joined the crowd in front of the Prospect House. He was dusty and travel stained and no one recognized him but Roy and Fanny, who, with Helen, were in the carriage next to Uncle Zach's chair.

"Oh, Roy,—there's Tom!" Fanny cried, as he passed them without looking up, so intent was he upon the forlorn old man sitting alone with his attendant behind him.

"If you please, this is my place," he said in a low tone to Sam, waving him aside so peremptorily that Sam had nothing to do but submit, which he did willingly, wondering who the stranger was and why he was so anxious for a job he did not fancy.

Uncle Zach was rather hard of hearing, and in the confusion of starting did not hear Sam's instructions, "Go easy over the stones; he's awful lame."

Tom nodded that he understood, and the funeral cortege started.

"Careful, now, Sam. There's a rut full of stones!" Uncle Zach said once, surprised at the deftness and ease with which the supposed Sam avoided the stones, almost lifting the chair over the worst of them, and showing a thoughtfulness he had never shown before. "It's because it's Dotty's funeral, he's so keerful," Uncle Zach thought, resolving to give him something extra when he paid him his next month's wages. "Get me as close to the grave as you can. I want to see her up to the last minute," he said, when they were in the cemetery.

Without a word Jeff wheeled the chair as near the grave as possible, every one making way for him and all wondering who he could be, except Roy and Fanny. Once during the committal he looked at them and in response to their greeting touched his hand to his uncovered head with a motion so natural that Alice, who was watching him, started with a conviction that she had seen him before, and when the next moment their eyes met and he smiled upon her she was sure that it was the boy Jeff. She could not speak to him then and when the ceremony was over and the people began to disperse there was a new diversion in the scene in the shape of a huge dog who came bounding over the grass and leaping upon Jeff nearly knocked him down. It was Nero escaped from the freight house at the station where his master had left him for a time in charge of a boy. Jeff's longing to see Ridgefield had grown in intensity until at last without any warning of his coming, he started east with his dog and travelled night and day until Ridgefield was reached. Hearing in the car of the funeral and fearing Nero might be in the way he had him shut up and went rapidly up the street he remembered so well to the Prospect House, reaching it in time to take Sam's place and wheel Uncle Zacheus to the cemetery. After many fruitless efforts to escape by the door Nero squeezed through a half open window and following his master's trail came upon him in the graveyard and in his joy at finding him caused a lurch to the chair which elicited a groan from Uncle Zach.

"Oh, Sam, are you in a hole, or what? You've nearly broke my back," he said; "and whose great dog is that cantering 'round as if he was goin' to jump on me. Go 'way, doggie, doggie; go 'way. Shoo! Shoo! Take him off!" he continued, as Nero showed signs of making his acquaintance, or at least finding out what manner of being it was wrapped in a shawl and looking so small and helpless.

Jeff did not reply till he got the chair away from the grave to a side path where they were comparatively alone.

"Where be you takin' me? I or'to go back with the procession. Folks'll think it queer," Uncle Zach said, as he found himself at some distance from the main road of the cemetery.

Stepping in front of him Jeff took off his hat and said, "Don't you know me?"

Uncle Zach's sight was dim and his eyes weak with the tears he had shed, but something in Jeff's voice and manner seemed natural. He, however, had no suspicion of the truth, and replied, "I or'to know you, of course, but I'm kind of blind, and my spe'tacles is at home. Who be you, and where is Sam?"

"If I were to turn a somerset or two, and stand on my head, do you think you would know me then?" Jeff asked, with his old merry laugh.

The effect was wonderful. Uncle Zach had not risen alone from his chair in months, but he sprang up now and stood firm upon his feet, with his arms outstretched.

"Jeff! Jeff! my boy!" he cried, "It's you, yourself, come back to me! Thank God!"

He could say no more, and sank back in his chair, shaking like a leaf, while Jeff said to him, "Yes, it's Jeff, come back, and sorry to find Mrs. Taylor dead, and you so helpless. Shall I take you home?"

"Yes, sir. Yes, sir. I'm all of a tremble, and so glad you've come, and so would Dotty be, if she knew," Uncle Zach replied; "and this is your critter?" motioning towards Nero, who, with sundry sharp woofs, was signifying his approval of affairs.

"Yes, this is Nero. He belonged to Mark, and I could not leave him in the mountains alone. He is a friendly, faithful fellow, and will guard you, or your property, with his life," Jeff said, caressing the dog, in whose eyes there was a human look as if he understood what was being said.

As a rule Mr. Taylor did not care much for dogs. Dotty had disliked them, and would never have one on the premises. They tracked her clean piazza and floor and trampled down her flower beds, she said. But Dotty was gone. Nero had belonged to Mark, and when he put his nose on Zacheus's knee and looked up in his face, the old man's heart was won and Nero adopted with Jeff.

"Doggie, doggie, Mark's doggie, you are welcome," he said, patting Nero whose bushy tail was in full swing and who, with the sagacity of his race, had seen that Uncle Zach needed care and had constituted himself his body guard.

Meanwhile Craig and Alice, and Helen and Roy and Fanny had been watching the scene at a distance. They were yet to be met and it was hard meeting them all. Jeff had seen Helen at Clark's when he took Fanny and Roy there after Inez's funeral. She had been rather reserved towards him then and said very little, but now her manner changed, and she was the first to go forward and meet him as he came near to them. Inez was dead and he could never claim any connection with Fanny. He would stay with Uncle Zach as his proper place, and she was very cordial in her greeting. Alice and Craig came next, the former doing most of the talking and both seeming so pleased to see him that he felt his spirits rising and had not been as happy in years as he was when at last he stood again in the house where he had spent his boyhood.

Roy was cordial, but could not forget Inez's dying words, which had betrayed so much, and every time he looked at Jeff he recalled the scene of the hold up which he had heard described so vividly that he sometimes felt that he had been an actor in it. Fanny was unfeignedly glad to see Jeff and kept him by her a long time while she questioned him of her father's sickness and death and burial. Helen, who sat near, made no comments, but she did not lose a word, and occasionally, when Fanny cried the hardest, her bit of linen and lace which passed for a handkerchief, went up to her eyes and came away with several wet spots upon it. With his friends around him, treating him as if he had always been an honest man, Jeff began to feel like one. He was glad Alice did not refer to the pick-pocket business, for he could not tell her that he had kept his promise to the letter. He had followed no one on the street, or in a crowd, but he could recall pockets in which his hands had been while the owners were pale as death and almost as still. That was buried in the Yosemite and here in Ridgefield, where every one was pleased to see him, the dreadful past was slipping away from him, and with a rebound his old life was returning. Nero, too, came in for a share of notice and petting. Craig, who was fond of dogs, offered to buy him, but Jeff said, "No, he is the only relative I have left in the world. I have brought him from beyond the Rockies and if Mr. Taylor does not object, I shall keep him."

"Object to the critter! Of course not. He was Mark's, and Dotty isn't here to care about his feet. They are pretty big. *Shoo, shoo,* doggie; not quite so friendly," Uncle Zach replied, shaking his fingers at the dog, who had taken a great fancy to him and persisted in laying his head in his lap and occasionally putting his paws on the wheel of his chair.

The next day Craig and Alice and Helen went home, but Roy and Fanny staid on to see to the new cottage. The ground for it had been broken a little distance from the old ruin, "but not so far away that Tina can't come across the grass to visit us if she wants to," Roy said to Fanny, who had no fear of Tina so long as Roy was with her. They staid in Ridgefield the rest of the summer with an occasional trip to New York, where Helen kept herself secluded until it was time for the fashionable world to come home and open their doors. Then she gradually made her way again into the society which she enjoyed. Sometime in September Roy and Fanny returned to Boston, leaving the cottage so nearly completed that it would be ready for them in June of the next summer, if they wished to occupy it so early.

CHAPTER XIX.

ODDS AND ENDS.

Six years later and it is summer again in Ridgefield. Uncle Zach has celebrated his ninetieth birthday, and except for his lameness is nearly as hale and hearty as he was when he first welcomed the Masons and the Tracys to his home. Jeff's presence has worked wonders in him and in the house as well. In a quiet way he assumed the role of master while nominally acting under Mr. Taylor's orders. The servants, who had become lax and worthless, have been dismissed, and others more competent hired in their place. The house has been thoroughly renovated and refurnished. Many of the former boarders, who had gone to the Tremont, have come back, and a few people from Boston spend the summers there.

"If Dot was only here, and I had my laigs it would seem like old times," Uncle Zach often says to Jeff, who is his right hand and left hand and feet and brains.

If kindness to an old man can atone for the past Jeff is atoning for it. He puts his master to bed at night as if he were a child and dresses him in the morning. Every pleasant day he takes him for what he calls a drive through the town, stopping wherever the querulous old man wishes to stop and wheeling him so carefully that his rheumatic limbs seldom receive a jolt. Nero is always in attendance and is as much a part of the turnout as Jeff himself. Uncle Zach no longer *shoos* him when he puts his head on his knees, but he sometimes has pricks of conscience as to what Dotty would say if she could see the big dog stretched on the floor of the piazza or wherever he choses to lie. Dotty's habits are deferred to by both Uncle Zach and Jeff, except the quarterly house cleanings. At these Jeff has drawn the line. Twice a year was sufficient, he said, for any house, and Uncle Zach agreed with him. Every three months, however, a dress coat and vest and little yellow blanket are brought out to air, the blanket so tender with age that Jeff scarcely dares touch it. "Johnny's blanket," Uncle Zach always says, with a tone very different from that in which he speaks of his swallow tail.

"Fool and his money soon parted," he said when telling Jeff what it had cost. "I never wore it but once and never shall again. The missionaries don't want it, nor the heathen. If you had any use for it I'd give it to you.

It seems a pity for it to lay there year in and year out smellin' like fury with that moth stuff you put in it."

Jeff laughed and thanked him as he folded up the garments and laid them away with Taylor's Tavern in the hair trunk. Once he brought the sign down for Uncle Zach to see.

"I can't git up them stairs and I'd like to look at it agin," he said, and when Jeff brought it and stood it before him tears ran down his cheeks like rain. "It makes me think of the time when I was young, and Dotty, too. The lalocks in the garden was blowin' and the apple trees was blossomin' the day it was sot up. I can smell the lalocks yet, though the bush has been dead many a year just as Dotty is. Take it away, Jeff, and you needn't bring it agin. I'm done with Taylor's Tarvern, and with everything else but you!"

Jeff took it back and felt the moisture in his own eyes at his master's reminiscences of a past which could never return. To the villagers Jeff was very reticent with regard to his western life. Of his change of name he made light. It was a fashion with some of the miners and he foolishly followed it, he said, but of what befel Tom Hardy he said very little. He was, however, paying so heavy a penalty for his misdeeds that he sometimes felt as if he must hide where no one had ever heard of him in connection with Long John and Little Dick. Fanny had told of the hold up of which he had been the hero, and of the other where he had been an actor, and it seemed to him people would never stop questioning him as to the most minute details. If he repeated the story once in the office he repeated it a hundred times to a breathless audience which never grew tired of listening and were always ready to hear it again.

"And they never got a clew to them, you say?"

"Never," was the question and answer, with which the evening usually closed, the people dispersing to their rooms or homes, while Jeff rushed out into the night overwhelmed with remorse.

"I believe State's Prison would be better than this," he sometimes thought when Uncle Zacheus had him on the rack.

He was inexorable and made Jeff tell the story over and over again until he ought to have known it by heart. Once when he was out for his airing he asked, speaking of the robbers, "Be they gone, root and branch?"

"Yes, root and branch. Neither Long John nor Little Dick have been seen since Inez died," Jeff replied.

It was not often that he spoke of Inez, and now at the mention of her name Uncle Zach rejoined, "Poor girl, and you was to have married her. I am sorry for you. And she was Miss Mason's sister and Mark was her father. Mark was a likely chap. I've nothing agin him except that he run away and let 'em think he was dead and changed his name. I s'pose he put you up to change yours, too."

"No, he didn't," Jeff answered quickly. "It was right the other way. I put him up to every bad thing he ever did."

Jeff was a little heated in his defense of Mark and pushed the chair over a rough place with less care than usual.

"Softly, softly, Jeff. My bones is older than they was once," Uncle Zach said.

This recalled Jeff to himself, and the rest of the journey was made with comparative comfort to the old man's bones. They were on their way to the Queen Anne cottage which had been built near the site of the old ruin and between it and the road. It was a very pretty and artistic affair, with bay windows and projections and wide halls and piazza, where Roy said 'Tina could sit and rest if she wanted to, when she made her nocturnal visits. The cellar was filled up and made into a terrace, or plateau, which was ablaze with flowers from June to September. A part of the orchard had been cut down and with the lane converted into a small park of green sward, flowering shrubs and shade trees. Here Roy and Fanny spent a part of every summer and were often joined by Craig and Alice, and occasionally by Helen, whose beauty was not greatly marred by the lapse of years and who was sometimes told that she looked nearly as young as her daughter. She was a grandmother now and two children played on the grass and picked flowers from the spot where 'Tina once had lived and loved and sinned. They were a sturdy boy of five years old and a little girl of three. The only real disagreement Fanny and Roy ever had was on the subject of the boy's name. Fanny wished to call him Mark Hilton, while Helen favored the idea. Roy could not tell Fanny that his son must not be named for one who he believed had been a highwayman, but he objected to the name and held his ground against Fanny's entreaties and the advice of Craig and Alice.

"Perhaps as you won't call him for my father you'd like to call him for yours," Fanny said, with as much spirit as she ever opposed to Roy.

"No," he answered, "not for my father either, but I'll tell you what we'll do. We'll call him for your adopted father, Walter Prescott. How will that suit you?"

"Not as well as Mark Hilton," Fanny replied, but she gave up the point and the boy was christened Walter Prescott.

When two years later a girl was born there was no

question as to her name from the moment Roy said to Fanny, "Would you like to see our little daughter *Inez?*"

They were bright, active children and Jeff was their slave. They were never happier than when with him, and always hailed with delight the sight of the wheel chair coming down the road, for that meant a ride after Uncle Zach was safely deposited upon the piazza with their father and mother.

On the morning when Jeff came near upsetting the chair in his defense of Mark they were on the look-out for him. They had come from Boston the night before and were watching eagerly for their *horse,* as they called him, while Nero was a *colt.* Craig and Alice were there and with Roy and Fanny were enjoying the freshness and fragrance of the June morning.

"There they come; there's Jeff and Nero," Walter cried, running to meet him, and "Dere's Deff and Nero," Inez repeated, toddling after her brother.

Both Fanny and Roy hurried to meet Uncle Zach, who was soon helped to a seat on the piazza, and his chair was at liberty and at once appropriated by the children.

"Where shall we go?" Jeff asked, and Walter answered, "To the woods."

He always wanted to go there, hoping to find a bumble-bee's nest, if not the hornet's his grandmother had told him about. Inez was satisfied to go anywhere with Jeff, whose face always brightened at sight of her and then grew sad as he remembered another Inez in her mountain grave. They found the spot where a hornet's nest had been, and saw a rabbit steal cautiously out from her hole and then in again as Nero started for her. They picked some wild flowers and ferns and then Inez grew tired of walking about and wanted Jeff to sit down and take her. When, as a baby of a year old, Inez had first held up her arms to him, he had shrunk from her with a feeling that he was unworthy to touch her. Roy, who was present, had something of the same feeling, for he never saw Jeff without a thought of the hold up. But the child's persistence had conquered his prejudice and subjugated Jeff, who loved the little girl better than any living being. Indeed, there was no one else for him to love. He respected Uncle Zacheus and admired Fanny and reverenced Alice as one of the noblest of women, but his affection was given to the baby Inez.

"Taky me; I'se tired," she kept saying in the woods until he sat down upon a log and took her in his lap.

"Now, tell us a story about Aunt Inez and the robbers," Walter said, coming up with the dog, who stretched himself at Jeff's feet while Walter lay down at his side.

The previous summer Jeff had told Walter of his home among the mountains and his life there with the other Inez, and his grandfather and Nero, and once Walter had heard his mother tell some one of the hold up and the robber, and boy-like this pleased him more than the cottage and the mountains. He had made Jeff tell him about it two or three times the year before and now insisted that he should tell it again, and begin where his Aunt Inez jumped over the wheel and Nero ran after the robber. Very unwillingly Jeff told the story, adapting it to Walter, who listened intently and did not allow him to omit any part of it which he knew.

"I wish I'd been there with mamma. Where was I?" he asked.

Jeff did not know, and with his respect for Jeff's

knowledge considerably lessened, he continued, "I'd have shot the robber."

Inez, whose arms were about Jeff's neck and who generally said what Walter did, replied, "I'd sot the yobber," and her arms tightened their hold, giving Jeff a feeling of suffocation and helping to smother the groan he could not entirely repress.

"Now, tell about Aunt Inez and where she lived," Walter said, and Jeff told him of the grand mountains and the waterfalls in the beautiful valley far away and the grave among the hills where his Aunt Inez was buried.

"Was she as pretty as mamma?" Walter asked, and Jeff replied, "*I* think she was prettier."

"I don't believe it. Do you, Nero?" Walter said, with a kick of his foot against the side of the dog, who answered by springing up and hurrying after the rabbit which had ventured from its hole a second time.

Walter followed the dog, and Jeff was left alone with Inez, who whispered drowsily, "Tell more of the bufiful valley far away."

Then she fell asleep, and bending over her Jeff whispered, "Oh, God, in this world my sin will always follow and torture me, but grant that in the next I may be pure and innocent as this child."

Something roused the little girl and opening her eyes, so like the eyes Jeff remembered so well, she lisped, "Ess, he will."

Then she fell asleep again, and with a feeling that he had received a benediction, Jeff, who had never kissed her before, kissed her now for the sake of the dead Inez, whose grave was in the beautiful valley far away.

THE END.

www.ingramcontent.com/pod-product-compliance
Lightning Source LLC
Chambersburg PA
CBHW032026220426
43664CB00006B/378